P9-BHY-177

THE NEW DANCE
OF CHRIST

DEMCO

THE NEW DANCE
OF CHRIST

Discovering Our Spiritual Self
in a New, Evolving World

Anthony T. Massimini

786-MASS

Copyright © 2000 by Anthony T. Massimini.

Library of Congress Number: 00-191459
ISBN #:   Softcover   0-7388-2795-9
All rights reserved. No part of this book may be reproduced or transmitted in
any form or by any means, electronic or mechanical, including photocopying,
recording, or by any information storage and retrieval system, without permission
in writing from the copyright owner.

This book was printed in the United States of America.

To order additional copies of this book, contact:
Xlibris Corporation
1-888-7-XLIBRIS
www.Xlibris.com
Orders@Xlibris.com

IN APPRECIATION

I write with special gratitude to three dearly beloved friends who have walked a long way with me: Bill Leahy, whose brilliance lit my way to so much spiritual understanding; Anthony Padovano, whose deep and clear spirituality illumines thousands in today's world; and Fred Ruof, who puts spirituality to work every day.

Jo Paolin, Bill and Eileen McNiff, Earl and Pat Martin, Bill Haggerty, Bob McGovern, Veryl Yoder and so many others, have taught me the full meaning of the hero's journey. Friend and colleague, Dr. John Elias, of Fordham U., helped me immensely in my understanding of the philosophies of education. Dr. Paul Mestancik has enriched me not only with his friendship but with psychoanalytic insight into what it means to be human. Theresa Padovano, wife of Anthony and mother of four wonderful children, is my role model for family spirituality. Jerry and Eileen Spinelli, superb writers for the young, keep my soul young and fresh. My own family, especially my sister Lucy and her husband Phil, flavors my spirituality like the best Italian spaghetti "gravy," while Mary's family, especially her sister Ann and her husband Harry, puts the lilt of Irish laughter in my heart, with a little German *Gemutlichkeit* tossed in.

Special thanks go to physicist/mystic Brian Swimme, who read the first draft of this book and whose comments and suggestions vastly improved the manuscript. His own book, *The Universe Story*, written together with Thomas Berry, inspired my telling of the story of the universe.

The image on the cover was created by Mary Massimini, who also improved the manuscript with her many insights, and who kept me going throughout the writing with an enthusiasm that only a loving wife could generate.

The excerpt from THE SECOND COMING, by W. B. Yeats is reprinted with the permission of Scribner, a Division of Simon & Schuster from THE COLLECTED POEMS OF W. B. YEATS, Revised Edition edited by Richard J. Finneran. Copyright 1924 by Macmillan Publishing Company, renewed 1952 by Bertha Georgie Yeats.

"i thank You God for most this amazing". Copyright 1950, © 1978, 1991 by the Trustees for the E. E. Cummings Trust. Copyright © 1979 by George James Firmage, from COMPLETE POEMS: 1904-1962 by E. E. Cummings, edited by George J. Firmage. Used by permission of Liveright Publishing Corporation.

STOPPING BY WOODS ON A SNOWY EVENING. From THE POETRY OF ROBERT FROST edited by Edward Connery Lathem. Copyright 1923, © 1969 by Henry Holt and Co., copyright 1951 by Robert Frost. Reprinted by permission of Henry Holt and Company, LLC.

Special thanks to Judi Kincaid for her gracious assistance in helping locate the copyright owners for the poems mentioned above.

The poem A GENESIS CAROL by Anthony Massimini, was first published in the National Catholic Reporter, December, 1985.

Scripture excerpts in this work are taken from the *New American Bible with Revised New Testament and Revised Psalms* © 1991, 1986, 1970 Confraternity of Christian Doctrine, Washington DC. Used with permission. No part of the *New American Bible* may be reproduced in any form without permission in writing from the copyright owner.

CONTENTS

TO MARY,
MY LUMINOUS WIFE,
MY LIFE'S DANCING PARTNER

86-MASS

ONE

Before the New Beginning

Everything has changed, except our way of thinking.
Albert Einstein

Surely, some new revelation is at hand.
W. B. Yeats

A fresh kind of life is starting.
Teilhard de Chardin

Be not afraid.
Jesus Christ

Imagine a family in ancient Athens about to go to the Acropolis to worship the goddess, Diana. One teen-age son announces that he is not going. His shocked parents ask him why. "My friend, Plato, has introduced me to his teacher, Socrates. He has a new way of seeing people and the world. I'm going to go listen to him."

Now imagine a diplomatic Roman family in first century Jerusalem. They are about to go to a temple to give honor and glory to Caesar and to their pantheon of gods and goddesses. But their daughter tells them she is not going. "My friends, Martha and Mary, have introduced me to a man named Jesus. He has a new way of seeing people and the world. I'm going to go listen to him."

Time passes. Imagine a medieval monk working in his scriptorium, illumining a map that puts earth at the center of the universe—a "fact" that adds great security and certitude to his faith. A visitor arrives and shows him a new map. "The earth is not in the center of the universe," the visitor says. "It is a small planet orbiting around its own sun in a solar system that's at the outskirts of a large galaxy. See, here is a new way to see earth and ourselves, and even our faith."

Now picture a woman talking to a psychoanalyst. She says she believes God is leading her to take a certain job in order to gain a particular satisfaction. The analyst shows her that it is not God who is leading her but her unconscious mind. She asks, "So, where is God?" He has no answer.

Finally, imagine a "Modern World" scientist who understands the universe according to the classic laws of Newton. A quantum physicist visits him. During their conversation she picks up an apple from his desk. "To you," she says, "this is a solid apple that you can objectively understand according to determined scientific and mathematical laws."

He eyes his apple. "To me it's a snack, but . . . yes, let's say that's how I understand it."

"But it's not solid. Its a localization of sub-atomic particles that are dancing around 99.9% empty space."

"Dancing? Empty space?"

"Beautiful, isn't it? Look at the way the light dances off its skin."

"Dancing apples!" the scientist blurts. "Are you a scientist or an artist?"

"Why not both?" Science and art are interconnected. We need both in order to understand this apple."

"Science and art are *not* interconnected," the scientist objects. "Science is objective, and art is subjective. True understanding comes only from objective science."

"Actually, science is not all that objective," his guest replies. "Our understanding of this apple depends on many subjective factors. It depends on the questions we ask, the way we think, the words we use, and even whether we like apples or not." She takes a bite. "Mmmm," she sings, "I just improved my understanding of this apple."

She continues. "In fact, our understanding of this apple ultimately depends on the fact that we're human. We're engaged in a human dialogue with it. God understands this apple differently. But now we also have a scientific way to see the divine understanding of this apple."

"The modern scientist throws up his hands. "You want me to be in a dialogue with this apple, as if it's alive. And you want me to provide a *divine* understanding of this apple!?"

"That's right. This apple—like everything else in the universe—is made of pure energy. We have no direct access to pure energy, so we can't understand it in itself; we can only understand it in the ways it shows up—for example, as this apple. Pure energy can show up as anything it wants. It contains untold numbers of possibilities. The more we see its possibilities unfold, the more possibilities there will be to unfold. Pure energy is like Mystery: the more we understand it, the more there is to understand—forever and ever. Mystery is one way to describe God, who created the universe and apples, and who can create anything he wants, anytime he wants, forever and ever. So you see, by getting in touch with pure energy and Mystery, today's science has gotten in touch with how God understands the universe—and apples.

The modern world scientist is newly baffled. "Now you're talking like a mystic."

"Yes. Art. Science. Mysticism. They're all interconnected. In fact, today's scientists are seeing, thinking and talking just as the mystics have done for over 2500 years. And they're experiencing the same awe and wonder that the mystics experience. Many of them, however, don't know this, and they even get angry when somebody tells them what they are experiencing and doing. Artists, of course, have always experienced awe and wonder and have always seen, thought and expressed themselves the way mystics do."

She then puts down the apple and leaves the Modern World scientist to ponder what she has said.

*   *   *

Science. Art. Mysticism. Something's afoot in the universe. A new world has been born, and with it, a wondrous new way to tell our story—the story of the universe, earth and ourselves. A new spark of Genesis has been enkindled. A new dance of Christ is being choreographed.

We are only beginning to hear the music of the new dance and to learn its new steps. We are only beginning to discover the enormity of the "new way of thinking," the "new revelation," and the "fresh kind of life," that is now being born. Einstein spoke his prophetic words on August 6, 1945, the day the atomic bomb exploded over Hiroshima. The great scientist saw that, along with that Japanese city, a whole world was being blown up. From its ashes a new worldview began to rise—a new way of seeing, organizing and valuing ourselves, others, the world and even God. On that historic day, many of our old views, ideas and values became obsolete, and so did our old religion. People began not only to see, think and value differently, but also to believe differently. The search for a new spirituality was born.

Up to that time, most Christians accepted what other people told them about God. They learned about God from their church authorities—many of whom were still caught in a pre-modern, medieval mindset. Little by little, an increasing number of people began to look for a way to experience God for themselves. That quest takes clear form today. An increasing number of people want to experience God personally in today's world of fast change, dazzling technology, consumerism, new possibilities for personal fulfillment, and new expectations for full justice and respect for women, for the various races, for the poor and outcast, and for the earth. They wanted a spirituality that will allow them to have an impact on today's society—on its education, politics, economics and its religions. The spiritual question today is not, "How can we be more pious and devout?" but, "How can we experience God in such a way that we can make ourselves and society more human—

more just, peaceful, free, joyful, hopeful and loving? And how can we do this without imposing our religion on others?"

These questions make a whole new spirituality necessary. Spirituality is our personal experience of God and the way we live our life in that experience. The new spirituality, born of science, art and mysticism, opens us to a deep and effective, contemporary experience of God, who is living and active within ourselves and the whole world. In Christian terms, when God is present and active within us and the world, God is referred to as Spirit. So throughout this book, we will speak of the indwelling Spirit. By this, we mean, that God—One and Trinity—is alive and active within ourselves and the world.

While God living within us has the name, Spirit, the new spirituality has no name. I'll simply call it the new spirituality, and invite the readers to think up a good name for it. More to the point, this book is an invitation to you to walk the new spiritual path with me, adding your own talents, dreams and insights along the way. It is an invitation to all to take part in the new dance of Christ and to add their own, personal "steps" to the dance.

While Christian, the new spirituality is fully ecumenical. It embraces all the human community's best and most beautiful truths, especially the truths of love and compassion, in whatever religion or tradition they are found. It is also historically ecumenical. It welcomes all the humanizing insights of ancient Mesopotamia, Egypt, Greece, Rome, the Far East, and the Incas, Aztecs and Mayas of Central and South America. With gratitude to Confucianism, Buddhism and Hinduism, it gazes with Eastern eyes into the human soul and contemplates its depth and richness. It stands on the firmness of the revelation given to it by Jesus' own people, our "elder brothers and sisters," the Jews. It echoes the beat of drums from Africa and the New World. Its imagination is thrilled by the sacred majesty of medieval cathedrals, and glows with the colors and textures of the Renaissance. It allows Galileo to show us our proper place in the universe; it invites Darwin and evolutionary science to show us new ways to grow and develop; and it lets Freud, Jung and others give us wondrously deep insights into our inner behavior and relationships with others. It breathes the earth's air, drinks her water, and eats her food. It cries with the oppressed and outcast and raises its eyes in hope with the developing nations. It encourages equality among the races and sexes; works for justice and peace, and creates new visions for education, politics, economics and religion. It stirs us with awe and wonder at the dazzling marvels of science and technology and moves us with the ever-fresh, transcendent poignancy of art. Finally, it looks forward to the untold galaxies of possibilities waiting to be discovered and developed by the human community.

All embracing and all-respecting, the new spirituality is fully alive, joyfully free, scientifically correct, intellectually clear, emotionally moving, poetically a-dance, artistically poignant, spiritually ecumenical, open to all space/time and eternity, and practical and applicable in the everyday world.

The new spirituality is not a road to Utopia. It will take us along a new path where we will die to our old ways of seeing, valuing and acting, and rise to new ways and new life. It sets us out on a new Hero's Journey, in which we will face our internal demons and external dragons before we meet our new life. Nor is it for ourselves alone. It is for ourselves and others—for our family, community, society and world, and for the earth. From within its galaxies of new possibilities, we will discover anew the one humanity that binds us together with women and men of all races, economic levels, religions and traditions. We will see how the Spirit of Christ is moving us today to collaborate with all people of good will, love and compassion to help create a new world of interconnected unity in which everyone can enjoy opportunities to live in justice, peace, freedom, joy, hope and compassion. It will not automatically give us a new world, but it will give us the mindset to create a new world.

The old world, that Einstein declared dead in 1945, was called "The Modern World." Born in the 16th century, it gave us an array of magnificent accomplishments—modern nations, exploration, modern science and technology, the industrial revolution, modern democracy, individual freedom and rights, modern medicine, psychoanalysis, and modern capitalism. But it also gave us child labor, modern colonialism and slavery, stark economic inequality, pollution, Nazism, fascism, communism, the most destructive wars in history, and a pathological individualism that often pushed people into anxiety, depression, irresponsibility and violence. A fragmented world, in the end, left us with fragmented selves and fragmented spirits.

With its mindset of radical individualism and fragmentation, the Modern World suffered from a built-in schizophrenia. People and institutions were locked up in their own, separate boxes, all "doing their own thing," and justifying themselves by looking at themselves. Business was business; politics was politics; religion was religion. The boxes themselves were divided into two worlds, the secular and the sacred. The secular world—business, politics, entertainment, public education—operated on its own, usually on weekdays. The religious world—belief and prayer—operated on its own, at home and on Sunday mornings. People lived and worked in one world, and believed and prayed in another. If they brought their religion into the everyday world it was in the form of their personal morality, as they tried to obey the rules of their faith. Spirituality, the personal experience of God, became the realm of special people, who usually lived in monasteries and convents, and had little or no relevance to the everyday, secular world.

THE MODERN WORLD

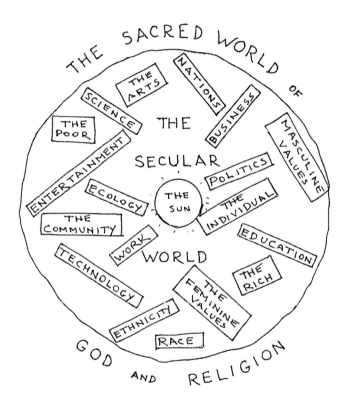

THE SACRED WORLD OF

THE ARTS

NATIONS

SCIENCE

BUSINESS

THE POOR

THE

MASCULINE VALUES

ENTERTAINMENT

SECULAR

POLITICS

ECOLOGY

THE SUN

THE INDIVIDUAL

THE COMMUNITY

WORK

WORLD

EDUCATION

TECHNOLOGY

THE FEMININE VALUES

THE RICH

ETHNICITY

RACE

GOD AND RELIGION

OF FRAGMENTATION

Some 20 years before Einstein saw the Modern World blow itself up at Hiroshima, poet W. B. Yeats prophetically foresaw the dying of the Modern World. Today we call that dying the "deconstruction" of modern society. In his famous poem, "The Second Coming, he said:"

> ...Things fall apart, the centre cannot hold;
> Mere anarchy is loosed upon the world
> The blood dimmed tide is loosed, and everywhere
> The ceremony of innocence is drowned;
> The best lack all conviction, while the worst
> Are full of passionate intensity.

Being the mystic he was, Yeats was not without hope. Looking forward to a new, "post-modern" world and spirituality, he added,

> Surely some new revelation is at hand.

In the 1950's, mystic/scientist Teilhard de Chardin, also saw that the Modern World was dying. Being the mystic he was, he pointed out that the Modern World was not dying by accident. Its deadly flaws of fragmentation and isolation were not aberrations of its design but were built right into it. He saw that it could not be fixed on its own terms. A new world had to be born, and like Yeats and Einstein, he saw that new world rising—a world of interconnected unity. In this new world, he saw a new Christianity being born, and a new Christian spirituality. "A fresh kind of life is starting," he concluded.

Where shall we find this fresh kind of life, this new spirituality? We shall find it within ourselves, where it is now pregnantly alive. From within our very souls, the indwelling Spirit is calling to us—groaning in labor within us to beget us anew as spiritually alive people who will become fully involved in rediscovering and re-creating ourselves and society. She is choreographing a new dance of Christ—a new way to see who we are, why we are here, where we are going—and a new way to get there. In the first few chapters of this book, we will start telling our story anew by going all the way back to the first flaring forth of the universe, to the Big Bang. Beginning with that exquisite moment of creation we will take a whole new look at the origin of the universe. From there we will move forward to today—and tomorrow.

De Chardin said that the "fresh kind of life," that is now being born is the greatest change the world has ever known. The new spirituality is a new dance on a new stage. The choreography calls for us to begin the dance by leaping into the arms of the Spirit. The stage is dark. We may be fearful that we may not leap well, or that the Spirit will not catch us. From across the stage, She speaks silently and persuasively to our very soul, "Be not afraid." In our hearts, minds and souls, we repeat her words, "Be not afraid." She stretches out her arms. We prepare to leap.

Let the new dance begin.

PART ONE

Invitation to the New Dance

86-MASS

TWO

In the New Beginning

On the first silent, holy night,
in a stable as big as infinity and as deep as eternity,
the Nameless One created and birthed forth a child.
The child was the universe,
immaculately conceived and created as good.

In the beginning, . . . God created the
heavens and the earth.

Gen. 1:1

The newborn universe was a single dot, perhaps no bigger than the period at the end of this sentence. Imagine. All the energy necessary to create the indescribably great galaxies, all the laws and equations that would tantalize scientists for centuries, all the trillion trillion "decisions" necessary to form all the suns, planets, black holes, our solar system, earth, and ourselves—all was contained in that single dot.

The grandeur and the beauty . . . the ultimate history
story, the history of the universe, is the story of how a single
kernel of energy could have become everything that is.

Timothy Ferris, TV Presentation
"The Creation of the Universe"

Before God inspired people to write the Bible, He wrote
His own book, the universe.

Thomas E. Clark
"The Way," Jan. 1989

Scientists call the dot energy. Poets call it fire. Eastern thought calls it Chi, or
Kundalini. The Bible calls it Dahbar, the Word of God—a pregnant expression that Christianity will later birth forth as The Universal Christ. (Cf. John 1:1). We'll unfold this insight throughout the book.

The earth [universe] was a formless wasteland . . .

Gen. 1:2

The tiny dot vibrated trillions of times a second—a formless, hyper-hot, black soup of unimaginable, churning, chaotic energy. Scientists say the dot was held together by infinite density and infinite gravity. Like an all-consuming black hole from which nothing could escape, the dot should have stayed eternally closed in on itself. But it didn't. Instead, it opened and expanded. Scientists don't know how or why the newborn universe began to expand. For this to happen, the dot would have had to be infused with a new energy—an "outside" energy—that was even greater than the infinite density and infinite gravity that was holding it together. But what energy can be more infinite than infinite? Our understanding is baffled. Scientists, doing the best they can, say that the newborn universe experienced a "one-time, anti-gravitational phenomenon." This is a statement of fact that explains nothing. The Biblical writers had a better idea:

A mighty wind swept over the water . . .

Gen. 1:2

Into the hyper-hot, black, chaotic soup entered the Infinite One, who at this time had no name and was imagined as a mighty wind. The wind was the power of the Spirit of God entering the newborn universe, creating a special, life giving union between God and creation. In response, the newborn universe awoke to the Infinite One who had come to dwell within it, and recognized the Infinite One's name, "I-Am-With-You." God became present within the universe, gifting it with tremendous love. Quickened by God's presence and love, the universe became pregnant with galaxies of wondrous possibilities. Being pregnant, it began to expand. To change the image, energy began moving in all directions like ripples in a stirred-up pond. Wherever the ripples crisscrossed, they vibrated, like the strings of a violin and produced different "notes." We call these "notes" of energy "sub-atomic particles," to which we give such names as electrons, quarks and photons. Although they are vibrating notes, or foci of energy, we often imagine these sub-atomic particles as dots.

At first, the energy particles were wild; all they could do was crash against one

another, bounce away, and crash again. In the stormy confusion, the notes formed no melody. All was cacophony and chaos. Electrons and protons, caught up in frenzied individualism, created an electrical charge that trapped the photons, the energy particles that we know as light. As long as the photons were trapped and unable to flow freely, no light was present in the newborn universe. All was dark.

. . . darkness covered the abyss

Gen. 1:2

For 300,000 years, the vibrating notes of the universe refused to come into sync. Slowly, patiently, I-Am-With-You nurtured them and soothed them, teaching them order and peace. In due time, the electrons and protons learned and responded. Now no longer chaotic and self-absorbed, they peacefully began to discover who they truly were. In their new self-knowledge, they learned that they possessed an amazing quality—they were attracted to one another. Instead of crashing about in chaotic individualism and mutual hostility, they learned that they could join together in loving marriage. Rather than shrieking with cacophonous noise, they could form a melody. This they did. In the universe's first "act of love," the electrons and protons joined together, married and formed atoms. Now newly alive, the tiny vibrations of energy played the first strains of the music of the spheres.

The new marriage bore fruit. Within the atoms, the electrons' electrical charge was reversed and the captive photons were set free. In the blink of an eye, glorious light filled the universe from end to expanding end.

God said, "Let there be light," and there was light.

Gen. 1:3

The writers of the Bible possessed no knowledge of particles, electrons, protons, atoms, or the flow and reversal of electrical charges. Yet, in their own way, they recorded the fact that universal light preceded the light of our sun.

Now the atoms discovered that they, too, were attracted to one another. The single notes that formed the music of the spheres were attracted to join together and form great harmonious chords.

Scientists call this universal attraction gravity. They know, of course, that gravity exists and they know how it works. But they don't know why gravity exists. In fact, they really don't know what gravity is. Perhaps they will never know. Perhaps only poets and mystics will know.

Poets call this universal attraction allurement and enchantment, and they love to sing of it. The attraction is truly universal. It occurs not only among atoms and molecules but among galaxies, stars, planets, and here on earth, among plants and animals. Plants express it in their cross pollination, and animals express it in their natural curiosity about their surroundings and in their herd instincts and maternal instincts. When this universal attraction reaches the human level, we call it love. Love, in all its expressions, is simply built in to the universe. In a very real way, the universe is literally made of love.

As the universe expanded, love continued to work her magic. For example, a law of thermodynamics, called entropy, says that as the universe expanded, the atoms should have arrayed themselves in one big, formless cloud. But that did not happen. Instead, the expanding universe formed itself into distinctive shapes and flared forth into the sweeping panorama of galaxies and stars that give us the poetic beauty of the night sky. The presence of divine love raises our scientific understanding of the law of entropy to a majestic new height.

While poets sing of universal beauty and love, and spirituality celebrates them, today's science gazes upon them in awe and wonder. As an example, we can look at Fermilab, the center for high energy physics in Batavia, Illinois. In its very architecture, it expresses the awe and wonder that today's scientists are experiencing as they see ever more deeply into the beauty of the universe and even into the love that shines forth from the heavens. Fermilab's Wilson Hall is comprised of twin towers whose design was inspired by a Gothic cathedral in Beauvais, France. Rising side by side from the prairie, the towers do not go straight up. Rather, as they rise, they approach each other to form what looks like two praying hands. Imagine. A contemporary scientific building that images prayer!

Also, outside Wilson Hall, straddling the road, stands an unusual, three-armed arch, named, "Broken Symmetry." Viewed from directly beneath, the three spans of the arch appear to meet perfectly at the top. This gives the viewer the symmetrical view that we could expect from the law of entropy. But from every other view, we can see that the three spans do not meet perfectly at the top. They come together in broken symmetry, just like the different galaxies come together to form the distinctive pattern of the night sky.

What today's scientists see as a beautifully luminous universe, the Biblical writers saw as a burning bush, luminous with an Interior Fire that makes it radiant without consuming it, (cf. Exodus 3:5). As today's scientists look in awe and wonder at the night sky, Moses looked in awe and wonder at the burning bush, and realized that he was standing on holy ground. He took off his shoes and thereby told us that wherever on earth we stand—wherever in the universe we stand—we too should "take off our shoes" because we are standing on holy ground. The earth and the entire universe, ever luminous with the indwelling presence of I-Am-With-You, is sacred.

The sacred universe inspires us with ever deeper awe and wonder. Today, we have come to realize that when I-Am-With-You entered the newborn universe, it not only began to expand but it also began to organize itself. Formless energy began to organize itself into vibrating "notes." Sub-atomic particles organized themselves into atoms; atoms organized themselves into molecules, and so on—all the way up to the universe's organizing itself into the great galaxies that spin in the sky. Self-organization is a sign of life. From its very beginning, the universe showed the sign of life. The pregnant possibilities of the newborn universe were *living* possibilities. One of the great breakthroughs—in science, art and spirituality—is the realization that the universe is a living reality. It is alive!

Our awe and wonder continues. If the universe is alive, then it possesses psychic, i.e., mental, attributes. By organizing itself into distinct forms—all the way up to its birthing forth of conscious life—the universe shows us that from its beginning, it was endowed with the seeds of consciousness. The universe was created, not just of energy, but of *conscious* energy. Universal energy is *consciously* organizing itself. In fact, is it now plausible to say that universal energy is not only conscious, but that it is *consciousness itself.* This conclusion is not all that far fetched. Let's keep in mind that the universe is the created image of the living, conscious God.

One more point. If the universe is conscious—in fact, if it is consciousness itself—then we can also say that it also enjoys a conscious, living *freedom.* We can say that the primordial vibrating notes of energy were, in their own primitive way, free to organize themselves into an electron, or a quark, or a photon, or any other particle. Some say that the primordial selection process was simply a function of randomness and chance. But just as our understanding of entropy has been raised to new heights, so today our understanding of randomness and chance is being refined and raised. We now know that chaos itself is actually a form of order. What appears to be randomness and chance can now be seen to be a deep form of conscious and free self-organization.

Nothingness. Creation. Life. Consciousness. Freedom. Vibrating notes. Self-Organization. Particles. Atoms. Galaxies. Suns. Planets. A sacred universe. Untold numbers of living possibilities. How easy it is to contemplate new vistas of awe and wonder for the universe, the world and ourselves. How easy to be attracted to the new dance of Christ.

Thus evening came and morning followed—
the first day.

Gen. 1:5

The Biblical writers were not referring to a day on earth. Rather, with no scientific knowledge to call upon, they were describing the first stage in the evolution of the newborn universe, a stage that occurred billions of years before the earth was formed. With mystical insight, they expressed thousands of years ago what has now become a scientific fact. And they also expressed evolution in a fascinating way. In our language and culture, we describe a day as running from morning to evening. The biblical writers describe it the other way around, as running from evening to morning. In his book, *Genesis and the Big Bang*, (Bantam Books, 1992), Scientist Gerald L. Schroeder, Ph. D., points out that in Hebrew, the word for "evening," *erev,* carries not only the meaning of being dark but also of being mixed up, thrown together, and disorderly. Conversely, the word for "morning," *boker,* carries the meaning of the first light that makes things distinct, discernible and orderly. By describing days as running from evening to morning, the biblical writers are telling us that creation is an ongoing, "daily," movement from darkness to light, from disorder to order. They are telling us that the universe was not simply created 15 or so billion years ago and left at that. Rather, in the beginning, the *process* of creation began. The process—the evolution of creation—is still going on today and it will continue to go on until the end of space/time. The new spirituality calls us to collaborate with I-Am-With-You in the daily creation and development of the world—to continue fulfilling the ongoing work of creation.

Another way of saying that the universe is in the process of evolving from darkness to light and disorder to order, is to say that it is evolving from chaos to cosmos. The word, "cosmos" comes from Greek, and means "beauty." (Note the word, "cosmetics.") When the ancient Greeks looked at the night sky, they saw that it was beautiful and so they called it *cosmos*, "the beautiful thing."

When the Biblical writers described creation as days of movement from darkness to light, or from chaos to cosmos, they anticipated by thousands of years the dynamic understanding of order and chaos that scientists have only recently discovered. Using today's science—and then going deeper—we can take a look at creation's movement from chaos to cosmos, and, for example, explain the deepest reason why we can see. Very simply, scientists say we can see because we have eyes and because light is present. By "light," they mean photons, the light particles that are streaming throughout the universe and literally striking our eyes. When we look at the moon, for example, the moon's photons fly across space and strike our eyes. We are literally moonstruck.

As we saw earlier, light first appeared in the universe when atoms were formed and the photons were set free. But what if atoms had not been formed? What if electrons and protons were still ensnared in chaotic hostility? Photons would still be locked up as they were at the beginning of the universe, and all would be totally dark. We would not be able to see anything or anyone. But atoms did form; photons were set free. Chaos did begin to give way to cosmos. Why? Scientists can give us no rational answer. Yet an answer is available. We can say that, ultimately, we can see because I-Am-With-You, the Spirit—One and Trinity—came to dwell within the universe, and brought it the order, peace and love that made light possible, and that made us possible, so we could see the light with our human eyes. If the Spirit were to withdraw from the universe, the forces that hold it together would dissipate. Gravity would disappear, as would electro-magnetism and the weak and strong atomic forces—the four basic forces that hold the universe together. Electrons and protons would separate, atoms would explode, photons would once again be trapped, and universal darkness would again reign. Stars would turn to dust. Plants, animals, mountains, machines and we would disintegrate. Primordial rage would return, and the whole universe would revert to hellish chaos.

Spirituality teaches us how to see. We can "see" God in the very fact that we can physically see. God, the indwelling Spirit, is present everywhere. But in this world, nobody sees God directly. We can see the indwelling Spirit only indirectly. Those who can see spiritually can see the Spirit in the luminous beauty of the night sky, in a grain of sand, in a tree, flower or animal, in the eyes of a loved one, in a job well done, in a community or economy well run, in a ballerina's leap, a child's smile, in the order of mathematics, in a soulful poem or piece of music, in someone giving a thirsty person a drink of water, in a nation striving for peace and justice.

This way of seeing has traditionally been beyond the scope of science. Scientists have traditionally seen their job as discovering and studying the physical expressions of the universe—from the microcosm to the macrocosm—and explaining them within a coherent system of natural laws. Other considerations, they would tell us, belong to poetry and spirituality. Yet many of today's scientists are learning to look beyond the traditional limits of science and are finding themselves standing in awe and wonder on common ground with poets, artists and mystics. After 400 years of sometimes hostile separation, science, art and mysticism are now opening us to astounding new insights into what the universe is, and into who we are. Physicist/writer Brian Swimme says we are in a position to reinvent the human person—by which he means we are also in a position to reinvent the universe and the world. We can add that we are now in a position to move Christ along on the road to greater evolution and development. Teilhard de Chardin was right; we are truly going through the greatest change the world has ever known.

Christ, of course, is Jesus' title. He is Jesus, the Christ. Here it will be good to explain what we mean by that title. "Christ" is the name we give to the union of God and the universe. It is a Greek word that means, "anointed." To anoint is to touch something or someone, usually with oil, usually for the purpose of making that thing or person holy or sacred. When God entered the newborn universe, he touched, or anointed it, at every point in time and place. He made the whole universe—past, present and future— sacred. The whole universe is anointed, sacred, Christ. This is the universal reality that Jesus took to himself. He is God-with-us, God in loving union with the entire universe—all centered in one person.

In him were created all things
in heaven and on earth [i.e., the universe].
. . . He is before all things,
and in him all things hold together.

Col. 1:16ff

[It is God's plan] to sum up all things in Christ, in
heaven and on earth.

Ephesians 1:10

We could say that by the time Jesus was born, the universal
Christ that he took to himself was already 15 billion years old.
Today, the same Christ is 2000 years older—and wiser. Christ will
continue to grow and develop until the end of time. On earth, as
the global Christ, he will continue to grow and develop especially
through his people—all those who live in good will, love and compassion. Teilhard de Chardin said that cosmogenesis is
Christogenesis. As the universe, earth and the human community
grows and develops, Christ grows and develops. The more we grow
in justice, peace, freedom, joy, humility, hope and love, the more
Christ grows. The more we learn what it means to be human, the
more Christ learns. The more we mature, the more Christ ma-
tures. The dance of the universe—especially the dance of the human community on earth—is the dance of Christ.

Jesus came to earth to be the fulfilling Christ. He came to
bring our union with God to its fullest possible development. But
because our union with God had been stained by the Fall, he also
came as the redeeming and saving Christ, who repaired the union
by his death and resurrection. If nothing had gone wrong, Jesus
would have come anyway, and he would not have had to suffer and
die. St. Paul tells us of Jesus,

. . . though he was in the form of God,
[he] did not regard equality with God
something to be grasped.

Rather, he emptied himself
He humbled himself,
becoming obedient to death . . .

Phil. 2:6-8

The new spirituality includes our own dying in order to live. To grow and develop, we will die many times to old ways and mindsets and rise again to new worlds of meaning and love. One day we will die to space/time and rise to a new world of eternal life and love unfettered by any space/time restrictions. The universe follows the same pattern of dying in order to bring forth new life. Five billion years ago, a very particular star was living its life in the sky. Its particles were joined together to form such elements as hydrogen and helium, and iron, lead, gold and other heavy metals. Though the star was indeed beautiful, it did not regard itself and its beauty as something to be grasped and held on to. When the fullness of its time came, it emptied itself and died a very special death. In its dying, it lit the sky with the brilliance of a supernova, like the glow of the Christmas star that would light our sky much later. Coming apart, the self emptying star filled millions and millions of miles of surrounding space with the swirling particles of its former self.

For a while, the separated particles "lay buried" in their tomb of disintegration and isolation. But even though they had been violently blown apart, they never lost their inborn gravitational "love" for one another. In time, they began to come back together again. A resurrection took place. In due time, the scattered hydrogen and helium atoms joined together to form a new star, a new sun. Then the heavier elements, having been thrown farther out in space by the explosion of the old star, spun themselves into nine new planets. So it was that 10 billion years after the first flaring forth of the universe, and five billion years ago, in Christ-like fashion, the old star gave its life and "rose again" as a new solar system, whose third planet out from the new sun came to be called, Earth.

THREE

The Beginning of Earth

Different cultures and traditions have different views as to where the earth came from and what it looks like. One ancient people told of a battle that their gods fought against a gigantic sea monster. In the battle, the monster was torn to pieces, and one of the pieces became the earth. Some Native Americans see the earth as the back of a giant turtle. They see life on earth as coming from a woman, who was carried down and placed on the turtle back by a flock of birds. Artists and astronauts see it as a beautiful blue and white sphere hanging delicately in a black sky.

The ancient Hebrews saw the earth as having been created by God in the shape of a pie, with a flat surface and mountains ringing its rim like a rippled crust. At first, the entire pie was submerged in water. Then God fashioned a blue metal dome and raised it above the surface of earth, the way a large tent is raised from the ground. As this dome rose, it pushed the water upward. Thus, between the earth's flat surface and the dome, space was created for the atmosphere.

God said, "Let there be a dome in the middle of the waters to separate one body of water from the other. And so it happened. God made the dome and it separated the water above the dome from the water below it. God called the dome "the sky."
Evening came and morning followed—the second day.
Genesis 1:6-8
You stretch the heavens out like a tent . . .
Psalm 104:3a

THE WORLD OF THE BIBLE

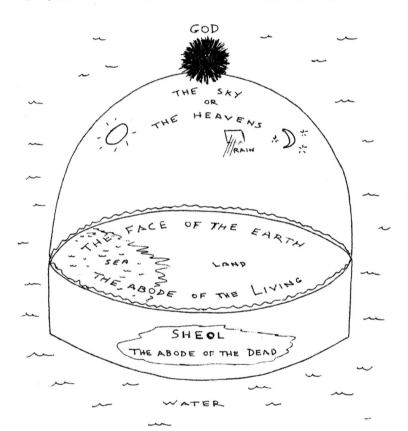

Another word for the sky among the Hebrews was "the heavens." The Biblical writers then tell us that God created the sun, moon and stars, and fixed them to the inner surface of the sky-blue dome. The dome turned once a day, so that for a time there was night and for a time there was day. God also put water gates or flood gates in the dome. Whenever they opened, the water that was above the vault fell through and provided rain.

It is easy to say that the Biblical description of the earth and sky is not scientifically correct. More exactly, it is not scientifically correct today. But it was "scientifically correct" when it was written. It represented the best understanding of the people at that time, just as our description of earth and the sky represents the best scientific understanding of our time. So when we say that the Bible's understanding is scientifically incorrect, we should keep in mind that our own scientific understanding is incorrect—or at least in constant need of being updated. If the Bible were written today, the writers would certainly not use the same scientific understanding that we find in the Book of Genesis. They would use the latest understanding of science today—which we can say is actually the latest update of the Bible's understanding.

In another context, however, the Biblical description of earth and the sky is beautifully correct. All we have to do is to go outside on a clear day, find a spot that gives us a sweeping view of the horizon and look up and around. From that vantage point, we could easily get the feeling of walking "the face of the earth" under the blue dome of heaven.

The Biblical writers didn't invent their picture of the earth; they borrowed it from an the earlier culture of the Sumerians. The ancient land of Sumer is today's Iraq. The Sumerians imagined a three-level world, patterned after a house with a basement, ground floor and upper floor. In the Hebrew view, living people occupied the ground floor. They "walked the face of the earth." Dead people were obviously different from the living. So the Biblical writers, who were poetic, story telling Hebrews, and not philosophical, abstract thinking Greeks, put the dead in a different "place" from the living. They put them in the basement of the house, or in the "filling" of the pie. This underground region, which existed only in the imagination of the ancient Hebrews, was called *sheol*, from which we get the word, hell. For the Hebrews, sheol or hell was the imagined place of the dead, not the place of the damned, as it later came to be for us. Jesus, after his own death, "descended into hell," i.e., he visited the dead in sheol to announce to them that they could now enter heaven.

To complete the picture, God, who is "superior" to us and the whole world, lives in a palace on the upper floor, on top of the vault of the sky, where there is water.

> You build your palace on the waters above . . .
>
> Psalm 104:3b

In the drawing of the world, God is depicted as dark, because the Hebrews knew that no one sees God directly. They saw God in everyone and everything on earth, even while they knew he was "up" above the sky. So when they prayed, "Glory to God in the Highest," they meant, "Give glory to God from the highest places on earth." They went up to their roofs and to the mountain tops to get as close as possible to "heaven" where God lived. Even today, many of us still look "up to heaven"—to the sky—when we pray, imagining that God is located up there. We also use this same image when we say that Jesus "ascended" into heaven. And many of us still imagine that after we die, we will go "up" to heaven and somehow fly about in the sky, e.g., as Michelangelo depicted on the ceiling of the Sistine chapel. Some atheists use this same image to deny the existence of God. In the 1950's, for example, Soviet astronauts orbiting the earth, dutifully reported to their atheist superiors that there were absolutely no sightings of God up there.

Getting back to our story, the appearance of the atmosphere was another step from evening to morning, from chaos to order and beauty. The primeval atmosphere churned with tremendous natural forces that produced torrential rains, which in turn created oceans. For a while, earth was divided between a single land mass, which we call, "Pangeia," and a single ocean.

> God said, "Let the waters under the sky be gathered into a single basin, so that the dry land may appear." And so it happened. . . . God called the dry land "the earth" and the basis of the water he called "the sea." God saw how good it was.
>
> Genesis 1:9-10

For a long time, the atmosphere was thick and dark, like an ever-present, heavy fog. The sun, moon and stars, though present, were not visible. Nevertheless, the light of the sun was able to penetrate the fog and do its evolutionary work in earth's water. The Biblical writers, of course, had no microscopes. They couldn't see that the newborn oceans, warmed by the sunlight, teemed with microscopic organisms that began the process of producing oxygen and aquatic plant life, and later, terrestrial plant life. How then, other than revelation from God, do we account for the fact that they saw and understood so much?

When the rising tides and breaking waves hit the seacoasts, the seeds of plant life were planted on earth's beaches. From the pregnant sea water, oxygen floated up into the foggy atmosphere. In time, youthful earth brought forth vegetation.

> Then God said, "Let the earth bring forth vegetation: every kind of plant that bears seed and every kind of fruit tree on earth that bears fruit with its seed in it. God saw how good it was. Evening came, and morning followed—the third day.
>
> Genesis 1:11-13

The Bible does not say that God created vegetation, plants and trees, but that God commanded the earth to bring them forth—a Biblical awareness of the earth's living, Spirit-directed ability to evolve and produce new forms of life. In the ancient Hebrew mind, creation is not something that happens once and is over; it is an ongoing process. Evolution is the ongoing, Spirit-directed process of creation, that is going on from within the earth herself. The Spirit is present within every one of earth's atoms, continuously making "mother" earth pregnant, and quickening her to birth forth new life as the fruit of her womb. There is no need to look at earth as a clump of dead dirt, and then to wonder where life came from. We are completely correct to look at the earth as having been alive from her very creation and therefore as containing within herself the seeds of all earthly life—even human life. If we look deeply, we will see that earth's evolving life is immersed in and being directed by the creative, healing and world-evolving life of the indwelling Spirit.

As earth's plants and vegetation produced even more oxygen, the very heavy atmospheric fog began to clear. Soon the sun, moon and stars appeared in the sky. Day and night became clearly distinguished.

> God said, "Let there be lights in the dome of the sky, to separate day from night. Let them mark the fixed times, the days and the years, and serve as luminaries in the dome of the sky, to shed light upon the earth. And so it happened: God made the two great lights, the greater one to govern the day, and the lesser one to govern the night, and he made the stars. God set them in the dome of the sky, to shed light upon the earth . . .
>
> . . . God saw how good it was. Evening came and morning followed—the fourth day.
>
> Genesis 1:14-19

The introduction of oxygen into the world was an event of the greatest importance. Oxygen helped make life possible, and helped us learn a deeply important lesson about life. The very organisms that produced oxygen could not themselves tolerate a great abundance of oxygen. So by living their own lives, they died. Though not "conscious" of what they were doing, they made life possible for others by living their own lives to their fullest, which meant sacrificing themselves for others. The universe, being the cosmic Christ, began to act even more like Christ. The Christ-dynamic of dying so that others may live, thus entered into earth's evolutionary process. In time, this deeply spiritual Christ-dynamic entered into the deepest levels of the human psyche.

Oxygen brought about a radical change of plants, rocks and the atmosphere. Like Christ, of whom it is a special expression, oxygen was a two-edge sword, destroying old structures and bringing new ones to life. It made respiration possible. The ability to breathe made such an impact on earth, and later, on the human psyche, that billions of years later, Hebrew nomads could look into their psyches and conceive of the living Spirit of God as the "breath" of life.

Within the bubbling, foaming, frolicking salt-bath cradle of life, microscopic life forms grew and developed. Early organisms reproduced themselves by dividing in half. In this way, they grew and developed to the limits of their inborn possibilities. When these possibilities were exhausted and their own DNA could take them no further, some of them learned to eat other life forms in order to get more DNA. The dynamic of the predator and the prey was born—a critical development that, when it entered into the human psyche, could go in the direction of compassionate self-giving and service to others, or in the direction of lying, stealing and murdering.

Soon afterwards, sexes became distinguished and sexual reproduction was born. Evolution, however, placed the sexual experience dangerously close to the predator-prey experience. Today's news tells us all too often of people, especially men, who confuse the two experiences and who pervert the loving wonder of sex into the violence of rape, wife-battering and child abuse.

As the evolution of life progressed, earth birthed forth the egg layers. Dancing with new life, fish swam merrily through the water, serpents slithered onto the land, insects buzzed and birds flew freely through the skies.

Here we can note an important point in our understanding of evolution and spirituality. Neither the Bible nor science says that lower species simply evolved into higher species. There was no smooth movement up the evolutionary scale. In the Bible, each anew species is called forth by a command of God.

God said, "Let the waters teem with an abundance of living creatures, and on the earth let birds fly beneath the dome of the sky."
. . . God saw how good it was.

Genesis 1:20-21

In today's scientific understanding, each new species simply appears "by surprise." Why "by surprise"? Because, of the millions of fossils unearthed, no "missing link" between one species and another has ever been found. Today, most scientists agree that these links will never be found because they do not exist. The gap between the species baffles human understanding. An old argument said that each new species is the result of some mutation. But that view commands practically no respect today. Mutations can account for changes within the possibilities of parents' DNA or genes, but no mutation can produce more DNA or genes in an offspring than already exist in the offspring's parents. In truth, in both the Bible and in science, new species simply appear by surprise.

The surprise, however, while scientifically baffling, is not completely beyond our understanding. Let's take it one step at a time. We can rule out that one day, for example, a primitive pre-equine animal simply gave birth to a horse. Like begets like. To beget "unlike" requires something new. So we must imagine a picture more like this: one day a primitive, pre-equine animal conceived. At that moment, or very soon afterwards, something happened that changed the unborn offspring into a new species. Into the pre-equine fetus, new energy was infused from "outside" the parent. Where did this new energy come from? The most logical answer is that it came from the vast reservoir of unformed energy that makes up most of the universe. This unformed energy represents the universe's vast, untapped menu of possibilities.

As a result of the infusion of new energy into the fetus of the pregnant pre-horse, a horse was born, formed partly of its parents' DNA and genes and partly of altogether new energy. The horse represents a surprise jump or leap from its non-horse parents.

Scientists use the expression, "punctuated evolution" to describe the process that produces new species by surprise. Life leaps forward in a punctuated manner, much like a word in a sentence "leaps forward" from the words that precede it, and like sentences and paragraphs "leap forward" from the sentences and paragraphs that precede them. In either case, the new word, sentence or paragraph, while carrying forward the meaning that precedes it, is the result of new energy infused into the writing process by the author.

Poets would say that life leaps forward in an ever surprising dance of joy. Spirituality can call it the dance of Christ.

Today, science, art and mysticism can agree that all that exists arises from the unformed energy of the universe. Every observable form in the universe—stars, planets, mountains, electrons, etc.— is the emergent, observable expression of the unformed energy of the universe.

As the process of creation continues, earth herself continues to show forth the wondrous unformed galaxies of possibilities that live within her. Earlier we saw that the newborn universe could have been expected to expand into a formless cloud of particles. But it didn't. It broke its monotonous symmetry and formed the wondrous array of stars that make up the night sky. Directed by the indwelling Spirit, earth followed the same pattern. Apparently defying the law of entropy which would have kept her locked into her simplest forms, earth began to make trillions of irreversible "decisions" that led forward to the emergence of ever more complex forms of life. In her own good time, she brought forth animals with spinal cords and nervous systems—a wondrously advanced organization over earlier life forms. Every new species that earth produced was a new surprise, a natural miracle.

> Then God said, "Let the earth bring forth all kinds of
> living creatures: cattle, creeping things, and wild animals of
> all kinds. And so it happened.
>   . . . God saw how good it was.
>
>   Gen. 1:24-25

There are still scientists who say that life on earth appeared by chance. Using the old paradigm that sees earth as a ball of dead dirt, they see no way that earth herself can be alive, and they see no need for an indwelling Spirit, to give earth form, direction, purpose and destiny. But reason, the very tool of science, seems to be against them. Even if earth somehow contained within herself the possibility of life, according to the laws of mathematics, it would take hundreds of billions of years for life to appear by the process of chance. The earth is only five billion years old, and life appeared on earth surprisingly early. Even granting the speeding up of the process by mutations (which we have already discounted), chance does not seem to be a reasonable answer for the arrival of life.

The stage is now set for life's greatest miracle. From the first moment of creation when the energy dot appeared, to the Spirit's entry into it, causing it to expand and take form, to the birth of atoms and galaxies, to the death of our own "Christ-star" and the birth of our solar system and our earth, to the birth of water, air, plants and animals—all was consciously and purposefully aimed— by earth herself in collaboration with the indwelling Spirit—toward bringing forth the human community, the most excellent expression (so far?) of creation and evolution. New dancers are about to enter the stage.

FOUR

Rediscovering Ourselves as Fully Human

> The Lord God formed man out of the clay of the
> ground and blew into his nostrils the breath of life, and so
> man became a living being
>
> Genesis 2:7

The ancient Hebrews imagined us as being formed from the dust of the earth. In their Biblical story, they write of the "Divine Potter," who takes some dry Palestinian soil into his hands, wets it and turns it into a reddish clay. The Hebrew word for clay is *adam*. In the story, the Divine Potter took the clay into his hands and began to shape it into the form of a human person. It was a job that would take many steps and many millions of years.

By shaping us out of clay or earth, God endows us with humility. The word, "humility" comes from "humus," soil or ground. To be humble means to be close to the soil, to be earthy. From both the Bible and science we can say that our bodies are formed from the earth. Our humble birth, however, is not cause for low self-esteem but for celebration. The earth from which we are formed is not dead dirt but the living, christed, sacred earth within which the Spirit dwells. When the earthy, humble Jesus directed us to be humble, he was telling us to be a joyful part of the earth, just as he was.

It is a living earth that is the dwelling place of God—of the living Spirit. The Spirit's presence within earth does not make the earth God. That would be pantheism and not Christianity. Rather, the Spirit's presence within earth anoints earth and makes it a union of the divine and created, and therefore makes it a "local" expression of the universal Christ. Like the universe, earth is experiencing constant, living evolution and growth. And, as Teilhard de Chardin said, as the universe and earth evolve, so Christ evolves and grows. In de Chardin's terms, cosmogenesis is Christogenesis.

Let's pick up the earth's evolution—and Christ's—by going back about 70 million years from the present. About that time, two pre-primate mammals came together and conceived an offspring. At that moment of conception, or maybe a little later, the indwelling Spirit infused new energy into the conceived creature. This new energy did not come from the two parents; it was completely beyond the possibilities of their DNA endowment. Rather, the Spirit took new energy from the vast pool of unformed universal energy. She then formed and focused this new energy into earthly energy, and infused it into the fetus. In due time, the pre-primate mother gave birth to a totally new creature—a primate. The primate offspring was similar to its parents in some ways, and yet surprisingly different from them. In fact, the offspring belonged to an entirely new species. The gap between the parents and this new species was not merely a physical one but a qualitative one. The new species was so different that it could not possibly be explained as any form of mere genetic mutation of the part of the parents. The parents simply did not have it in them to produce such an offspring.

Time passed, and the indwelling Spirit directed earth to produce even more surprises. New pregnancies occurred, and when they did, the Spirit took new unformed, universal energy, focused and localized it and infused it into new fetuses. New primates appeared—gibbons, orangutans, gorillas and chimpanzees—each surprisingly different from its parents.

Then one day, following the Spirit's infusion of yet more new universal energy into a pregnancy, there appeared a particularly interesting new species: pre-human hominids. They had larger brains than their primate "cousins" and a "personality" that allowed them to sense the gap between themselves and the others. So they moved apart from the others and went off by themselves.

About 4 million years ago the Spirit again infused new energy into a fetus, and hominid parents, who lived in southern Ethiopia, brought forth a special offspring. It was a female, whom scientists have named, Lucy. Though not human, Lucy represents a very special, new form of the living clay that the "Potter" was shaping. DNA taken from people all over the earth can be traced back to her. With her, our primal, bodily experience of who we are begins to come together in earnest. Thanks to the new and different energy infused into her, Lucy's possibilities were greater than those of her parent hominids. Her brain was larger. Though she still swung from trees, she also walked on two feet, so she could look around at the florid, buzzing, chirping earth, and up at the bright, blue sky. Her new abilities quickened her sight and focused her attention in a new way, deepening her sensitivity to her environment. From Lucy we pick up our first sense of feeling "at home" in the forest, with its flowers, trees, animals, sounds and fragrances, and under the sky. In and through her, a distinct appreciation of the diverse richness and free movement of life was born. Today, in the deepest parts of our bodies and psyches, we feel the far off echoes of Lucy's experiences and development.

In the hands of the Potter, evolution leaped forward, revealing new surprises and new facets of the earthy face of Christ. New hominids moved out of the forests and into the open savanna areas. Their eyes achieved frontal focus and their countenance changed. Their hands became more adept at grasping, and soon, their hand-eye coordination developed—the same coordination that later would help us write a word, paint a picture, fly a plane and hit a baseball. Their throats, tongue, teeth and lips were refined in preparation for the gift of speech. But they were not yet human.

Another infusion of new energy into existing DNA by the Spirit, and still new hominids learned to shape tools with their hands and to define their work. The period of childhood was prolonged, necessitating a longer period of parental care. From their primal experience of work and caring parenthood arose the first stirrings of awe and wonder. This in turn flowered into the fashioning of artistic items and emotional communication—all of which we eventually inherited.

Some 2.6 million years ago, new energy caused our clay ancestors to leap another gap of evolution. New hominids hunted animals for food and clothing, and developed the experience of being predators. Deep within their psyches, they became conscious of having cosmic authority to kill. With this new consciousness, they experienced the adrenaline rush of the hunt and the terror that arose when they confronted dangerous animals. In a very special jump forward, they learned to control fire, thus experiencing a whole new kind of power over nature. In the beginning of creation, the Spirit had entered the fire that was the primal universe and had allured electrons and protons to join together to form atoms. Now, billions of years later, the Spirit allured the developing hominids to join together around a hearth fire and form social groups for cooking and eating. Thus the early hominids endowed our psyches with our first consciousness and appreciation of the importance of being together in families and community—after the manner of protons and electrons that live together as atoms. Even today, we refer to families and certain groups as "nuclear communities." Yet, even as these hominids took ever more wondrous shape and form, living now in families and communities, they still were not human.

Later, the Neanderthal and Cro-Magnon hominids appeared. Thanks to their surprising new energy and consciousness, they were endowed a primal sensitivity to the changes of the seasons and to the ebb and flow of life. They experienced, and passed on to us, a respect for death and the dead, an awareness of a power greater than ourselves, the meaning and importance of rituals and sacrifices, and the first stirrings of religious consciousness. Also from these advanced clay ancestors arose our primeval mythic consciousness—not the English word, "myth" as a story that is not true, but the Greek *mythos*, an imaginative way to tell the truth. It is from our mythic consciousness that emerge our imaginative, emotional, poetic, musical, artistic, narrative, "right-brain" flow and expressions of ourselves and our lives. (By contrast we also have a *logos* consciousness, from which emerge our "left-brain," intellectual, scientific, mathematical, philosophical, theological and prosaic expressions of ourselves and our lives. It is the *logos* consciousness that dominates today's culture.) The birth of mythic consciousness gave us the cave drawings of our hominid ancestors. Yet, even considering the religious and mythic sensitivity of the Neanderthals and Cro-Magnons, they still were not human.

The Divine Potter was now ready for his almost final shaping and forming of his clay—adam. Once again, the Spirit infused unformed energy into a hominid and caused another jump across a gap to another species. Homo Sapiens was born—the pre-human hominid we most closely resemble—and to whose level we are often reduced in those areas of our culture where spirituality is missing, e.g., Modern World science and public education. Homo Sapiens inherited all the endowments given them by earth and all their ancestors—minerals, organisms, plants, animals, Lucy and all the ancestral hominids. Also, they now had all the DNA and genes necessary to make up a human person. With new layers added to their brains, they developed new skills. Their oral communication improved and their ornamentation became more expressive than that of previous hominids. Their minds awakened with primitive thought; their emotions were refined, and their wills were better focused. Yet, Homo Sapiens were still not human.

Finally, after millions of years of loving, "hands-on" work, the Divine Potter had sufficiently shaped and formed his clay. Its features were sufficiently refined and its DNA and genes were sufficiently endowed with galaxies of new possibilities. Everything was ready for a totally unexpected new jump. Everything was ready for the biggest surprise of all.

> Then God said, "Let us make man in our image,
> after our likeness. Let them have dominion over the
> fish of the sea, the birds of the air, and the cattle, and
> over all the wild animals and all the creatures that
> crawl on the ground."
>   God created man in his image;
>   in the divine image he created him;
>   male and female he created them.
>   Genesis 1:26 and 27

In an entirely new and unexpected act of creation, the indwelling Spirit infused into Homo Sapiens a final, great surprise. Instead of infusing new, unformed universal energy, she infused Homo Sapiens with her own divine energy. Without making Homo Sapiens divine, the indwelling Spirit anointed—christed—Homo Sapiens with a special spark of divine energy. Immediately, the pre-human Homo Sapiens ceased to exist and a new creature was born, Adam-Eve, the human community, male and female. It is into this human community that we are born, and it is from this human community that Jesus was born.

On that graced day, the human community awoke, looked around and asked the questions that forever echo in our souls, "Who are we? Where did we come from? Why are we here? Where are we going?" And from within the great galaxies and supernovas that light the night sky; from within earth's air, mountains, seas and meadows; from within the birds, fish, plants and animals; from within all history— past, present and future—and from within our own anointed consciousness, came the indwelling Spirit's answer.

"You are not Homo Sapiens or some enfleshed machine. You are Adam-Eve—unique,

individual members of the human community; my beloved daughters and sons, sisters and brothers to one another. You are my specially created and endowed human word, my human image and likeness, my special expressions of Christ. In you the Spirit of Christ—God, One and Trinity—dwells in creating, healing and transforming intimacy and love.

"Like me, your Creator, you are creative—filled with galaxies of possibilities, able to know yourselves, earth and me with loving intimacy; free to build the world into a more luminous expression of Christ. Like Christ, your Redeemer and Savior, you are humble healers and peacemakers. Like the Holy Spirit, you are capable of loving in a way that can refresh the face of the earth and transform the world.

"You are artistic, passionate, poetic, story-tellers and singers, dancers, painters and sculptors. You are mythic, intuitive and insightful, intellectual and reasoning, understanding, philosophical, wise, skillful, cultural, believing, hoping, joyful, prayerful, morally free and responsible, visionary, mystical, prophetic, loving and worshipful. You are endowed with both space/time and eternal dignity, integrity, meaning, purpose and destiny."

Born from a new spark of Genesis, we know in our hearts and souls that we are not merely Homo Sapiens or some enfleshed machine, with some "extra features," like grace and faith added on, which we can accept or reject and still be human. While we have the same DNA and genes as Homo Sapiens, we are immersed in a transcendence that makes us different from our clay ancestors by a distance so vast that it cannot be explained in any terms of mere physical, genetic or chromosomal mutation. Firmly and humbly placed on earth and in space/time, we soar like eagles into eternity/infinity. (Earth, plants, animals, etc., are also immersed in eternity/infinity. The difference is that we are immersed in a human way, a self-reflexive, free, etc. way.) While all creation is the image of God, we are the image and *likeness* of God, made of a special infusion of divine energy into creation. Creative, healing and loving like God, we gather into ourselves the entire universe, all earth and nature, and make them greater images of God and expressions of Christ. To remove the transcendent radiance of our special endowment of divine energy—to reduce ourselves merely to our genes, or our environment, our net worth, or even to our minds and souls—is to destroy our very humanity. We are specially luminous creations of God!

As images and likenesses of God, we are human expressions of God, who is both One and Trinity.

Like God, who is One, each of us is a unique individual, endowed with luminous dignity and worth. Like God, who is Community-in-Trinity, each of us is a living, inter-acting member of the entire human/earth/universal community.

Like God, our Creator/Parent, we are creative and life giving, called and empowered to continue the work of creation by building up ourselves, others, society and earth.

Like Christ, our healing Savior, we are healers, called and empowered in the Spirit of Christ to serve and heal ourselves, others, society and earth by being instruments of forgiveness, reconciliation and peace, in our individual and families lives, and in the institutions of our society.

Like God, the Spirit of unifying and transforming love and compassion, we are called and empowered to be loving and compassionate—to go beyond the requirements of justice and peace and to extend self-giving, and when necessary, self-sacrificing love and compassion to all we meet or influence.

Our identity and empowerment as creative, healing and loving images and likenesses of God gives us our luminosity and sets us on the spiritual path to growth and fulfillment in collaboration with the indwelling Spirit. In this way, we give contemporary meaning to what St. Iraneus said in the 2nd century, "The glory of God is the human community fully alive!" In and through our luminous humanity all creation is gathered up and joyfully sings to God the universal hymn of thanks and praise, "I am! I am! I am! I am with you!"

FIVE

Re-Membering Ourselves to Earth

Being human means living on earth and with earth. Our bodies are made of the earth and we are destined to live on earth, not only while we are in space/time but also, as we will see later, forever. Even in eternity, we will be people of earth. On the last day, the earth will die but it will not end. It will rise again along with us— changed, as we will be, beyond our imagination. We will live on earth forever.

One of the basic spiritual flaws of Christianity has been to disconnect us from earth. To be holy, many Christians believe, we have to separate ourselves from earth and nature. We were taught that we are only pilgrims, passing through earth on our way to our true destiny, which is heaven. This meaning of heaven puts it up or out in space somewhere, away from any life on earth. It dis-members us from earth and easily leads to our failure to care for it. A Secretary of the Interior once sold beautiful wilderness to a lumbering company because, he said, the world was going to end soon, and we would have no need for the forest. Until recently, ecology has not been a mark of Christianity.

Twenty-first century spirituality reconnects—re-members— us firmly back to earth, of whose atoms our bodies are made, whose air we breathe, whose water we drink, whose food we eat, and whose sunsets fill our very souls with stirring beauty. Our bodies are the clay that the Divine Potter worked in his hands, touching us and shaping us so lovingly for millions of years. When we arrived, earth became conscious and loving, as we are. In and through us earth fulfills the purpose of her creation as our natural home and nurturing mother. We gather up in ourselves all of earth's life and history. When we arrived, all life on earth—past, present and future—changed. In and through us, earth looks around and gazes in wonder at her stately mountains, rushing waters and swirling night skies,. She enjoys the aroma of her fragrant flowers, and delights in the sounds of her buzzing insects, singing birds and her barking, meowing, mooing and roaring animals. In and through us, amoebas squirm purposefully, fish swim knowingly, plants grow decoratively, insects pollinate industriously, whales splash their fins thunderously, birds sing praisefully, and animals meow, bark, moo and roar proudly.

In and through us, our pre-human ancestors take on new life and look at the world with a new sensitivity. They walk upright with a new purpose, hunt with new vigor, conquer fire with new power, gather together in families and communities with new emotion, grow crops with new appetite, paint images with new vision, respect life and death with new awe, and kneel ritually with new spirit.

> God blessed them, saying: "Be fertile and multiply; fill the earth and subdue it. Have dominion over the fish of the sea, the birds of the air, and all the living things that move on the earth." God also said: "See, I give you every seed-bearing plant all over the earth and every tree that has seed-bearing fruit on it to be your food . . .
> . . . God looked at everything he had made and he found it very good. Evening came and morning followed—the sixth day.
>
> Genesis 1:28-31

Our earthy roots help give us our "instructions" on how we are to "subdue" the earth. We are not to ravage her, exploit her or pollute her. We are to care for her—to work creatively to fulfill her possibilities; to heal her hurts with a Christ-like compassion; to collaborate with the Spirit who dwells within her to help her become an ever more luminous expression of God's creative wisdom, an ever more luminous expression of Christ. We are not earth's kings and queens but her nurturing caretakers. Though our minds and souls take us into infinity and eternity, earth is and always will be our natural home. She is our *oikos*, our "household," which we are responsible to care for and manage. The Greek word, *oikosnomikos*, which gives us the word, economics, means not just the care and management of money, but the care and management of the whole household—earth included.

How close are we to earth? Here's one way to answer the question. How old are you? You will, of course, answer by giving your age in years. Actually though, all your muscles, tendons, blood vessels, bones, etc., are renewed every few weeks, so they are younger than you are. Now your body is made of atoms—the same atoms that make up all the earth. In a very real way, we can look at mountains and trees, birds and animals, and say, "You are atom of my atom, flesh of my flesh and bone of my bone." Earth is five billion years old. The atoms that make up your body were formed when earth was formed, following the explosion of our Christ-star. So your atoms are five billion years old. You are truly made of star-stuff. Finally, the atoms that make up your body are themselves partially made up of electrons. The electrons that make up your body are 15 billion years old, having been formed just after the initial flaring forth of the newborn universe. How old are you? In part, you are as old as the universe and as old as earth herself. Part of you has actually participated in the history of the universe and in the history of earth. Possibly—probably—your own electrons were once part of dinosaurs, mountains, birds, bacteria, oceans, lions, and other people's bodies. Take a deep breath. According to the laws of physics and mathematics, you have just inhaled about 400 electrons that were once part of Julius Caesar's body from when he was alive. Take another deep breath and breathe in another 400 electrons—this time from Jesus' body from when he was alive.

Scientists tell us that electrons "remember" every place they've been and every person they've touched. So we are all free to wonder where our electrons have been and what they remember. We can even wonder, does this explain how some people remember "past lives?" Our point here is that your body, in a very special way, is an "eye witness" to the history of the whole universe—from all its chaotic scrambling in its first few minutes, to its "surprise" when it began to expand and take on order, through all its irreversible, self-organizing, forward moment; to all the peace and joy of being able to form beautiful expressions in the glowing night sky. All history is present in your body. In you all that has ever happened is gathered up, localized, focused, humanized and made luminously conscious and self-reflective within your psyche. Imagine all the experiences and possibilities that are whirling, spinning and dancing within you. Imagine all the possibilities the history of the universe is giving you right now. Imagine the creativity, healing and world-transforming love that is pregnant within you!

Part of the wonder of who we are is our personal, individual integrity. For all the places our electrons and atoms have been, for all the people whose bodies they once helped to form, for all the psyches they have stirred, for all the memories and echoes that resound within us, nevertheless, each of us is distinctly our own person. Even though our bodies are made up of "used" or "preowned" material, each of us is a fresh, new, individual person—unique and unrepeatable—within the human community. No one has ever been the same person we are, and no one will ever be. (Even a clone of ourselves would be a different person.) Each of us can look in the mirror and say to ourselves and the world, "Appearing here and now, in person, one time only!"

How much God-like power must we possess in order to hold together the localized energy that we are? How much power holds us together as unique individuals, who can feel and think and believe all the way from earth to eternity. How much power permits us to take materials that have been around for literally billions of years—or to take new materials made by today's medical science—and make them personally and uniquely our own. We can take atoms, food and even metal or plastic medically made body parts, and elevate them to the level of a living person. The answer to how much God-power we posses is beyond all imagination. Consider the energy that is holding together the paper of the page you are now reading. If extracted correctly, it would be enough to heat and light your house for years. The energy that makes up only a few ounces of plutonium, if released all at once, can destroy a city. How much energy, then, does it take to hold together a human person? How much power must you possess to be able to see this page, to read and understand it, to be educated, to love another person and all people and earth, to form a family, do a job, join with others to build a bridge, create peace (or fight a war), design a culture, change a paradigm and renew a value system, and create and live a new spirituality?

What is this awesome power that holds us together so magnificently? It is love, the power that holds the whole universe together. Love holds the earth together, holds each one of us together, holds societies together, and holds the world together. The absence of love is the definition of disintegration. Later we will consider the tragedies that we bring upon ourselves when we fall short of love. But before we can appreciate the power of disintegration, we have to appreciate the commanding power of the love that gives us our human integrity and meaning. Love is not something we have; it is what we are. We are human images and likenesses of God, of Divine Love. We are enfleshed love, love incarnate, in human form.

Little wonder then, that 15 billions years into the universal flaring forth, in the boondocks of a very average galaxy, on a speck of dust thousands of times smaller than the smallest star, earth awoke in human form, and newly born people looked around and asked, "Who are we, that you should be mindful of us?" (Adapted from Psalm 8:5). The human dance of Christ had begun.

SIX

Rediscovering Our Luminosity

I first spoke publicly of the new creation story and the new dance of Christ by delivering guest lectures on the new spirituality at several colleges. The presentation I will describe in this chapter is an excerpt and composite of many presentations, and the students are composites of many of the young people I've met, and who have enriched my life beyond measure.

In each case, I began by taking a moment simply to look at the students in front of me. I gazed at their youthful beauty—I always make it a point to tell young people they have no idea how beautiful they are—and I envisioned their wondrous possibilities. I then looked deeper until I saw what I was looking for. Then I started to speak.

"At this moment," I began, "I'm looking at you—at your beauty and youth, at your energy, and all the way inward to your very atoms."

The students smiled at being thus "undressed."

I continued. "I see every one of you as luminous."

"You mean, we're all lit up," one student quipped.

"O. K." I smiled, "If that's what you want to call it. I see your atoms whirling and buzzing and expressing the energy that you have—that you are. I see you as made up of energy. And to make your energy visible to myself, I see it as light. To me, you are made of light. All your atoms, cells, muscles, bones, organs, features—all are made of light. All your feelings, thoughts and actions are made of light. Each of you is an individual expression of universal energy or light."

I paused to give the students a moment to digest what I was saying. They liked being seen as energy and light and smiled at one another and at me.

I continued. "Further, when I say I see you as individual expressions of universal energy, which I see as light, I mean that I see each one of you as constantly emerging from universal energy. In my view, you are therefore constantly in touch with all the energy and light of the universe. Now, universal energy can become anything it wants to become; it is filled with galaxies of possibilities. It can become a star, or an atom, or a lion, or an flower, or anything else, including a person's body, mind and soul. So by being in touch with universal energy, each of you is in touch with a universe of possibilities. Who knows what possibilities live within each of you for wondrous development toward your own personal fulfillment and the fulfillment of the world.

"Of course, there will be individual limits to your possibilities. Your physical and mental, and even your social and financial situations, will influence your possibilities. But never forget that you are in touch with the whole universe of possibilities, so never be quick to cut your possibilities short, or to cut yourselves off from some aspect of fulfillment you might achieve.

"When I speak of your fulfillment I mean your taking advantage of every opportunity to become more luminous persons, especially by being ever more luminous expressions of creativity, healing and world-transforming love and compassion."

The students laughed. Some shook their heads.

One said, "I've never heard anything like that before. What kind of religion is that?"

Another student spoke up. "I'm a Quaker. I've heard something like that before. I've heard of the inner light."

Another student called out, "I'm a Catholic, and all through twelve years of Catholic school, I never heard that."

Another student called out, "I never read anything like that in the Bible."

The Quaker turned to him, "Its got to do with mysticism. It is in the Bible, if you read it correctly."

"I do read the Bible correctly," he shot back."

I took back the floor. "There's even more about your luminosity. I see your light shining with a very special brightness and intensity because I see a Light within your light. The greater Light that is making you specially luminous is the Spirit of God, dwelling within each of you, animating, shaping and directing you toward the best possible fulfillment of who you are. In fact, if the Spirit were not present within you, you would not even exist. Her presence is ultimately what makes you human, what makes you alive, and what makes you who you are. And all the while that she is directing you toward the fulfillment of your best possibilities, she is keeping you free to collaborate with her or not.

"How can we be directed and free at the same time?" a student asked.

"That's part of the great mystery of being human. The indwelling Spirit is the Spirit of transcendent love. In her love, she is calling you to herself, she is calling you to discern her presence and to collaborate with her, but if she didn't see to it that you are free to answer her or not, then you wouldn't be human. You'd be a puppet.

No one commented on the fact that I was referring to the Spirit in the feminine, so I continued. "I see the indwelling Spirit touching you at every point throughout your person—your body, mind and soul. And at every point where the Spirit is touching you, she is anointing you and making you sacred. And at every point where you are being touched by her, I see you not only as sacred, but as immaculate. Each one of you, deep within yourselves, is immaculate. Of course, by the time we work our immaculate luminosity to the "outside," by the time it shows up as who we are and how we act in the everyday world, our immaculate luminosity has dimmed. For some of us, it shines very brightly; for others, not so brightly. For a few—I hope it's a few—it is not bright at all; in fact, it is quite dark. I'm thinking of Hitler and people like child abusers and serial killers. Yet in everyone, the luminosity never goes out. The Spirit never leaves us. She is always touching us, anointing us, making us sacred. So we are always, at some point within ourselves, luminous and immaculate.

Finally, since the Spirit is touching you at every point of your being, she is making you a loving union between her divinity—between God—and your humanity. That makes each of you, in my eyes, an expression of Christ, who is the total loving union between God and all humanity, centered in one person."

My words were greeted with a classroom full of mixed comments and shaking heads, as the students loudly chorused their surprise and disbelief in what I had said. As I waited for the din to subside, one particular student caught my eye. She too was shaking her head, but not the way the others were. She was moving her head very slowly, expressing deep sadness. I looked back at her. She lowered her eyes and I looked away. When the students grew quiet, I repeated that as a Christian, I saw each one of them as luminous expressions of Christ, and as immaculate at every point of contact with the indwelling Spirit throughout their person—while emphasizing again that I did not expect the atheists and non-Christians to agree with me. I added that the new Christian spirituality finds substantial common ground with other religions and traditions and fully respects them—but that would be another lecture.

After my presentation, a group of students gathered around me. The student who had shone such deep sadness was among them, but she hung back a little, letting the others grab my attention. Another student approached me and spoke up with anger. "I'm a good person," she announced firmly. "And I'm an atheist. I don't need any God or anyone to make me good. I can do the job all by myself." She paused, and then added, "I don't need anyone! I'm all right by myself."

"Are you doing a good job of being good?" I asked.

"Yes, I am. I study hard and I help people whenever I can, as long as they don't try to influence the way I live." She spoke with strength and anger. "So then," she concluded, "what about this Spirit and the luminosity you talked about. Why do I need them?"

I took a moment to let her emotions subside a little. Then I answered, "I would like you to look deep inside yourself to see what is making you study hard and help other people. I mean I would like you to look really hard and deep. Can I count on you to do that?"

"For how long?"

"For as long as it takes."

She smiled knowingly. "For as long as it takes for what? What should I look for?"

"I'll leave that up to you." I left it at that. It would do no good to press her further. She had just made it clear that she didn't allow anyone to influence the way she lived. I could only hope that she would some day look deeply into herself and see that her goodness was rising not only from herself but from Someone other than herself who dwelled within her. I hoped—I prayed—that she would experience her own goodness as a gift she had received from God and that—to her own credit—she had developed.

Another student volunteered that all he was interested in was business administration. I goaded him a bit. "You mean, you're interested in having a career in business administration and making a lot of money from it."

"That's it," he answered brightly.

"But what about being human? I mean, even business administrators should learn what it is to be human, shouldn't they?"

The student hesitated for a moment. "Well," he said somewhat thoughtfully, "Being human would be nice, but I think I'll wait for others to become human first. In the meantime, I've got to make money. After that, maybe I'll learn to be human."

I looked at him, hoping he was joking, at least a little. He wasn't.

When everyone else had left, the student who was hanging back approached me. I looked at her and simply said, "Yes?"

With deep sadness, she said softly, "No one ever told me I was immaculate inside." Before I could say anything, she walked away.

Standing there alone, I watched her go out the door and disappear. There was such sadness in her eyes—and even in her walk. What had she been taught? What had happened to her? In my years of spiritual counseling, I have met many Christians who were told from a very young age that they were corrupt sinners in constant need of repentance. Some of them needed psychotherapy to get over the depression that such a spirit-devastating message had caused them. Had this happened to this young student? Had she possibly even acted upon her terrible misinformation? If young people are told often enough—by adults they love and respect—that they are corrupt and dirty, they sometimes act that way. Had she done something destructive to herself or to someone else? I prayed that the Spirit would break through to her and tell her how interiorly beautiful and luminous she was.

These three composite students exemplify some of the great difficulties that spirituality is facing in today's society.

The atheist student was adamantly on her own, fully in charge of herself, solely responsible for her human meaning and purpose. She had adopted a radical individualism that isolated her from God and from others. Even those she helped, she seemed to keep at a distance. "I don't need anyone!" she had proclaimed. She didn't want anyone influencing her life, having any say in her choices. I could see her helping others strictly on her own terms, without really touching those she helped. And I feared that in dismembering herself from God and others, she had also dismembered herself from herself. Her manner and her voice showed me that her overly-strong affirmation of herself was also a statement of angry loneliness. How well did she really know herself and accept herself? How sensitive was she to her human need to be interconnected with others? What had cut her off from herself and others? To whom or what would she reach out to overcome her loneliness?

The business administration student had disconnected himself from his own humanity. He saw himself only as a money making machine. And he saw his college only as a job training center. Becoming fully human was not a value to him. (I wondered if it was a value to his college.) For him, business administration will generate activity only for income or profit; it will never dance the dance of life.

The student who had never been told she was immaculate inside had been cut off from her true human beauty, worth and dignity. I could not imagine her looking into herself, because she already knew that all she would see was corruption and darkness. For her, there was no poetry, no joy of life, no vision to open her to the Light and Love that glowed within her making her luminous. Without some change in her life, she could find no path to true fulfillment and happiness. Maybe someone would come along to love her enough to make her take a different look at herself. Maybe that would be the way the Spirit would break through to her.

When I look at the obstacles that block our way to our fulfillment as luminous human persons—radical, isolating individualism, secularism and consumerism, and the devastating sense that God is not with us because we are corrupt and dirty—I think of author Thomas Berry. Berry says that obstacles like these are so deeply implanted in us by our culture and certain kinds of religion, that they may now be said to be "genetically encoded" into us. If we follow his insight, we see that before we can begin our path to the new spirituality and our fulfillment in it, we will have to perform some "genetic surgery" to remove the obstacles that lie in our way. First, we will "diagnose" what went spiritually wrong with the Modern World, and then we will excise the great spiritual mistakes that Christianity has made over the past centuries. This will open the way for us to become whole in the new dance of Christ.

PART TWO

Why the Old Music Died

SEVEN

The Loss of Spirituality

What Went Wrong

Spirituality opens our eyes not only to our luminosity but also to the darkness that lives within us. The farther we walk along the spiritual path, the more clearly we see the corrosive forces within ourselves and the world that are working against our luminosity.

Yet, spirituality does not simply tell us that something is wrong within ourselves and the world. That is the job of morality. Spirituality goes deeper. It lets us see first our human luminosity, and then it shows us the corrosive influences that live within ourselves and the world and that work to darken our luminosity. It gives us our deepest and clearest insights into ourselves and the world, and moves us to gather up and strengthen our spiritual energy so we can act to intensify our luminosity.

We can see the difference between morality and spirituality when, for example, Hitler was coming into power. The world could see that something immoral was brewing, but it was not spiritually insightful enough to really see with any clarity what Hitler was about to spew upon the globe. As we look back, we can now see that the Nazi horror was foreseeable. But the world, in its spiritual weakness, did not see clearly enough what was about to happen and so did not act in time to prevent the horrors of Nazism without violence—or at least with minimal violence. By the time the world woke up and saw what was happening, it took vast Allied armies and worldwide death and destruction to overcome Hitler and the holocaust.

Spirituality, then, not only teaches us to see and foresee, but it also lets us look back and see again what we could have seen, and should have seen. We can use our spiritual hindsight to look back at the Modern World's pattern of brokenness, with the intention that what we learn about the past, we can apply to foresight into the new world that is now being born. The Modern World came into existence in the 16th century, following the Renaissance and the Reformation. It attained its full form in the 18th century, in accord with the insights of Sir Isaac Newton (1642-1727). In fact, the Modern World mindset, or paradigm, is often called the Newtonian paradigm. Very simply, the Modern World's way of seeing, organizing and evaluating was patterned after our solar system, with its sun and nine orbiting planets. Each planet was seen as a solid object flying through space around the sun, with the whole system being held together by gravity. This view gave the Modern World a choice. It could focus primarily on the system as a whole, i.e., on the community, or it could focus on the individual planets. It chose to focus on the individual planets. Each planet was seen primarily as an individual in its own right, orbiting along its own path, following its own momentum, moving toward its own goals. The gravity exerted by the sun could have been seen as the pull toward community; instead it was seen as a threat to the individuality of each planet's movement and purpose. In the Modern World, the individuality of each planet developed into a radical individualism, and the community—especially as represented by the government and the church—came to be seen by many as a threat to the individual.

The modern "guy meets girl" story typifies the Modern paradigm of radical individualism. The story opens with the guy and the girl orbiting in their own, individual space toward their own, individual goals. In one way or another, they meet and begin orbiting side by side. This kind of orbiting has a name; it is, "relationship." In almost every story, "relationship" includes a sexual relationship, and sometimes, nothing else. The guy and girl have sex and tell all their friends about it. They practice the Modern

World version of "safe" sex, i.e., they give their bodies to each other without the risk of giving themselves to each other. They become an "item," but never really a couple. They continue to live their individual lives, following their own orbits toward their own goals, taking care to protect and develop their own self-esteem along the way.

As the story progresses—after a few commercials—the guy and girl begin to feel the pull of gravity. "Commitment" looms on their horizon. But commitment is outside the meaning of relationship. It means becoming one, uniting and wedding together at a deep, self-giving level. To these Modern World individuals, uniting and self-giving mean being swallowed up by the other person and losing one's individual freedom, interests and goals. This is too much. Individual freedom, interests and goals are the whole meaning of life. To fall into commitment is to cease being an individual; it is to die. One of the great clichés of any Modern World story is "the fear of commitment." Some friends may tell the guy and girl that oneness and self-giving are really a path to greater self-realization and fulfillment. But the guy and girl don't buy it. They reject commitment by trivializing marriage, reducing it to some old-fashioned custom or to a meaningless signing of a piece of paper. Instinctively, the guy and girl realize that marriage is both a private act and a public act—it tells the community that two people have become one and that from now on, they will help build the community as a married couple and later as a family. But the guy and girl have no real community to relate to, so becoming a stable part of the community "doesn't compute". After a few more commercials, the story ends—actually it just runs out— with the guy and girl breaking up and going back into their own individual orbits.

In the Modern world, other people are not only fellow "orbiters," they are also dangerous competitors, vying with us for both our individuality and our material goods. "I don't want anybody telling me what to do!" and "I want to be Number One!" became the battle cries of the Modern World. With telling insight, Jean Paul Sartre wrote his famous line about the Modern World, "Hell is other people." In such a hell, competition is the principal value—siblings compete for affection, co-workers compete for pay and position, students compete for the greatest opportunity for career success, political parties compete for power, entertainers compete for the greatest attention. Nations also compete for position and power, and churches compete for the truth. "Dog eat dog" competition was carried on outside the unifying and humanizing concept of community.

As the Modern World ended, raw, dehumanizing competition began to wear some people out. They looked around for some effective or compelling alternative, but finding none, many of them fell into the spiritual darkness of disengagement. They simply "dropped out." In the 1960's many young people separated themselves from mainstream society, and then confirmed their separation by turning to different styles of dress and music, drugs and free sexual expression. The "Woodstock" generation dreamed of creating a new world and a new spirituality. The movie, "Easy Rider" symbolized the new world and the '60's spirituality as a motorcycle ride across the country. The ride itself—whizzing past the everyday world at every turn—became the whole story. There was no destination and no need to have one. Moving, "orbiting," existed for itself alone; the only value was to keep on riding. Along the way, the riders stopped only long enough to pick up some companions, so they too could enjoy the ride. The riding just went on and on, leaving the riders with the constant need to fill their nagging emptiness by being, "on the road again."

We can now see that the Modern World was eternally adolescent, and its adolescence redounds even into the present day. Comedian Jerry Seinfeld gained great success with his TV sitcom about four people who lived as friends on the surface but who, underneath, were isolated and so frightened of any adult commitment to life that they never grew out of their prolonged adolescence. Fittingly, they ended their series imprisoned.

Even more frightening is the insight that the Modern World was schizophrenic. Individuals and the institutions of society were locked up in separate, air-tight compartments or boxes, with little or no way to unite themselves into one overall, functioning community. More and more people lived in their own individual box— their city box or suburban box, their economic box, their secular box or their sacred box. The races lived in their separated boxes, as did the sexes, school departments, churches and nations. The competitive, adolescent, schizophrenic Modern World endowed us with a great ability to make a living, but left us with little ability to make a life.

By the 20th century, the Modern World's built-in flaws were diminishing its life and spirit to the point where Yeats could look at it and see that it was falling apart, that its "center could not hold." The Modern World was losing its grip on life itself. Two World Wars had unleashed unspeakable death on the world, and religion had been unable to prevent it. A new way of seeing and living was needed, a new world need to be born, and with it a new spirituality.

Philosopher Albert Camus poignantly expressed this need in 1948, when he addressed a group of priests and bishops in Paris. While he was still an atheist, he challenged the Catholic church to join him in his own spiritual quest toward a better world. "Maybe we can't create a world in which no children suffer, but we can at least work to create a world in which fewer children suffer."

While the new spirituality looks at the corrosive influences that are at work in ourselves and the world, and still prays, "Lord have mercy on us," it focuses its eyes on the deep luminosity with which the Spirit graces us and the world. It prays with renewed hope, "Lamb of God, you have taken away the sin of the world." While we still live in a world where sins are present, Christ has taken away the root sinfulness of the world and revitalized the world's deep, immaculate luminosity. We can realistically pray and work for a world that is marked by fewer sins and less suffering.

As we look back over the spiritual decline of the Modern World, from the split between the secular world and spirituality, all the way to that fateful day when an atomic explosion was judged to be necessary to stop a horrific war, our "diagnosis" reveals three specific spiritual ills that have to be excised through "genetic surgery." The first is Christianity's encouragement—and even sponsorship—of the domination of men over women and of masculine traits over the feminine—which was the spiritual breeding ground for all forms of domination, e.g., of one race over another, of Christians over people of other religions, of the rich over the poor, of the powerful over the weak, and of humans over the earth. The second ill is Christianity's false separation of the body and soul, which is the spiritual root of materialism, secularism, consumerism, and of atheistic science, education, politics and economics. The third ill is the separation of Christians from the everyday world, which is the spiritual root of Christianity's fall into irrelevance—from modern science all the way to its irrelevance in the 1960's, to its lack of credibility in so many quarters today.

With our diagnosis in hand, let's begin our genetic surgery.

EIGHT

The Christian Madonna-Whore

"If you drag a hundred dollar bill through a trailer camp, you'll pick up all kinds of trash." This remark was made by a friend of President Bill Clinton, after the President had been accused of seducing a young women when he was still Governor of Arkansas. The degrading remark against women was really not new; it echoes all the way back into history. The President's friend could just as well have said, "If you drag an apple through the Garden of Eden, you'll pick up all kinds of trash." To correct a long standing cliché, the world's oldest profession is not prostitution but the disparaging and trashing of women by men. Throughout Christian history, women have been held up to the ideal of the virgin-mother "Madonna, " while at the same time being seen as seductive whores. This ancient, "genetically encoded" perversion has been infecting individuals, institutions, cultures and religion from the very beginning of history. So our genetic surgery will have to be radical. We will have to get to the root of the disease.

Many excellent books are available that tell in detail the history of sexism from many points of view, e.g., social, cultural, economic and religious. Here I will focus on the deepest roots of sexism—the spiritual roots. When we look at sexism from the viewpoint of the indwelling Spirit, we see that while this aberration includes political, social, psychological and economic aspects, it is deeper than all of these. It is a spiritual illness that lives in our very souls.

God created the human community—men and women—not only as good but also as equal in humanity and dignity. All Biblical scholars agree that the Bible expresses the human equality of men and women by saying, in its own ancient language, that men and women are bone of one another's bone and flesh of one another's flesh (Genesis 2:23).

The prophet, Ezekial, has God saying this to all men and women,

> You were stamped with the seal of perfection,
> of complete wisdom and perfect beauty . . .
> Blameless you were in your conduct from the
> day you were created . . .
>
> Ezekial 28:12 and 15

Sexism, then, was not built into creation and was never God's intention. It is a pollution that men brought upon the human community. How did this happen? What went wrong? Ezekial tells us,

> Until evil was found in you . . .
> Ibid.

Nobody knows what actually happened. But something did happen; something went wrong. The human community fell from grace, and sexism is one of the fundamental results of the Fall. Let's look at the familiar old story with new eyes. As we do, we'll keep in mind that while the truth that the story carries comes from God, the language and culture that carry it to us are not God's, they are those of the ancient Hebrews. This distinction is of the greatest importance.

The story of the Fall is a classic example of *mythos,* a very imaginative story that carries the truth. The truth that the story of the Fall carries to us is that the human community—men and women—was created by God. There is no information whatsoever that says there was only one man and one woman at the beginning of humanity. The two individuals, Adam and Eve, are creations arising from the imagination of the ancient Hebrews. The truth is that God could have infused divine energy into the entire race of Homo Sapiens and created a large community of humans right from the beginning. The truth also includes the fact that when the human community fell, everybody fell.

The truth goes on to show us that the human community enjoyed the special grace and favor of God. The ancient Hebrews expressed this insight by placing the first humans in a lush, green garden—strikingly different from the dry, arid land of Israel. Also, our special grace and favor is expressed in the truth that we humans can know who we are. We can know that we are humans and not animals. We can also know that we are humans and not God. What we know, we can freely affirm and confirm. In fact, our dignity is so great that we can—in fact, we must—knowingly and willingly affirm ourselves as humans—as not animals and not God—but humans. To express this essential requirement of our self-affirmation as human, the ancient Hebrews made up a story,

> The LORD God gave man [the whole human community, men and women] this order: "You are free to eat from any of the trees of the garden, except the tree of knowledge of good and bad. From that tree you shall not eat; the moment you eat from it you are surely doomed to die."
>
> Genesis 2:16-17

To affirm ourselves as humans, we are required to affirm that we can tell the difference between good and evil. We know this difference, however, as humans, i.e., in a limited way. We do not possess the absolute knowledge of good and evil that God alone possesses. Nor do we possess the absolute degree of knowledge that God alone possesses. The test of Eden was God's requirement to all humans to affirm themselves as fully human—a little less than God (Psalm 8). To affirm ourselves as equal to God, as possessing absolute knowledge, would be to step out of our humanity and to fall into absurdity. The ancient Hebrews, in their deep wisdom, saw that this very temptation to affirm ourselves as God lived within the human psyche. It still lives within us today. Why was it put into us?

Physicist/mystic Brian Swimme, in his wonderful little book, *The Universe is a Green Dragon*, explains that such a temptation has to be there in order for us to be free. Being humans, Swimme notes, we are created as free and self-reflective, able to know ourselves and our wondrous possibilities, and able to enjoy our own beauty. In creating us this way, God took a chance. We are free to accept that our human freedom, knowledge and beauty come from God, or we can abuse our freedom and absurdly declare that our freedom, knowledge and beauty come from ourselves alone. If we did not have this freedom—and the ability to abuse it—we would not be human; we would be passive, unknowing puppets dangling from divine strings. The first humans had to say, "Yes, we know who we are; we know we are human and not You. We know this and we gratefully and lovingly accept ourselves for the humans that you have made us." That was what the first humans were required to do. That was the test that brought them face to face with the temptation that lived within them, and that lives within everyone of us.

Enter the snake. In the culture of ancient Israel, the snake represented temptation and evil. In fact, it represented Satan himself. Most unhappily, it also represented women. So in the minds and culture of the ancient Hebrews, Satan, temptation and evil were placed in affinity with women. To the Biblical writers, then, it was natural that when temptation came, it came to the woman.

> The serpent asked the woman, "Did God really tell
> you not to eat from any of the trees in the garden?"
>
> Genesis 3:1

Satan's approach is insidious. He does not present himself openly, because Eve would recognize him and repel him. He approaches her tangentially, by misquoting God. He is tempting Eve not to commit a sin but to tell the truth. She falls for his ploy. In her own commitment to truth, she corrects him.

> The woman answered the serpent: "We may eat of the
> fruit of the trees in the garden; it is only about the fruit of
> the tree in the middle of the garden that God said, 'You shall
> not eat it or even touch it, lest you die.'"
>
> Genesis 3:2-3

Without the benefit of modern psychological studies, the ancient Hebrews had the wisdom to understand the nature of temptation very deeply. Temptation must be rejected as soon as it appears. When Jesus was tempted in the desert, he immediately rebuked Satan. Eve, instead, fell into the lethal mistake of getting involved in a conversation with temptation, with Satan. She tried to tell the truth to the Father of Lies. The advantage was entirely his. The rest is history.

The story tells us that instead of accepting reality and confirming themselves as human, the human community stepped into unreality and absurdity, and tried to confirm themselves as God. As a result, the human community broke itself apart. People separated themselves from themselves, from one another, from earth and from God. The paradigm of fragmentation was introduced into the world.

Was the Fall a woman's fault? No. That's simply the way the story was written by the ancient Hebrew culture. Was it a man's

fault? No. The opposite extreme is not true either. The truth is
that the Fall was the fault of the entire human community. Whatever happened happened to all people and for all time.

On the other hand, some people today doubt that a Fall ever
took place. Yet, everybody knows that there is something wrong
with the human community, and that this problem is very deeply
ingrained. Some scientists say that humans simply evolved in an
imperfect way and that we are still working out our full meaning
and purpose. There is some truth to this view, but this truth is not
deep enough. In fact, spirituality sees it as a shallow and dangerous answer. What's wrong with the human community is not merely
a matter of working out our evolution. It is some flaw that touches
our very souls, something that misdirects us against our best understanding of ourselves, no matter how well evolved we are. It is
something within us that diverts our best efforts to make the world
more just, peaceful and compassionate. What's wrong is something spiritual. Certainly, our flaw influences our psychological,
sociological, educational, political and economic efforts—and even
our religious efforts—to make ourselves and the world more human. But it is deeper than all of these. It lives in our very souls. So
the solution must be equally deep. It must touch our souls and
animate and energize our efforts in every aspect of our lives.

To get back to our point, the Biblical story of the Fall of the
human community blames the woman because it was written
within a broken culture that was marked by a male-dominate
mindset. The ancient Hebrews simply could not have blamed a
man, or men in general, for the Fall and for what is wrong with the
world. Spiritual insights opens our eyes to the truth. We don't
know how long humans have been on earth. We don't know when
Adam-Eve, the human community, was born. We don't know when
the Fall took place. But all this certainly happened a very long
time before the Hebrew nation arose. So the ancient Hebrews themselves were children of the Fall. They inherited its blindness and
weaknesses, just like all other nations. When God revealed the
light of his saving truth to them, they received it in their own

dark, fallen way and recorded it in their own dark, fallen way. Nothing in the Bible says that God protected his chosen people from the aftermath of the Fall. Just the opposite. The prophets constantly pointed out that the Hebrew people were continuing to carry forward the effects of the Fall in their lives and social activities. The light of God's revelation, on one hand, and the darkness of the fallen Hebrew culture on the other hand, explain why Genesis contains great contradictions. On one hand it reveals the truth of God that men and women share human equality and dignity. On the other hand, it expresses the deep flaw of male domination over women. Spirituality sorts out the light of God's truth from the cultural darkness that carries that truth—not only for the Genesis story but for our own society today. It is God's pure, revealed truth and saving message—that we sort out from the dark aspects of Hebrew culture—that makes the bible shine with infallibility.

We can imagine how the ancient Hebrews might have told the story of the temptation and Fall of the human community, if they had not be caught in the darkness of male dominance of women. Let's imagine the temptation coming to Adam, and we'll imagine it happening in terms that fit "today's man."

"Yo, Adam! What's this stuff about not eating the fruit from that tree. You're not looking too good here. Where's your testosterone!? Grab the fruit. Go for it! Be Number One!"

If nothing else, our little re-interpretation shows that the Fall was the result of humans falling into absurdity by confirming that they were God. In the male dominant culture of Genesis, Adam, who represents all men, was certainly lording it over Eve, who represents all women. In his male pomposity, which would have been silly were it not so destructive, we see that the words of Ezekial fit him more than Eve.

> You became haughty of heart because of your beauty;
> for the sake of splendor you debased your wisdom.
>
> Ezekial 28:17

In the Biblical story, however, the skewed version of the Fall continues. The first result of the Fall is recorded as this curse,

> To the woman, [God] said,
> "I will intensify the pangs of your childbearing;
> in pain shall you bring forth children."
>
> Genesis 3:16

If we read it literally, it looks like the curse is brought down upon Eve and all women who will follow her throughout history. Is this so? No. A spiritual reading sorts out God's revelation from the way the Hebrews expressed it. With spiritual eyes, we see that this curse refers to the coming history, not of women alone, but of the entire human community. God is not cursing women to painful childbirth, but telling the entire human community—men and women—that because we freely broke ourselves apart—from ourselves, one another, earth and Him—we have also broken ourselves apart from every new generation that will be born. Pain will accompany the birthing forth of every human generation throughout time—not mere physical pain, which modern medicine can rightfully and morally remove—but the pain of anxiety and worry over whether the new generation will learn to live humanly or will repeat the faults and fragmentation of previous generations. No sexism here, but rather the true human condition of being born into a fallen and fragmented world, and the need for a deep and effective, healing and unifying spirituality.

Let's unravel another sexist curse:

> Yet, your urge shall be for your husband
> and he shall be your master.
> Ibid.

Many Christians read this curse literally as God's statement of what *should* be. God, they say, has ordained that husbands must control their wives by being their masters. In Biblical language, the opposite of "master" is "slave." If we take the Bible literally, then wives should be slaves to their master-husbands. But this is not God's statement of what *should* be. It is a statement of what actually happened after the human community broke itself apart. Male dominance over women became the curse of the human community—not the will of God. It is what men did—and do—to women *against* the will of God. Very importantly, it is a curse whose roots Christ removed from the world. Again, only a deep and effective spirituality can overcome this tragic absurdity.

The curse of male domination has expressed itself especially in the way men see their attraction to women's bodies. Throughout history, including the history of Christianity, women's bodies have been seen as the seductive cause of men's sins. The old affinity between Satan and women still lives in many psyches. Women's bodily functions, such as menstruation and child bearing, place them close to nature, to our living, "mother earth"—which the ancient Hebrews also placed in affinity with women and Satan. In masculine-dominant, sexist eyes, women's natural beauty, their menstruation, and their child-bearing makes them dirty. In Biblical times, childbearing made women not only physically unclean but also morally unclean. New mothers had to be "purified." Until recently, Roman Catholic women went to church following childbirth to be "blessed." This was actually a ritual intended to remove their moral uncleanness for having had sexual intercourse—

with their "innocent" husbands. Throughout church history, the perfect woman was presented to Christians as the Madonna, a mother, who nevertheless was a virgin. Eve, and all her sisters who married and had sexual intercourse, were really considered to be whores.

Shame now enters the story of the Fall,

> They realized that they were naked.
>
> Genesis 3:7

Many Christians know that the Fall did not come from a literal eating of a piece of fruit. (The fruit didn't become an apple until Medieval times. The Latin word for "apple" is *malum*, and the adjective for evil, in its neuter form, is also *malum*. So the apple is a play on words, the *malum malum,* or, "evil apple."). The true sin, many Christians say, was a sexual sin, namely, Eve's seduction of Adam. Yet Adam and Eve are portrayed as husband and wife. In their married love, they saw each other's naked beauty and attractiveness without shame (Gen. 2:25). Their marriage was not an occasion for sin. Even after the Fall, they were still married, and sexual intercourse was still good and pure.

So how do we explain the shame of their "nakedness?" This shame is a lesson directed to all of us. Because of the Fall, our minds are dimmed and our eyesight is shallow. We often do not take the time or effort to look deeply into ourselves and others—to see down to our very souls, where the full light of our human dignity shines. All too easily, our sight is only "skin deep." The Fall did not make our bodies dirty; it made our view of our bodies dirty. In our brokenness, we can separate our bodies from our minds and souls. We can covet each other's bodies (as we can also covet each other's status, money, reputation, etc.). When Adam and Eve were ashamed at seeing each other naked, they were not ashamed of what they saw but of the way they saw.

We can also look at Adam and Eve's shame in another way. When they saw their naked bodies, they realized with startling new clarity that they were truly human and not God. They saw with new and chastening insight how absurd they had been by trying to make themselves God, and for this they were humbled and ashamed.

Yet, the literal, sexual curse continues. Many men still see women as dirty, or as sex objects. The curse can also be contagious. How many women also see themselves that way? Remember the student who said, "Nobody ever told me I was immaculate inside." She was truly living a cursed life.

The absurdity continues. According to the skewed male-dominant paradigm, in a world where women are fallen and men are innocent, only men are capable of straightening things out. Men and the masculine human traits must dominate all societies—and the earth. Men don't have to listen to women or respect feminine traits such as nurturing, caring, listening and reflecting. They simply have to do their masculine thing—be aggressive, exploitive, competitive and expansive, and everything will work out.

Even at that, men don't have it so easy. Eve caused a curse to be brought down upon them too!

> "Because you listened to your wife . . .
> "Cursed be the ground because of you!
> In toil shall you eat its yield . . .
> By the sweat of your face
> shall you get bread to eat."
> Genesis 3:17 and 19

Now we finally know why the world is in such a mess—because a man listened to his wife. Poor, innocent-victim Adam. If he were alive today, he would no doubt sue Eve for damages. Eve's sin cursed Adam to a life of hard work. But not to worry. Men took care of this curse themselves. They turned hard worked into a virtue. The world admires men who work hard—not so much physically any more, since machines and computers have taken over that part of the job—but in their devising of plans to take power, sell goods and make money. The business executive who doesn't work day and night is a wimp. Even physical hard work is still good—at the gym. And men especially admire those men who work hard and sweat a lot while wearing athletic uniforms.

With the curse of hard work removed from men, the only curses remaining are those imposed on women. But, as we noted earlier, Christ has removed the root of all sin from the world, and in doing so, he has removed the root of all the curses that we have imposed on ourselves. Once and for all, men are not to dominate women. The masculine traits are not to dominate the feminine ones. Such domination was wrong from the first moment of creation; it is even more wrong after the coming of Christ.

Jesus related to women in a revolutionary way, as his human equals. He took the time to become aware of women's daily lives and tasks, and thereby give them importance (Mt. 13:33; Lk. 15:8ff; Mt. 25:1ff). He performed miracles at women's requests (Mt. 8:14ff). He was close friends with Martha and Mary (Lk. 10:38-42). He accepted anointing by Mary, and even defended her against criticism (Jn. 12:3ff; Mt. 26:10). He listened to women and learned from them (Mk. 7:24-30; Mt. 15:21-28).

Most striking of all was his conversation with the Samaritan woman at the well (Jn. 4:7ff). The very fact that he spoke to her at all was revolutionary. The Jews would never think of speaking to a Samaritan man, let alone a Samaritan woman. In any case, whenever a Jewish man spoke to any woman, he spoke only of necessary family matters, and beyond that, only of trivial things. Jesus, however, spoke to this woman not of trivial things or even of ordinarily important things. Rather, he spoke to her of the deepest concerns of her soul and of universal faith. With compassionate understanding, he sympathized with her for having been divorced five times. In his culture, this meant that she had been thrown out, with no say on her part, by five men who "owned" her. She was now owned by a sixth man. For all this, she was an outcast, even among the woman of her town. Jesus met her at the well at noon, the hottest part of the day. Women usually went to the well in the morning, when it was still a little cool. This woman had to wait until the other women had left. She went to the well alone, at the wrong time of day. Jesus accepted her and went on to reveal to her truths of faith that the men in his society would say no woman could possibly understand. Could this have been because the men were high and mighty while this woman had been brought low?

Yet, even despite Christ himself, today's Christianity still has trouble relating to women and listening to them. The genetic encoding runs deep. It showed from Christianity's very beginning. On the one hand, women were honored members of the newborn Christian church (Acts 1:24; 12:12). Who could have been a more honored member than Mary? Women enjoyed a variety of charisms, i.e., Spirit-given gifts of service and leadership. They gave instruction (Acts 18:26), they prophesied, i.e., spoke in and for the indwelling Spirit of Christ for the building up of the church (Acts 21:9 and 1 Cor. 11:5). St. Paul says that the women who prophesied had a gift that was greater than the gift of tongues. Other women ministered in the church (Rom. 16:1, 3, 6, 12). Recent research shows that women were ordained deacons, a major holy order just below that of priest.

On the other hand, in the very same letter in which St. Paul praised the women who prophesied, he said that women should be silent in church (1 Cor. 14:34). (We must wonder, did St. Paul or anyone else tell Mary to be silent?) The snake of sexism bit even this great foundational teacher of Christianity. Once St. Paul got into conversation with this temptation, he fell all the way. A few years later, he imposed total silence on women and decreed their submission. His "reasoning" is frightful.

A woman must receive instruction silently and under complete control. I do not permit a woman to teach or to have authority over a man. She must be quiet. For Adam was formed first, then Eve. Further, Adam was not deceived, but the woman was deceived and transgressed.

1 Tm. 2:11

St. Paul's fall into the darkness of the curse of male domination is especially confusing in light of his ringingly clear declaration that,

> . . . [in Christ], there is not male and female, for you
> are all one in Christ Jesus.
>
> (cf. Gal. 3:28)

Biblical scholars "explain" that St. Paul and the male leaders of the early church were traditionalists who didn't want to upset the public mindset of the time by setting women free. Preaching Jesus Christ crucified and risen from the dead was revolutionary enough, the scholars say, without adding the revolutionary teaching of treating women as human equals to men. This "explanation" does not even begin to justify the church's spiritual fall into a continuing policy of degrading women—a policy that has continued even into our time. That the church's fall was spiritual is shown, for example, in the church's vicious treatment of Mary Magdalene. She was a visionary woman, who accompanied Jesus during his ministry and supported him financially. It was she who was chosen to announce the resurrection to the apostles. She became a distinguished and prominent leader in the early church. Apocryphal literature tells of her being very close to Jesus. Yet Christianity, until very recently, felt it necessary to wrongfully portray her as whore—albeit a penitent one.

Christianity's loss because of its insistence on holding on to the curse of sexism is immense. Karen L. King, professor of New Testament Studies and the History of Ancient Christianity at Harvard University Divinity School, lists a series of views that were put forth by early Christian women. How different Christianity would have been if it had taken these views to heart:

— Jesus was understood primarily as a teacher and mediator of wisdom rather than a ruler and judge.

— Direct access to God is possible for all people through receiving the Spirit of Christ.

— Those who are more spiritually advanced, freely give what they have to all, without claim to a fixed, hierarchical ordering of power.

— An ethics of freedom and spiritual development is emphasized over an ethics of order and control.

— Both women and men could exercise leadership on the basis of spiritual achievement apart from gender status and without conformity to established social gender roles.

— Overcoming social injustice and human suffering are seen to be integral to spiritual life.

We can read the above list with both sadness and hope. In our day, Christianity has begun to listen to the women of old as well as to today's women. The "genetic surgery" is taking place. We pray that it truly cuts to the quick, and that from now on, in the one Christ, in whom there is neither male nor female, or better, in whom there is both male and female, Christianity will have no room for male domination over women or for the degradation of women in any way, or for all the other forms of domination that were spawned by this primary curse. May women finally be free to collaborate openly and fully with the indwelling Spirit of Christ and thus make their unique contributions as human equals with men in the work of creating, healing and transforming the world in the love and compassion of Christ. As it was in the beginning and was re-confirmed by Christ, women and men share equally in human luminosity, integrity, dignity, meaning and purpose. And so may it ever be.

NINE

The Spiritual Mistake of Saving Our Souls

I remember years back when on Saturday afternoons I went to confession. I would walk the few blocks to my parish church, find the shortest line and tell my sins to the priest. After receiving absolution and saying my penance, I would walk out of the church into the world of temptation. All the way home, I kept my ears closed and looked neither right nor left, lest I would hear some dirty word or see a girl who would tempt my weak body and upset my pure soul.

Throughout the history of Christianity, the human body has traditionally received "bad press." Christians certainly respect the soul, which most mistakenly believe to be supernatural, good and pure. The body, in contrast, is seen as natural, of lesser worth than the soul, and as the source of temptation and sin—almost not worth saving. Yet, the soul is as natural as the body. We'll see more about this in a later chapter. We can note here that pride, greed and envy, for example, are temptations and sins of the soul. The mindset of the pure soul vs. the impure body gives a false meaning to the Christian expression that our goal is to save our souls, because it can mislead us to think we should save *only* our soul, while we remove ourselves as much as possible from our body, with its temptations and weaknesses. This mindset serves, in effect, to dismember our soul from our body—with tragic consequences for Christian spirituality. It is now time to re-member our soul to our body. We can look to the Bible for help.

The ancient Hebrews were concrete, passionate, earthy people, who lived close to nature at every turn. When they looked at a person, they did not see a body and a soul but one, whole, living person. In fact, their language did not even have words for "body" as separate from the soul, and for "soul" as separate from the body. Whenever they referred to the body, or the flesh, they were referring to the whole person. For example, in Psalm 136:25, we read, "God gives food to all flesh." This means that God provides food for all people. In our language, we also use the word, "body" to mean the whole person when, for example, we say, "Was anybody there? Yes. Somebody was there."

The ancient Hebrews did have a word, *nephes*, which is often mistranslated as "soul", in the way that we mean soul, i.e., as separate from the body. This is not what the Hebrew word means. *Nephes* means life, or self, or person. It refers to the whole person. We see this use of the word, "soul" in our language when we say, "There were one hundred souls aboard that ship."

When the Hebrews referred to a person as a body, they were seeing the person as sensitive and emotional, as one who has desires and passions, and who is mortal and subject to illness and death. When they referred to a person as a soul, they were seeing a person as the image and likeness of God, as a child of God. Obviously, both terms could refer to the same person. Psalm 16:9 uses both terms together,

> Therefore my heart is glad, my soul rejoices; my body also dwells secure,

In our language we would say, "Therefore, *I* am glad; as the image and likeness of God, *I* rejoice; as one who has emotions and passions and who is weak and mortal, *I* also dwell secure." What a difference in the richness of meaning!

In the New Testament, the separation between the soul and body could be mistakenly understood when we read in English such statements of St. Paul's as this one,

> For if you live according to the flesh, you will die, but
> if by the spirit you put to death the deeds of the body, you
> will live.
>
> Romans 8:13

Biblical scholars tell us that St. Paul is not referring to the body as separate from the soul, as we would take his words in our language. And he is not disparaging the body. He is writing in Greek, which indeed, does have separate words for body and soul (that's where we get the mental separation) but he is thinking in Hebrew. He is telling us that if we give in to the corruptibility that lives within us, within our entire selves—body, mind and soul—we will die. But if we work in the power of Christ to overcome our corruptibility of body, mind and soul, we will live.

The Bible tells us that there is a corrosive influence living within us. But this corrosive influence is not living only in our bodies and not in our souls; it is living is us entirely—body, mind and soul. If it were living only in our bodies, then we would have to suppress our bodies so they would not contaminate our "pure" souls. In fact, the history of Christianity is filled with many such exhortations for us to suppress our bodily pleasures for the sake of saving our souls. This focus on the impurity of the body quickly narrowed itself to sex, which was generally considered to be only a "body" expression, and always close to sin, if not a sin in itself. Some early Christian writers even considered the sexual pleasures of marriage to be at least a venial sin—for which they blamed the woman. St. Augustine, who had his own sexual problems, was so overwhelmed by what he saw as the evils of the body and sex that he would not permit himself to be alone with his own mother. Even today, the Roman Catholic church considers marriage and parenthood, because of their "body" aspect, to be a secondary expression of spirituality in comparison to the primary honor it gives to celibacy. In this view, married people cannot fulfill their humanity and be as spiritually excellent as can celibate people.

In contrast to St. Augustine, St. Thomas Acquinas taught that we do no good at all by suppressing our body and our passions. Spirituality calls for us to fulfill our passions by expressing them reasonably. For Thomas, a reasonable expression of our passions was also a moral expression of them. Yet, despite this eminently sensible teaching, Christian spirituality continued to stress the suppression of our passions.

Today, we see more clearly that the so-called bodily appetites, e.g., for food and water, air, exercise, sex, and good health, are appetites of the whole person—body, mind and soul. My body alone doesn't experience passion; I do, as a whole person. Spirituality, then, focuses not on any separation of body, mind and soul, but on the luminosity of the whole person and also on the corrosive influences that live within the whole person. Our spiritual struggle is not simply to get our body under the control, but to make our total person more luminous. The indwelling Spirit is calling us and inviting us to look into ourselves and discover our God-given talents, interests and possibilities. She then calls and invites us to collaborate with her in working to fulfill ourselves and make our luminosity brighter and more visible. This involves fighting against the corrosive force that lives within us—body, mind and soul—and that would detract from our luminosity. With the Spirit, we live to fulfill ourselves—body, mind and soul—and we learn how to balance the needs of our body, mind and soul, so we grow as full persons and as ever more luminous expressions of Christ in and for today's world.

TEN

The Spiritual Mistake of Avoiding the World

Helga knelt in church and prayed. In accord with her pastor's constant exhortations she devoutly asked God to protect her from the outside world and all its temptations and dangers to her soul. After a while, her piety refreshed, she left the church and walked out into her German village. It was 1933. Helga was not interested in what was going on politically. Her pastor never spoke of such things. Her mind was firmly fixed on getting to heaven, not on living in the world. Twelve years later, now a war widow with two young children, she joined with her fellow villagers and told the American interrogators that she never had any idea what was going on down the road at Dachau.

At the same time, the Protestants in Germany and the pope in Rome were sadly wondering what more they and all the world's Christians might have done, if only they had realized in time. If only they had been able to act with any real influence in the world of the 1930's and 40's. In the Middle Ages, Christianity had ruled Europe and had acted with great influence in the everyday world. In the 20th century, after 400 years of decline, Christianity was so removed from the everyday life of Europe that it was unable to foresee or do anything to prevent a human tragedy of biblical proportions. With horrific consequences, the light of the world had gone dark.

Our genetic surgery now focuses on excising the roots of another great spiritual mistake—the Christian avoidance of the everyday world. Modern world Christians certainly knew that they were living in a "secular" world. It was the place where they lived and worked, but not where they believed and prayed. In fact, the church was often seen as their oasis of relief and protection from the secular world. From within the church's protecting confines, they could look out at the everyday world and lament the dishonesty, materialism and greed that afflicted them at every turn. Surely, the everyday world provided them with food and shelter, but not with any important spiritual goods. It was a world of sin and sorrow, a vale of tears. Some day, death would remove them from this world, and their souls would find happiness in heaven with God.

The new spirituality re-members us to the everyday world, and makes us and the world spiritually whole, as Jesus and his world were. Jesus, being a Jew of his times and culture, was deeply involved in his everyday world. He preached the kingdom of God by using images and terms that fit the pastoral, agricultural people of his first century society. He told concrete, everyday stories, e.g., of a good shepherd and his sheep (Jn. 10:1ff), a vine and its branches (Jn. 15:1-7), a sower and his seeds (Mt. 13:1ff), weeds among the wheat (Mt. 13:24ff), mustard seeds (Mt. 13:31ff), and yeast (Mt. 13:33ff). His referral to the kingdom of God evoked the loving and fatherly thoughts and feelings that David had raised in the Jewish people.

Later, the apostles went out into the world at large and repeated Jesus' stories. But as they met people of different cultures, they changed the terms of the Gospel to suit their new listeners. They created a new language and a new mindset, without changing the substance of the Gospel. The Gentiles, for example, did not speak of kingdoms, and did not value David, as the Jews did. So when St. Paul preached to them, he changed the image of the kingdom of God into the body of Christ, a more philosophical image that better suited the Gentiles' world, while still carrying the same truth. The words and image were different; the reality was the same, and Christianity was made to fit into a new world of new cultures. Especially beginning with St. Paul, Christians learned that their religion could fit into any and all cultures of the world. It could be made relevant throughout the globe while still retaining its substance and truth. There was never a question of avoiding the everyday world, but of animating it and trans-

forming it in the light of Christ, while respecting all that was good
and human in every culture and tradition. This is a lesson that Christianity is learning anew today.

The need to change Jesus' pastoral and agricultural images
arose in earnest when the Christian preachers reached the great
academic centers of the ancient world. There, the teachers and
philosophers listened to the stories of shepherds, sheep, and mustard seeds and asked the Christians the ancient equivalent of the
question, "What are you hicks talking about? We don't talk about
shepherds, sheep and mustard seeds. We talk about ideas. We talk
about Being, simplicity, unchangeability, immateriality, soul, and
perfection." As the pagan educators and philosophers spoke, the
Christians recognized an opportunity to fit the Gospel into a philosophical structure that educated pagans would recognize and respect. Some Christian teachers objected to "marrying" the Gospel
to Greek philosophy on the grounds that it would paganize the
Gospel. But the urge to spread the Gospel to the world won the
day. Christian teachers began reconciling the Gospel with Greek
philosophy. At that time, Greek philosophy meant Platonic philosophy, the thought system of Plato (c.428-c.348 BC). Unfortu-
nately however, for all the greatness of Plato's thought, his philosophy carried the roots of a disdain for the body and the world, and
this disdain worked its way into the Christian psyche.

Enter St. Augustine (354-430 AD). St. Augustine was the greatest thinker of his day, and one of the greatest thinkers of all history. It
was he who, better than anyone, restructured the Gospel to fit into
Plato's structure of reality. The spirituality of "saving our souls" owes
much to Augustine's use of Platonic thought. Even today, Christians
can easily recognize the influence of the Platonic philosophy that
caused St. Augustine to develop a Christian spirituality that is "other-
worldly."

Basically, Plato said that we are souls—*only* souls. As souls, we
pre-existed in the "Place of Intellectual Perfection," that is up in
the sky, away from earth and the everyday world. Only this Place
is real. It is the Place of perfect ideas. Up there, we waited to be

born. At birth, we left this Place, came down to earth, and were imprisoned inside a body. The shock of being born was so great that we forgot the ideas that we had before we were born. According to Plato, our lives on earth are lives of dark imprisonment, both in our body and in the world. Our body is not truly real. Earth is not truly real. The world is not truly real. Only our soul is truly real—and it has forgotten all the ideas it once had. Here on earth, the closest we can come to reality is through remembering our forgotten ideas. Our idea of a tree, for example, is closer to true reality than any tree we might ever come across on earth. Our idea of love is greater and more real than any love we might enjoy.

THE WORLD OF PLATO

TRUE REALITY
THE WORLD OF IDEAS
THE SPIRITUAL WORLD
THE SOUL

THE SHADOWS OF REALITY
THE MATERIAL WORLD
THE BODY AND NATURE

Plato explained the unreality of this world through his famous allegory of the cave. Our life on earth, he said, is like living in a cave. In this cave, we are chained against a wall in a sitting position and restrained so we can only look straight ahead at the wall on the other side of the cave. Behind and above us is a platform, on which a fire is burning. Passing in front of the fire are cut-out forms of people, trees, mountains, animals, plants, etc. As these forms pass in front of the fire, their shadows are cast onto the cave wall in front of us. In this life, all we ever see are shadows. We do not see true reality but only shadows of true reality. The shadows, of course, are real but their reality is so removed from true reality that they can be considered to be not real. Soon, however, we begin to think that these shadows are true reality. We begin to believe that what we see with our eyes, e.g., trees, mountains, animals, etc., are real. We begin to believe that our bodies are real. We even begin to believe that our real home is here on earth. The shock of being born has made us forget that we live in a shadow world and that our real home is not in our bodies or on earth but in the Place of Intellectual Perfection, which is for our souls alone and which is elsewhere.

If we want to see true reality, Plato taught, we have to break out of our chains, turn away from the shadows of this world, walk out of the cave and look up at the sun. The sun represents the Place of Perfect Ideas, the place of true reality. If we want to live in true reality, we have to turn away from our bodies, especially from our emotions and passions, turn away from nature and from the everyday world, and learn to contemplate ideas. This will aim us toward achieving perfection—by which is meant an other-worldly perfection.

Finally, once we see true reality, we have the responsibility to go back into the cave, into the everyday world, and tell the people who are still there that they too can break out of their chains, turn away from their bodies and the world, and come out of the shadow world into the sunshine of true reality and other-worldly perfection.

Jesus believed none of this. Possibly, he even knew about Platonic philosophy. Recent archeological digs have uncovered a heretofore unknown Roman-Greek city of Cefarus, only 4 miles from

Nazareth. It is easy to speculate that the young Jesus spent some time there picking up carpentry jobs. He would have had to know Greek and would have learned some Greek thinking. But whatever we speculate, we can surely conclude that Jesus rejected whatever Greek thought and philosophy he may have learned, and stuck with his Jewish thought and culture, which was earthy, concrete and very close to nature and the everyday world.

Yet it is very easy to see how the Platonic mindset influenced Christian spirituality. It was easy for Christians to learn to say that God is the Totally Perfect, Supreme Being who lives "up there" in heaven, the place of all perfection. Plato's influence helped them adopt the view that in our lives on earth, we must strive to get away from our bodies and passions and from this world, as we prepare to return our souls, i.e., ourselves, to God in heaven.

In fairness, this is not really what St. Augustine had in mind when he helped create this Christian adaptation of Platonic thought. But the other-worldly attitude of Platonic spirituality was so great that it worked its way into Christian spirituality and remained to the present time. Other-worldliness even influenced the way Christians understood Jesus' own attitude toward the everyday world. If we read the Bible while wearing "Platonic eyeglasses," it could easy appear that Jesus himself taught that we should avoid the everyday world.

> The world . . . hates me, because I testify to it that its
> works are evil.
>
> Jn. 7:7

> The world . . . neither sees nor knows [the Spirit of truth].
>
> Jn. 14:17

> The ruler of this world has been condemned.
>
> Jn. 16:11

In these and similar passages, it could seem that Jesus is refer- ring to the everyday world of education, work, business, politics, medicine, science, art, entertainment, etc. It appears that he is saying all these institutions and human pursuits hate him and are evil. Obviously then, we should stay away from them. Our example of Helga and her pastor, and of the Christians and the pope of the 1930's and 40's, bears out how Christians were influenced by this understanding of Jesus' teaching.

Jesus, however, was completely immersed in his own everyday society and world. He was known and accepted as the son of Mary, as a carpenter, as a young, itinerant rabbi, as a good friend, and as a companion of fishermen, tax collectors, and even an ex-terrorist, Simon the Zealot. (In today's terms, we could say that Simon had been a "guerrilla," who ambushed and killed Roman soldiers in the Jews' fight to overcome the Roman occupation.) Jesus directly related to the political powers, both Jewish and Roman, confronting the Jewish leaders on one hand; and telling people to pay their taxes to Rome on the other hand. He worked to make his world more human and compassionate. Most luminously of all, he so loved the whole world that he died for it.

What then, is the "world" that Christians must avoid and even condemn? It is not the everyday world of the institutions of our society. It is the corrosive force that lives within the everyday world and the institutions of society. Society and its institutions are the individual writ large. The corrosive force that is present in society and its institutions is the same corrosive force that is present in every person. It is the force that moves individuals and institutions to create egotism, sexism, racism, greed, arrogant authority, collapsed educational standards, oppression of the poor; mediocre and self-serving politics, maximized profits at the expense of people and earth, war, and degraded art and entertainment. It is the Anti-Christ that lives within every person and every institution, including religion. This corrosiveness is the "world" to which Christians must not conform. (Rm. 12:2). If, for example, we judge a political or economic policy to be evil, we must distinguish between politics itself or economics itself, which are good and necessary, and the corrosiveness that lives within them. Christian spirituality does not dismiss politics or economics or any of the institutions of society; it works to make them all more luminously human. The Spirit, for example, is moving us to get more fully involved in our form of capitalism while at the same time working to root out what is corrosive within it. It is a mark of spiritually mature persons to be able to get involved in the everyday world, to touch its corrosiveness and help heal society without getting infected by the corrosiveness they touch. This requires that we rediscover ourselves as the mystics and prophets we already are. As the mystics we already are, we are able to discern the Spirit living within us and the institutions of our society, and in her light, we are able to distinguish what is healthy and what is corrosive. As the prophets we are, we are able to collaborate with the Spirit and get hold of the corrosive energy that lives within society and crucify it by reworking and reshaping our institutions into more luminous expressions of humanity.

But because so many of us have been raised to be other-worldly Christians, we haven't been taught how to recognize ourselves as mystics and prophets in our everyday world. We haven't been taught how to see the Spirit's presence and intentions in our institutions, or how to get hold of the world the way Christ wants us to. Other worldly spirituality puts us in a position of dealing with society from the outside. It puts us in danger of reducing the Word of God, i.e., the full, world-transforming involvement in society, into mere words. From the periphery of everyday society, we can preach and create documents calling for justice and peace, but we do very little hands-on spiritual transforming. We don't get inside our public schools, or our politics or corporations with a spiritual presence. The new spirituality requires us to get intimately involved in transforming our schools, political parties, corporations, etc., without imposing our religion on any of them. How many Christians know how to do such a thing?

On its part, the everyday world does not take being spiritually reformed easily. Our getting hold of the world and crucifying it in order to transform it will result in our being crucified by the world. Mystical and prophetic Christians are called to "comfort the afflicted and afflict the comfortable". In the process, they themselves can be afflicted. It is easier to stay within our other-worldly spirituality, or to go along with the crowd—or with our congregations or parishes—than to get involved in our schools, or in our political-economic system. In the 1930's and 40's, there were some mystical and prophetic Christians in Germany, and they put themselves in mortal danger. Today, the same is true in Central and South America. In our society, the dangers are not nearly as great, and the opportunities are immense.

Jesus empowers us to have the insight and courage that we need, and that he had. He directly faced the corrosiveness of this world and broke its power.

> . . . Take courage, I have conquered the world.
>
> Jn. 16:33

In the Spirit of Christ, we can also "conquer the world," e.g., by working to ensure a truly humanizing education for our children, to bring justice and peace to politics, fairness and ecological care to economics, and justice to all women and all races; by working to create uplifting art and entertainment, and by making ourselves able to foresee and prevent the next global holocaust.

We are greatly helped in our efforts to get involved in the everyday world by the teachings of St. Thomas Aquinas (c. 1225-74), who recast Christian thought into a different paradigm. Thomas discovered Aristotle, who was Plato's student, and who disagreed with his teacher, saying that the human person is not just a soul but is both soul *and* body. Aristotle taught that the whole person—body, mind and soul—is not a shadow of reality but is real. He also taught that earth is real. Nature is real. The everyday world is real. There is no need to appeal to a world of ideas for reality. Reality is right here, in this world, on earth. Everything and everyone is real.

St. Thomas took Aristotle's teaching, adapted it to the Gospel, and gave birth to the Christian philosophy and theology that came to be called Scholasticism, because it was taught in the schools of Europe. He brought reality "down to earth," and helped bring forth the scientific method of "hands-on" inquiry, experimentation and research that flourished in the Modern World. Yet, though Scholasticism became the official philosophy of medieval Catholic Europe, Christian spirituality remained Platonic and other-worldly.

Platonic Spirituality

THE SACRED WORLD

THE SECULAR WORLD

THE NATURAL WORLD

For most Christians, God and truth were still "up there" in the sky, and the church reigned "above" the everyday world. The soul was still supernatural and pure while the body was natural and sinful; men still dominated women; masculine values still overran feminine values; and devout Christians still stayed away from the "world," even though they lived and worked in it. Christian spirituality withdrew from the world and went to live "up above the world" in monasteries and convents. In *The Imitation of Christ*, a devotional book that is still widely read today by devout Christians, a medieval monk wrote: "Every time I go out among men, I return less a man."

The feature of Platonic spirituality that placed God, the soul, and spirituality outside or above the everyday world, also gave great strength to the monarchical structures of the Middle Ages. In Medieval Europe, God reigned supreme above the world. In the political world, kings, who saw themselves as God's substitutes, reigned supreme by divine right above their courts and above the peasants of the land. In the church, in direct contradiction to Christ's teaching that his leaders were to serve the church and not to rule over it, the pope reigned supreme as Christ's substitute above the royal court of bishops and priests, and above the devout peasant laity. Whether it was a question of a peasant's right to make a decent living, or Galileo's right to explore the truth, the kings and pope had the final say as to what was real or unreal, true or false, good or evil, beautiful or ugly. In our day, this same paradigm was used by Hitler and Stalin, and is still being used by the leaders of Chinese communism and by dictators in other countries.

In contrast, a man named Francis, from Assisi, lived a life of simplicity, joy and poverty, with a refreshing and liberating closeness to earth and nature and a great love for them. So clearly did he see God in everyone and everything that he could call the sun and the moon, plants and animals, his brothers and sisters. The "poor little one" of Assisi stands in luminous counterpoint to hierarchical, world-disdaining spirituality. But Francis' spirituality was a minority one in contrast to the dominant Platonic, other-worldly spirituality. Francis was such a great example of spirituality against the prevailing mindset that in our day, Einstein praised him as a spiritual "heretic."

Then something happened that changed the world. The Medieval world began to stir. Trade grew. Peasants began making money. The middle class developed. Some "ordinary" people got rich. Banks were started. Local politics began feeling its oats. Emphasis began shifting away from God and an all-powerful, otherworldly church, toward people and the everyday world. A new world was born, the Renaissance world, with its great outburst of artistic, political and economic humanism. Along with the new world, a new image of Christ was born, pregnant with galaxies of new possibilities, as business people and politicians began putting God and the world together in new and egalitarian ways. Instead of dedicating all to the glory of God, as medieval people did, Renaissance business men wrote at the top of their ledgers, "To the glory of God and good profit."

The Renaissance gave us the art of Botticelli, Uccello and Fra Angelico; the sculpture of Donatello and Ghiberti; the architecture of Brunelleschi; and the special magnificence of Leonardo da Vinci and Michelangelo, as well as Raphael, Bellini and Titian. They and others rediscovered classical Greece and Rome, along with the laws of perspective. A rebirth of interest in things human and worldly took place. Along with their Christian works, Renaissance artists began painting scenes of mythical gods and goddesses. They once again glorified the human form and rendered humanistic expressions of nature, and scenes of the hunt with newly killed animals draped over groaning sideboards.

For a golden moment, Christianity was on the verge of gathering up the immense riches of the newly discovered and celebrated humanity and nature, and uniting them to divinity to form a new, magnificent, Renaissance image of Christ in and for the everyday world. It almost happened. But because of its other-worldly spirituality and authoritative structure, Medieval Christianity was not able to fully embrace the Renaissance's love affair with humanity and the world It chose instead to keep its authoritarian distance from the people and its unchristian disdain for the everyday world. In Germany, an Augustinian monk began writing theses to correct Christianity's spiritual errors. Unintentionally, he initiated a storm that would break Christianity apart in a new way and help render it increasingly irrelevant to the secularized Modern World.

ELEVEN

Christ vs. Humpty-Dumpty

Martin Luther looked out on his church and saw that it was in spiritual trouble. The pope had become a medieval lord and king, with a regal court of bishops, and with political and military power. Even worse in Luther's eyes, the pope was selling indulgences— the forgiveness that would hasten people's exit from purgatory and entrance into heaven. As far as the young Augustinian monk was concerned, spirituality was very far from Rome. He set out to fix his church. But he had a spiritual problem of his own.

Like St. Augustine, whose spiritual son he was, Luther had his own personal, spiritual demon. Augustine's demon was women and sex; Luther's was forgiveness. No matter how sincerely he confessed his sins, Luther had trouble feeling that God had forgiven him. In search for help, he turned to St. Paul. In Paul's letter to the Romans, the great apostle writes that we are justified by faith and not by law. Luther took this idea to heart and mind. To counteract the pope's crass selling of indulgences, and to overcome his own nagging feeling of guilt, he created a teaching that he thought would restore a sound spirituality to both the church and himself. He said that we are saved by faith alone and not by any actions on our part. Salvation, he taught, flows to us from the compassionate love of God, expressed in and through Jesus Christ. Nothing that we do—no obedience to rules, no good works, no purchased indulgences—can save us. We can add nothing to our own salvation. The reaction against Luther was strong. The Catholic church did teach that salvation comes only from God. But it insisted on defending what it saw as Luther's attack on human dignity and freedom. Just as we had to freely acknowledge that we are human, and thus contribute to our own humanity, which God gave us, we can and must freely contribute to our own salvation. We do this, first, by freely accepting the grace of salvation that God offers us. (All Christians agree that we can freely *reject* God's grace.) And we also contribute to our salvation by living lives of justice, peace and love. In all cases—accepting God's grace and living good lives—the Catholic church agreed that the grace to do all this comes from God alone. In sum, Luther and the church authorities got caught in a theological argument that could have been resolved on the spot. But it wasn't. Instead, a spiritual civil war engulfed Western Christianity—a war that raged for over 400 years.

In 1962, Pope John XXIII called the Second Vatican Council. As the council was about to open, he met with the Protestant representatives who had been invited to attend as observers and respected brothers in faith. The first thing he did was to come down off his papal throne and greet his guests. "I am Joseph, your brother," he said, using the name his parents had given him. Then he added, "We will be tempted to start arguing over the Reformation. Let me end the argument right here. It was our fault."

The council went on to say that the entire Christian community is the people of God, and that all Christians have access to the Spirit, who dwells in the whole world. It is the job of the whole Christian community to discern the Spirit's presence and intentions, and to come together to collaborate with her. It is the job of the Christian leaders to gather up, clarify and formulate what the entire community discerns, and to lead it—in humble service—as it collaborates with the Spirit. In all this, the Roman Catholic church was saying substantially what Luther had said over 400 years earlier—and what Christian women had said almost 2000 years earlier. In 1999, the Lutheran church and the Roman Catholic church formally acknowledged that their teachings on salvation were substantially the same. The war—at least officially—finally ended.

To get back to Luther, other reformers took his teaching and moved it to an extreme. The impact they had on spirituality continues into today's world. John Calvin (1509—1564) and others, for example, said that because of the Fall, we are radically and totally corrupt. No good remains in us. Our free will to do good is destroyed. The only thing we can choose on our own is evil and sin. We are saved only because God chooses not to see our corruption. This extreme teaching said, in effect, that Jesus did nothing for our lives here on earth. Only in heaven will Christ's saving work do anything for us—if God chooses us to be among the saved. This view makes spirituality unnecessary, in fact, impossible. We cannot discern the Spirit dwelling within us because, for all practical purposes, she is not present—or at least her presence in us is not effective. If we are radically corrupt and can will to do nothing good, then there is no way we can collaborate with the Spirit and help fulfill creation, develop our possibilities, build a world of greater justice, peace and compassion, or make ourselves and the world ever more luminous expressions of Christ. In this mindset, the only thing we can really look forward to is the end of the world. In fact, many Christians who follow this teaching are constantly looking for signs that the world is about to end.

Against this teaching, the Roman Catholic church taught—and some other Christian churches agreed—that even after the Fall, some good remained in every person. Our dignity and freedom, though weakened, remain intact. Every person in the world—even unbelievers—can still do some good here and there, but because of the Fall no one can live a life of *consistent* good will and love without God's grace. Jesus' redeeming work does count here on earth. He has overcome the grip of the Fall here and now. While we are still sinners and obviously not yet in heaven, we are holy and sacred—luminous—here on earth. Here and now we can live in the Spirit of Christ and we can live lives of consistent good will and compassion—and we can get credit for using our human freedom and dignity to live such lives by accepting the grace to do so from God.

While the theological wars tore Christianity apart, yet, on both sides, Christian spirituality continued to influence individual Christians in their private lives, though it did not work its way into the general mainstream of the world in any effective way. On the Catholic side, St. Theresa of Avila (1515-1582) and St. John of the Cross (1542-1591) were outstanding examples of a mystical spirituality that stressed contemplation and a very sensitive awareness of our union with God, here and now. These two great mystics taught the classical three-step path to a full spiritual life: The Purgative Way—clearing away our sins and faults; The Illuminative Way—learning about God and Christ; and The Unitive Way—living in intimate, loving union with God.

On the Protestant side, Luther himself had a sensitive awareness of God's presence. Jakob Boehme (1575-1624), a German Lutheran shoemaker, mystically saw the universe as the manifestation of God, and he wrote devotional works named, "The Way to Christ." George Fox (1624-1694), founded the Society of Friends, or Quakers, and gave us his teaching of the Inner Light.

The Reformation, and the spiritual corrections it offered, could have given Western Christianity a chance to enter the Modern World with a newly invigorated and effective, everyday spirituality. But Western Christianity was totally absorbed in its own civil war, and everyday spirituality, despite the shining light of some individuals, was thrown back into the Middle Ages. Spirituality withdrew from everyday society and locked itself up in monasteries and convents and in the privacy of one's devotions. In the everyday world, a spiritual vacuum formed, and in that vacuum, a whole new world arose—the secular Modern World.

The effects of the absence of spirituality from everyday life haunt us even today. For example, many Christians condemn public education as being Godless. A growing number of Christians either send their children to religious schools, or home-school them. Could it be, however, that the "Godlessness" of public education may be due to the fact that so many Christians themselves are not involved in their public schools—not to make them Christian, which contradicts the Constitution, but to make them more human, more fully alive—which involves making them more academically excellent. In the chapters on education, we will see how spirituality opens the way for public schools to make their education and their students more luminously human and more academically excellent without interfering with anyone's religion or with the separation of church and state.

Also, in the Modern World, Christianity and the new-born modern science lived side by side, with two opposed views of truth. Christianity saw truth as something that is given from above and firmly established. In the 16th century, for example, the Catholic church "knew" that God had placed the earth in the center of the universe, where it enjoyed a privileged position among all the stars. If anyone saw anything different from this view, they were automatically wrong. So when Copernicus (1473-1543) put forth the notion that the earth and other planets orbited around the sun, and that the earth is not the center of the universe, the church rejected his insight. Galileo (1564-1642) fared even worse. He was met with condemnation and house arrest by the church, and he was threatened with eternal damnation if he insisted on following what his eyes and mind were showing him to be true.

Science, as Copernicus, Galileo and others showed, saw truth as something to be constantly discovered and developed by means of reasoned investigation and research. Whereas in religion, a new discovery would be rejected if it contradicted an already established truth; in science, a new discovery, uncovered by research, was welcomed and celebrated as an advance in understanding the truth.

Christianity could have opened itself to the new discoveries of truth and let cosmogenesis be Christogenesis. It could have developed a dynamic, new Modern spirituality that would have helped make the Modern World a magnificent expression of the one, harmonious, living body of Christ (leaving people of other religions to see it their way). Instead it withdrew from the Modern World and allowed it to end up looking like Humpty-Dumpty. In such a schizophrenic world, the sacred and spiritual went one way, and the secular went another. With no one to put Humpty-Dumpty back together again, a wall of separation, and even hostility, was built.

The Humpty-Dumpty World

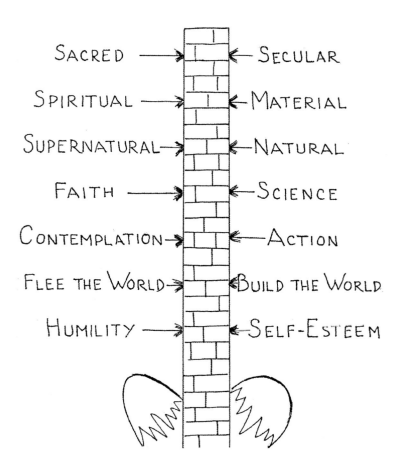

Sacred →	← Secular
Spiritual →	← Material
Supernatural →	← Natural
Faith →	← Science
Contemplation →	← Action
Flee the World →	← Build the World
Humility →	← Self-Esteem

These separations helped form the spiritual basis for the Modern World's separations between men and women, between masculine traits and feminine traits, and between various races, various nations, the First World and the Third World, the rich and the poor, and between people and the earth. All these contributed to the spiritual vacuum that we suffer from today.

The Modern World was not without those who saw the fragmentation and tried to put Humpty Dumpty back together again. Rene Descartes (1596-1650), a Christian, a mathematician and a scientist, saw the split that had occurred between faith and science and between the soul and body, and he tried to rejoin them. But he himself was a "Humpty-Dumpty" person. On one side of the wall, as a Christian, he adhered to a Platonic spirituality that moved him to see God as an unreachable ideal. On the other side of the wall, as a scientist, he was a secular materialist, who saw the universe and earth as nothing more than a giant machine, with no mind or soul. To him, scientists could use their minds to stand apart from the universe and objectively understand how the great, mindless machine works. The human soul had no importance at all to science. It belonged to religion.

What he saw as true of the universe, he also saw as true of the human body. Like the universe, the human body was nothing more than a machine, separate from the person's mind and soul. The body, therefore, could be treated and scientifically studied like a machine. We see this mindset, for example, in the way many Modern World physicians looked at their patients. Descartes also saw animals as machines, without minds and souls and with only feelings. The cry of a wounded animal, he stated, is nothing more than the screeching of a broken machine. This mindset is the basis for what has happened in many research laboratories.

Descartes the believer, on the other hand, looked out on the disconnections and wondered if they could be reconciled. Could the body-machine be reconciled with the mind and soul to form an integrated human person? Could faith be reconciled with science? But with the materialist "scientific" start that he had, he had nothing to work with. The best he could do was to say that a person's body and soul were somehow held together by God—in a way that is not understandable to us. The same was true of the dead machine that is the earth and the life that we see on earth—somehow they are held together by God in a way we don't understand.

His "explanation" didn't work. Try as he may, Descartes reconciled nothing, but rather confirmed for all the Modern World the fragmentation between the universe and life, between the body and soul, and between religion and science. Where Christ could have shone forth in all his luminously human integrity, dignity and beauty, Humpty-Dumpty reigned.

Sir Isaac Newton, who was an Anglican clergyman and who was trying to show how God ran the universe, nevertheless also helped confirm Humpty Dumpty. He did this by giving intellectual and mathematical clarity to the fragmentation of the modern world. Thanks to his genius, the universe-as-dead-mindless-machine became the accepted view of Modern science. Using his mathematics, scientists could understand and even predict all the laws of the universe. Under Newtonian scrutiny, the laws of gravity and motion lost any relation they may have had with God and came under the power of human understanding. Newton himself had no intention of separating the universe and science from God and faith. But he could not explain how God could relate to a universe that was totally understood and controlled by human scientists. Despite his good intentions, Newton, the scientist, helped push God out of the universe. In Biblical times, God had been placed "up there," above the flat earth and beyond the firmament, though at the same time, God was "I-Am-With-You," always with his people on earth. In the modern world, God was placed "out there," beyond the round earth and beyond the farthest boundaries of the universe, and was no longer here with us. The more we came to know and understand about the universe, the farther out we pushed God. Without God, Modern World science began to become intellectually arrogant. In the early 20th century, for example, some scientists discouraged students from studying phys-

ics because they were sure that by mid-century, they would understand all there was to understand about the universe, and physics
would become unnecessary. Humans were about to know it all.
This mindset caused special trouble with religious schools and
universities. How could they teach science when every advance in
scientific understanding pushed God farther away? Many of
them settled the question by simply teaching science and their
faith side by side, the way Descartes taught, thereby doing
justice to neither.

The new spirituality gives us a different point of view. It opens
us to experience God *within* ourselves, others, the world and the
entire universe. Every advance in knowledge and understanding,
far from pushing God farther away, reveals a clearer insight into
the presence and intentions of God, who is dwelling within everyone and everything. Faith does not reject science; it needs science
to help us understand ever more clearly the people and world within
which God is living, so we can recognize the indwelling Spirit
more clearly, along with her intentions for us and the world. And
science needs faith to help it stay human, humble and truthful in
the face of the great Mystery of reality that it is constantly prob-
ing. But learning about God, experiencing the indwelling Spirit,
and working with the fullness of reality were very difficult in the
Modern World.

The great philosopher, Immanuel Kant (1724-1804), for example, was a major influence in building the Modern World's
mindset. Following the other-worldly pattern of Platonic thought,
Kant said that God is unreachable and that we cannot know God
or truth in themselves. We can only know for sure what we can see,
hear, taste, touch and smell. God is beyond our senses; he may be
real but there is no sure way to know this.

Modern science removed God from the universe; then Kant
removed God from our certitude. Christians, of course, say that
their faith gives them certitude that God exists. To the Modern
World and Kant, however, the certitude of faith simply "floats" in
its own orbit, outside of scientific truth and even outside of our

personal logic and intelligence. In the Modern secular mindset, faith does not influence nature. It does not, for example, tell nature what is right or wrong. On the natural level, what is right to me may be wrong to you, and there is no way to tell who is correct. Finding the truth is a case of everyone for him or herself. Under Kant's influence, which had a powerful effect on the Modern World's secular way of thinking, agnosticism and the sense of God's absence took greater hold of the everyday world.

Kant tried to correct his fragmentation and find some unity that would bind all people together. He said that even though we can't know for sure that God exists, or what is right or wrong, we should choose to do what we would want everyone else to do. If I would like everyone to be honest, for example, I will be honest. But I can also say that if I would like everyone to be in killing competition with everyone else, I will be in killing competition with everyone else. This teaching simply doesn't work on a community basis.

As the influence of Descartes, Newtonian science, and Kant spread, the world and God became more separated, as did the body and soul. People became more unsure of how to agree on what is right or wrong, and became more isolated from one another. Today's debate over abortion gives us a clear example of how the separation of faith from reason and science, the separation of body from soul, and the inability to agree on what is right or wrong influence today's mindset. If we want to justify abortion, a good way to do it is first to say that faith is a private matter and that it has no influence on our reasoning or on our scientific understanding of who we are. We then separate a woman's body from her soul. We look at her body as a machine, a thing. Next we declare that the "fetus" within her to be also a thing. (We cannot, of course, call it a baby, because that would push the discussion in an entirely different direction.) The "fetus" is a thing that is growing within a thing. (It is ironic that women fought so hard not to be viewed as bodies or things.)

The woman shows her radical individualism by declaring that she alone is in charge of her body and of the thing that is growing in it. "It's my body and I can do whatever I want with it." She has no sure way of knowing if abortion is right or wrong. Neither does anyone else. The only absolute truth involved in this matter is the woman's right to choose what she wants to do. Her choice is totally her own. It does not involve the man who made her pregnant, her parents or family, her friends, the government, or any church. Nor does she consult the accumulated wisdom of the human community because she has no way of telling what is right or wrong. She is alone, utterly alone with her choice. She does not have to justify her choice, because there is no way to justify it. In this mindset, whatever she chooses will be correct, simply because she chose it.

Another great influential force in the creation of today's spiritually bereft, Humpty Dumpty world was philosopher Martin Heidegger (1889-1976). He was an agnostic and a great admirer of Hitler's—because Hitler overcame fragmentation and brought "unity" to Germany and almost to the world. Heidegger taught that if God exists, he is experienced today only as absent. With no experience of God to turn to, people are left with a deeply felt, existential urgency for some way to fulfill their human meaning. They urgently feel the need to be humanly authentic. To exist and to be authentic, Heidegger said, does not mean simply to be, but to *have* to be. Yet, we are headed for non-being. We are nothing more than Toward-Death-Beings, he said. This puts in us a deep dread of not existing. Heidegger called this dread, *Angst*. We even feel *Angst* when we realize we are not living deeply enough but are living shallow lives. We cannot escape the nothingness of death, but we can at least try to escape our shallowness. We find shallowness everywhere in the Modern World, he said. We find it in the noise we constantly create. We find it in the chatter we engage in over the latest personalities and news events. We see it when we replace true, critical thinking with data processing. To overcome our shallowness, he called for us to engage in thoughtful silence, reflection and meditation, by which we could learn how to live authentic lives—even though we are headed for nothingness. But for all his calling to meaning and depth, his thinking was shrouded with the ultimate pessimism that in the end our lives would mean nothing.

Prodded by some scholars, Heidegger came close to breaking through the dark forest of his agnosticism, but he didn't make it. Theologian Karl Rahner, for example, took Heidegger's thoughts, enlivened them with the light of the indwelling Spirit, and opened the way to a luminous, contemporary theology and spirituality of courageous commitment to deep meaning and effective involvement in the everyday world, with the sure hope of our eternal fulfillment in heaven. But Heidegger himself left us only with an ultimately meaningless world, where people are always on the lookout for the next juicy item, where the news is filled with mind-numbing violence, and where cars and space ships explode on TV and movie screens with dull regularity.

Beginning with the Reformation and following the birth of modern science and philosophy, the everyday Modern World declared Humpty-Dumpty the victor over Christ.

TWELVE

Today's Spiritual Hunger for an Absent God

The story is told that in 1991 after President George Bush decided to go to war with Iraq, he called in the bishop of his church and asked for a blessing. The bishop is reported to have said, "George, don't do it." He then left the White House, went across the street and joined some peaceful demonstrators. President Bush then called in the Rev. Billy Graham, who prayed with him.

The story typifies what we call the "American Religion," or American spirituality. We could describe it as, "Tack-on" spirituality. First, we make decisions and do things on our own, and then we "tack on" God and ask him to bless what we have already done. Every political speech follows this pattern. The speaker says, "Follow my plan and we will have peace and prosperity. We have the 'know how' and the 'can do' to get the job done." Finally, having extolled his or her abilities, and having cajoled the listeners into cheering the plan or program, the speaker adds, " . . . and God bless America."

The founders of America intended to separate any official religion from the government—a policy with which almost all Americans agree. The separation of the institutions of church and government arose from two main sources. First, the founders of our country wanted to distance America from the religious oppression that many Europeans suffered from various churches. Second, the founders were influenced by a movement called the Enlightenment. The Enlightenment, or the Age of Reason, was born in the 18th century—the product of journalists and educated men, such as Gotthold Lessing (1729-81) in Germany; Isaac Newton, and philosopher John Locke (1632-1704) in England; and Denis Diderot (1713-84) and Voltaire (1694-1778) in France.

The main point of the Enlightenment was to declare the primacy of reason and nature over faith and the supernatural. The Enlightenment used reason and nature to attack faith and do away with spirituality. The full force of this attack on faith and spirituality was shown in the French revolution, which overthrew—beheaded—both the government and the church. In place of these two institutions, which were the traditional foundations of community, the revolutionaries set up the primacy of the individual, and declared that individuals enjoy freedom, rights, and mutual equality. Modern individualism was born, one of the most magnificent—and yet, spiritually dangerous—ideas in history.

Throwing off the Catholic church as oppressive, the Enlightenment also threw away faith. Reason alone was declared to be the instrument for progress and prosperity, and the only guiding light and "savior" of the world. It is reported that some devotees of the Enlightenment enthroned a naked prostitute on the high altar of Notre Dame Cathedral in Paris and proclaimed her the goddess of reason. Again, the ancient curse of female degradation hissed through the ages and found its way into the Age of Reason, as a degraded woman was brought to church by "reasoning" men and humiliated under the guise of being worshipped. In the Enlightenment mindset, the earth fared no better than women. Men saw the earth as a miserly provider that had to be dominated and tamed (and that could be polluted) for the sake of income and profit. Finally, the Enlightenment promulgated a policy of toleration for all views.

Many of the founders of the United States were educated in the ideas of the Enlightenment. Thomas Jefferson, Benjamin Franklin and Thomas Paine were among those who helped build these ideas into the American structure and psyche. Like France, America also rejected the sovereign powers of king and church (but not God), and based itself on individual freedom, rights and equality. All men, our founders declared, are endowed by their Creator with the right to life, liberty and the pursuit of happiness. (We are now, of course, painfully aware that women, non-property owners, and slaves were not included in that "all.")

Enjoying great freedom, people in this wondrous new country vigorously began to compete socially, politically and economically to have their "truth" come out on top. To go back to the Newtonian paradigm of the solar system, everyone worked hard to get themselves into the position of the sun, around which all others orbited. In such a self-centered, hard competing, secularized mindset, discerning the Spirit's intentions became increasingly difficult. Spirituality began to dim.

From the beginning, the separation of church and state was never clearly understood. Questions arose that are still argued today. While the American government is free from any particular religion, is it free from any code of morality? If the government is to be moral, whose morality should it follow? The founders answered these questions by fostering the kind of Christianity that many of them adhered to. It is called Deism.

Deism is the religious tradition that sees God as removed from the everyday world. It holds that God created the world and then withdrew to heaven and left the world free to run itself. The Deistic God is often described as the "Watchmaker," who makes the watch, winds it up and then lets it run on its own. In true Deistic terms, America was founded as one nation, *under* God. God is "up there" in heaven, and we are "down here," under God, on earth. An important separation between God and America is built into this paradigm. Because of this separation, those Americans who base their spirituality on an intimate relationship with God who is here with us and within us, find themselves strangers in their own land.

Deism helped create what is called the "American religion," the tradition that is most often practiced in public life. It goes something like this: with the United States having been created by God, who is now in heaven, we are left to ourselves down here, where we use our Yankee ingenuity to develop industrial, technological and economic wonders. We work as rugged individuals for peace, prosperity and happiness according to our own individual talents and desires. Individualism and competition are our everyday values. We unite only in times of crisis, e.g., in a war, or a natural disaster, or when terrorism strikes, such as the bombing in Oklahoma City, and high school shootings. In both foreign and domestic troubles, we tend to see ourselves as the "Lone Ranger" with the white hat, who, like the Deistic God, rides into town, straightens everything out, and then departs.

In the American religion, one sure sign of God's blessing is financial success. If we work hard enough, God will bless us with big money. In our push for financial success, we can take advantage of sweat shop labor, pollute our environment, downsize to maximize profits while overworking the employees who are left, etc. Also, since the poor are obviously not blessed by God, they must be doing something wrong. A continuing American debate centers around whether the poor are "deserving" or "undeserving." The great aim of this "religion" has shown itself to be runaway consumerism.

The Enlightenment rejected faith and the supernatural, and taught that human reason alone was supreme. In 1905 a man was born who lost his faith very early in life and who also accepted human reason as supreme. But after World War I, the shaken young man declared that human reason had been murdered in the trenches of France. Atheist Jean Paul Sartre (1905-1980) went on to popularize the absence of both faith and reason from the world, in the movement called, "Existentialism." To Sartre, all is absurd. We are born with no meaning into a world that has no meaning. In classical philosophical terms, we are born with no essence. We can say that we exist, but we cannot say that we have any given meaning. We can call a cabbage a king, or a king a cabbage. In a world without any given meaning, we are left only with our own individual freedom to make our own meaning—even though that itself is without meaning. Life, Sartre stated, is a useless passion.

The only way to live an authentic life is to have the courage to make our own meaning in this absurd world.

In striving to be authentic, we are completely on our own. We must guard against anyone who would want to give us meaning, for they would take from us our freedom to give ourselves meaning, and they would make us inauthentic. The only thing we have is our freedom—along with the courage to use it. We must especially guard against loving anyone or having anyone love us. In either case, we would lose our freedom and begin to live for our beloved, putting ourselves in danger of taking meaning from them. The only "community" that is possible is a grouping of individuals who have their backs to one another, guarding against anyone who would try to give them meaning.

Most of all, we must resist believing in God. In fact, there can be no God. If there was a God, he would give us our meaning and thereby remove our freedom to make our own meaning. Worse, he would love us totally, and thereby totally destroy us. To live as authentic individuals, we must reject God, faith, reason, community and love.

A pale version of Existentialism was imported into America, mostly without any reflection, in the 1960's by the "Hippie" subculture. Borrowing from astrology, they introduced, "The Age of Aquarius," in which young people rejected their parents and families, education, marriage, government, religion, and everyone over 30 years of age, and went on a "trip" to "do their own thing" and "let it all hang out." In their quest for authenticity, they embraced drug highs, free sex and rock concerts as substitutes for religious experience. The Beatles became the "gods" of the 1960's, causing John Lennon to note ruefully, "We're more popular than Jesus." Timothy Leary, a Harvard professor who exemplified the collapse of higher education, offered young people LSD and taught them to, "Turn on, get high, and tune out." Somehow a new spirituality was supposed to arise amidst the fumes of this self-centered haze. But instead, the Age of Aquarius was born dead—or stoned. Even the Beatles themselves noticed the spiritual vacuum that had developed in America and England, and they went to India to study eastern spirituality. In a short time, however, they returned, disillusioned and frustrated.

The revolutionary tumult of the 1960's was so great that it almost drowned out a quiet, counter-movement toward spiritual wholeness. The 1960's were the time of the Civil Rights movement in America, with its long overdue move toward equality for Blacks and for women. It was also the time when Existentialism began to grow into a positive spiritual resource. Albert Camus (1913-1960) was a friend of Sartre's who at first agreed that all was meaningless and absurd. Then an insight dawned within him. The story is told that one day, during World War II, Sartre and Camus were sitting in a Paris café having coffee. The café was filled with German soldiers, and Camus and Sartre were members of the French Resistance. The two existentialists weren't all that patriotic; they opposed the Nazi occupation because it was imposing meaning on them. During their conversation, a thought struck Camus. "Everything is absurd," he said. "No matter what we do, it is meaningless." He looked at Sartre. "Isn't that so?"

Sartre agreed.

"Then," Camus continued, motioning secretly toward the German soldiers, "turn me in. Tell them that I'm a member of the Resistance."

Sartre recoiled. "Are you crazy!? They will kill you."

"Then," Camus concluded, "your concern for my life must have some meaning. Our friendship must have some meaning. Turning me in is not meaningless; it has meaning in itself. There *is* meaning in the world that is outside us—that is greater than we are."

Sartre recoiled again. "Be careful, my friend," he warned, "you are beginning to believe in God."

Soon afterwards, the two men ceased being friends.

Camus continued to discover meaning in the world beyond himself and within himself. Soon he courageously rebelled against the absurdity that he saw, and against the temptation to declare ourselves innocent bystanders in a meaningless world. If all is meaningless, he said, then we are free either to stoke the fires of the Nazi crematoriums or to devote ourselves to caring for lepers. Or we could commit suicide. It would all make no difference. But, he reasoned, this cannot be true. He went on to see that there is a difference. People and the world are not meaningless and absurd. They mean something. To do this thing or that thing means something in itself. All is not indifferent; we ourselves can make a difference. In fact, not only *can* we make a difference, we *have to* make a difference! We can make ourselves and the world better and we have to try to do it. Sartre was right. As Camus found his own meaning, he also found his spirituality and was on his way to finding God.

As we noted earlier, in his spiritual journey, Camus looked to the Catholic church for help in caring for the world. Addressing a group of priests in Paris, he said in substance, "I share with you the same revulsion from evil. But I do not share your hope. You have your heaven, where, you say, everything will be put right." (He was referring to the church's pious habit of telling people to "offer up" the sufferings that the world inflicted upon them, rather than try to do something about them, because everything will be all right in heaven.) He went on. "I continue to struggle in a world in which children suffer and die. For a long time, I have waited for the great voice in Rome to speak up. I, an unbeliever? Yes. Because I know that the Spirit will be lost if it does not utter a cry of condemnation with force. It has been explained to me that the condemnation has been voiced—but in the style of encyclicals, which are not understood."

To use a word that became very popular in the 1960's, Camus found the church irrelevant to the everyday world. As a voice for the suffering world, Camus cried out to the church and all Christianity to get involved in the everyday work of caring for the world. "Perhaps we cannot make a world in which no children suffer. But we can work to help create a world in which fewer children suffer. And if you don't help us, who else in the world can help us do this?" In desperation he ended his plea with the poignant cry, "All your heaven is not worth the tears of one suffering child here on earth."

Camus came close to finding the spirituality he was looking for. He started with his novel, *The Stranger*, in which he depicted a world in which all was meaningless and absurd, including the death of the main character's mother and finally, the main character's own conviction and execution. He then moved on to *The Plague*, in which he moved past meaninglessness and described himself and others as innocent victims in an evil world. When the plague breaks out, a doctor tries his best to treat the afflicted, but a priest goes around blaming the people's sins for it. Then a little boy dies of the plague. The doctor asks the priest if the boy's sins killed him. The priest has no answer. He stops accusing people of sin and begins to help victims. In time, the priest dies. Did he die of the plague or not? Camus is reluctant to give the church credit for getting that involved in the world. He has the priest's body tagged, "Doubtful Case." Finally, he wrote *The Fall*, in which a man stands by and watches a young girl jump off a bridge and commit suicide. By this time, Camus has come to see that rather than being innocent victims in an evil world, we are the ones who create the evil world. We are so caught up in our guilt and flight from responsibility that we need an "outside" Savior. The main character is named Jean Baptiste Clamance, "John the Baptist Crying Out." Camus was crying out for spiritual insight and close to finding the Savior he was looking for. Then he was killed in an automobile accident.

We are left to wonder what he would have thought of the Roman Catholic church's Second Vatican Council, that opened two years after his death. Pope Paul VI, who presided over the council after Pope John XXIII died, was an avid reader of Camus. How much was the thoughtful pope influenced by the passionate existentialist? In the council's document on the church and the modern world, we can almost hear Pope Paul VI answering Camus' plea. The document starts out, "The joys and the hopes, the griefs and the anxieties of the people of this age, especially those who are poor or in any way afflicted, these too are the joys and hopes, the griefs and anxieties of the followers of Christ." It was a good start, but since the Council ended in 1965, the Catholic church has turned in on itself, fighting battles over authority and sex, and retrenching back to its Medieval mindset as it tries to do battle with the fragmented secular world. Even this battle, however, has come too late. In the 1960's the Catholic church, along with many other Christian churches, tried to catch up to a Modern World that Einstein had already declared dead in 1945. A new world is being born, and as Christianity looks at itself, it sees that it is as fragmented as the Modern World had become. In the 16th century, Christianity had entered the Modern World in its own state of brokenness and spiritual turmoil. Sadly, several significant segments of Christianity appear to be equally unprepared to enter the new world.

These segments cover the Christian spiritual prism. On one extreme stand the Fundamentalist Christians, whose attitude toward the secularized world is based on anger and fear. They see the world as radically corrupt and look forward to its end, whose date they constantly predict. In the meantime, however, they are working to take over the world's power—by placing their members in political offices, school boards, etc., and to thereby impose their brand of morality upon society. In their literal interpretation of the Bible, they teach that men should dominate women, wives should be subject to their husbands, and only Christians are saved. Their literalism and their view of the world's radical corruption tend to rule out any experience of the Spirit as present and active in the world. The Fundamentalist spirit appears to be caught up in a deep psychological need for certainty and security that preclude openness and thought. With no real hope for the future, Fundamentalism appears to have opted out of the new dance of Christ.

Evangelical Christianity is committed to strong family life, ministry to the poor and sick, and an upbeat attitude toward religion. These qualities make it attractive to many young people and to some conservative members of the so-called mainstream churches, such as the Lutheran and Roman Catholic churches. It tends toward Biblical literalism and suspicion of the world, which moves its members to home school their children in increasing numbers. While not showing the anger that Fundamentalists show, Evangelical Christianity does not seem to hold out much hope for the Spirit's presence and activity in the world. Yet, it has greeted with some enthusiasm such spiritual writings as Richard Foster's, *Celebration of Discipline, A Path to Spiritual Growth*. We can also note that Jim Wallis, of the Sojourners group in Washington, DC, is an Evangelical Christian who is prophetically involved in society in a deep and persuasive way, though he sees himself as an exception to the general Evangelical mindset.

The largest segment of Christianity is the so-called mainstream. It includes the "parish" Christians such as the Presbyterians, Methodists, Lutherans, Episcopalians, Orthodox Catholics, Roman Catholics et al., who continue their very generous ministry to the poor and sick, while they cling to old pieties and mindsets and are caught up in internal struggles, especially over sexual issues. In heavy measure, mainstream Christians still believe and worship on the periphery of everyday society, and many still see their churches as safe "oases" from the burdens and onslaughts of the "outside" world. They bring their personal morality to their jobs and look for morality in their leaders, but lack the spiritual education and mechanisms to get mystically and prophetically involved in society in an effective way. They live in a sort of spiritual schizophrenia which shows, for example, in the Christian corporate executive who sued a newspaper for revealing that he is a Christian. When asked about his Christian education and the morality of maximizing profits to the detriment of the community, he answered that his Christian education had nothing to do with his business decisions. In another example, a high ranking office holder in Washington, DC was asked in a television interview what influence his Christian faith had on him. He answered that it consoled and sustained his personal life but said nothing about how it influences his political life and decisions.

For all its good will, this segment of Christianity is struggling under the weight of its spiritual inertia. Still clinging to the past, and still marked by passivity and the mindset of "offering up the world because things will be better in heaven," it cannot enkindle its members to become engaged in helping make the new world more luminously human and a clearer expression of Christ. Significantly, this segment of Christianity is having trouble attracting young people. In Philadelphia recently, the new leader of the Presbyterian church began his term by lamenting that his church is not attracting the young because it is so stuck in its old ways.

In great part, then, Christianity is in a state of spiritual turmoil and unpreparedness that is similar to the state in which it entered the Modern World in the 16th century. While Christianity does possess the theological and spiritual resources necessary to renew itself and the world, it is struggling to find a way to use these resources effectively. In the meantime, an increasing number of Christians, as well as others, are hungry to experience God in themselves and in the new world that is now being born, and are looking for ways to make a spiritual difference—for themselves and for society. But they are not being fed with the spiritual nourishment they need from churches that they increasingly find to be not credible. Many have simply walked away from their churches, or have not joined a church.

Finally, polls taken around the world show that an increasing number of Christians are awakening to the new world and taking up the spiritual challenge to find ways to get spiritually engaged in society and to serve it in the love of Christ in a new and persuasive way. Still, for the most part, considered outsiders by mainstream Christianity, these Christians have heard a new music and are accepting the invitation to the new dance of Christ.

PART THREE

*Dancing the New Dance
of Christ*

THIRTEEN

New World—New Vision

A new world is being born—a new, evolving world within which possibilities are flaring forth in a profusion unknown in human history. It is as if another Big Bang has occurred. The new world is filled with luminosity, from which are emerging unimaginable new galaxies of possibilities for self development, family life, education, science, technology, medicine, human rights and peace. The new world gives us a mindset and vision that overcomes the fragmentation and separated boxes of the Modern World. Every person, thing and event is inter-connected and inter-related with every other person, thing and event in a luminous web of wholeness. While individuals, families, communities, nations, education, politics, economics, businesses, religions, ecology, etc., retain their full unique individuality and possibilities, they grow and flourish in community with all others and with earth. Gone also is the central core of secular interests and activities, while the sacred is relegated to the periphery. In the new world, every person, thing and event is emerging from the same luminous source. All are luminous and all are sacred.

THE NEW WORLD OF

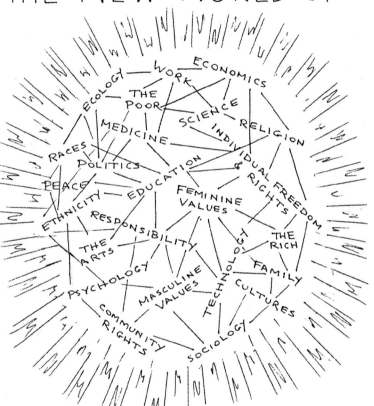

ECONOMICS
ECOLOGY — WORK
THE POOR
MEDICINE SCIENCE — RELIGION
RACES INDIVIDUAL FREEDOM
POLITICS EDUCATION & RIGHTS
PEACE FEMININE VALUES
ETHNICITY — EDUCATION
RESPONSIBILITY THE RICH
THE ARTS FAMILY
PSYCHOLOGY TECHNOLOGY CULTURES
MASCULINE VALUES
COMMUNITY RIGHTS SOCIOLOGY

LUMINOUS WHOLENESS

Some of the dynamic features of the new world are already emerging from the efforts of people who are answering the invitation to the new dance. These efforts include the Global Declaration of Human Rights, Liberation theology, the fight for full equality and respect for women, the fight against sweatshops and special concern for the poor and outcast throughout the world, work toward nuclear disarmament, new movements toward democracy among peoples of the developing world; debt reduction; fairness in monetary policies and trade policies throughout the world; an ever increasing ecological sensitivity; and various movements for church renewal, etc.

More and more Christians are seeing that the new world is birthing forth a new spirituality. They see that the luminosity that fills the new world is the light of the indwelling Spirit. All the features that are emerging and all the possibilities that will emerge, are flaring forth as created expressions of her light. In the new world, Christians see every individual as luminous with the indwelling Spirit—to one degree of intensity or another—as well as every family, community, the arts, science, education, politics, economics, etc. Christians see all the diverse expressions of the world as various expressions of the one, universal Christ—even if some of these expressions show us the suffering Christ. Our eyes are also opened to the extent that we give full respect to the right of others to see the new world with different eyes and different faith.

Here it is important to point out that the new world and new spirituality do not put us a road to Utopia. They offer us a new opportunity, given to us at this time of history by the Spirit of Christ, to help build a world that is more luminously human—a world in which more people will have greater opportunities to discern and fulfill their best possibilities. Christians are at a new beginning, with a new mindset and vision that now has to be "enfleshed" into everyday reality through mystical insight and prophetic action—in collaboration with people of other religions and traditions. Thus will the spiritual hunger be satisfied that afflicts so many Christians and others today.

We must emphasize that we are not naïve. The new world could collapse and die. We can fall back to the world of Humpty-

Dumpty and spiritual hunger. The new spirituality calls us to a new journey to discover our spiritual self in a new evolving world. Along the way we will have to face our demons and dragons. The journey lies before us. It is truly a hero's journey.

FOURTEEN

The Hero's Journey to Personal Fulfillment

Today, many of us find ourselves, along with others who are spiritually hungry, standing around like the town folks in the classical American cowboy story. The "bad guys" have had their way and we are standing at the edge of town, peering into the desert for the hero with the white hat to come and straighten things out. After a while, we see a dust cloud in the distance. Our spirits perk up. The hero's coming! But as the dust moves closer, from out of the cloud we see a stagecoach. Disappointed, we watch it arrive and we open its door and look inside. There are no passengers. There is only a hat box. We take the box out and open it. Inside is a hat, not white but multi-colored—everybody's color, and everybody's size. The hero we are waiting for is not coming; he is already here. The hero is each one of us.

The journey into the new world and the new spirituality is a new hero's journey that each of us is being called to take. In this chapter, we will take the hero's journey toward discovering our new spiritual self, one step at a time. As we move along the journey, we will also see how Christ walked the same path and continues to walk it with us today. Along each step of the way, we will pray a part of the Hero's Prayer. It is a prayer that I wrote. I invite you to write your own version of it. I also invite you to take this journey by supplying some details from your own life.

At the beginning of the journey, the hero is masculine. This is because, at this point, he represents that aspect of our personality that urges us forward to face a challenge and seek a goal—the aspect that has traditionally been identified as the masculine aspect. Everyone—women and men—have this aspect in their personalities. On the psychological level, the spiritual journey is the journey of our masculine aspect to find our feminine aspect, so we can become a more full and complete person. Spirituality deepens the psychological aspect and makes it luminous, making the journey one that moves us toward ourselves as fuller expressions of Christ. It is a journey that never ends throughout our lifetime.

Step 1: The hero becomes aware of trouble.

We feel our spiritual hunger and we long for a more meaningful life. Like the deer in the forest (Psalm 42), we sniff through the tangles of the everyday world for the scent of the fresh water of new life. Our experience of spiritual hunger is our way of hearing the Spirit within us, calling us to a more full, more meaningful and more luminous life.

From eternity, **Christ** sees our need for healing and wholeness, and for the luminous fulfillment of our lives here on earth.

The Hero's Prayer

Spirit of Christ dwelling within me,
in a world filled with good things
and many troubles,
I am aware of my spiritual hunger.

You are calling me to set out on a journey
into a new world that you are now birthing forth,
and there to discover new possibilities, new healing
and new transforming love for myself and others.

As I begin, I ask you to give me the light and courage
to walk the way with you.
Let me become a clearer expression of Christ's
creativity, healing and love,
for myself, others and the world.

Step 2: The hero sets out on his journey.

We begin our spiritual journey. At first, we don't quite know
how to proceed. We can begin by taking walks along a beach or in
some woods, or any place where we can find silence and peace and
make the commitment to move forward.

Christ sets out on his saving journey by being conceived of the
Holy Spirit and born of Mary into the world.

My first steps are small ones.
I feel a little strange,
like a child in a new world.

Step 3: The hero meets a guide, usually a woman, who will help him on his journey.

We don't have to make our journey alone. Others are also walking the path. We seek them out, talk with them, listen to them
and learn from them. We can read books on spirituality, join a
spirituality group, or find a spiritual friend or counselor. We can
join a Bible study group. Along with others, we begin to grow in
knowledge of the Spirit and we begin to see and experience her
wisdom.

The hero's guide is depicted as a woman. The Bible depicts
God's wisdom as feminine. The indwelling Spirit is the Spirit of
wisdom, and so I refer to her in the feminine in this book. The
feminine guide symbolizes the wisdom that the hero seeks—that
we all seek—in order to find new life. She symbolizes the love that
guides and impels the hero onward toward new life. In *The Divine*

Comedy, Dante has the poet, Virgil, lead him part of the way, but it is his beloved Beatrice who takes him to heaven. With new life as his guide, the hero can move forward with confidence.

Jesus becomes aware of the divine wisdom that lives in him. He is attracted to wisdom and opens himself to be guided by her. Divine wisdom calls him to follow the advice and teaching of his mother Mary, and of Joseph. He studies the Scriptures and learns from the Jewish leaders. He works at a trade and familiarizes himself with his society and with the condition of people, especially the poor and outcast. In so many ways, he grows in age and wisdom.

**Spirit of Wisdom, dwelling within me,
open my eyes, mind and heart
to recognize you with new insight and love.**

**Let me see anew my oneness
with all others and the world.**

**Guide me to those who will help me
along my way to you,
to the new possibilities
that live within me,
for new life in you.**

Step 4: The hero enters a dark forest.

All beginnings are difficult. The spiritual journey inevitably leads us into a "dark night" of strangeness and risk. We may feel that we don't know if we are headed in the right direction. The need to be a true hero now grows. We enter a new and strange land with courage, trusting that the Spirit is with us.

Jesus leaves his home and family and begins his public ministry as a young, wandering rabbi named Yeshua.

Even with your help the path is dark.
I am often afraid.

Give me the courage to step into the new land
with faith and trust that you are with me
every step of the way.

Step 5: The hero encounters demons and dragons:

Our demons are all our internal forces that fight against our growth and development. Our dragons are all the external forces that the world throws against us. We will begin with our demons.

Our demons include our immature images of God, e.g., as the Great Scorekeeper in the Sky, akin to Santa Claus; or as a King, with ourselves as uneducated, medieval peasants; or as a Shepherd, with ourselves as passive sheep. We overcome these demons by developing a more mature image of God, an image that frees us to become fully ourselves. The best image of God is that of Jesus. Some people prefer to do away with any image of God and just let God be God, with no image.

Our demons also include our biases and prejudices, and our tendencies toward pathological individualism, sexism, racism, consumerism, secularism, and all forms of superficiality. All of these will have no place in the mindset of the new world and new spirituality.

Our demons also include any psychological problems or addictions we may have.

Here is where psychology can come to the help of spirituality. First, it can help us know and understand ourselves better, e.g., through such instruments as personality inventories, a Myers-Briggs Test, an Enneagram, journaling, relaxation exercises, etc. Second, if necessary, we can enter into psychotherapy to "untie the knots" in our psyches that are acting as obstacles to our personal growth. By untying the knots in our psyches, psychotherapy opens us to a better life. (Medicine, law, politics, a job, etc., also open us in their own way). Once the knots are untied, we are free to gather up the new life that births forth within us and build it—often under the guidance of a spiritual friend or counselor—into the life in abundance that the Spirit wants us to have. I stress this point because many people in the field of psychology present themselves as spiritual guides, and conversely, many spiritual counselors and members of the clergy have become psychotherapists. Such professionals are wearing two hats, and they and their clients have to know clearly which hat the professionals are wearing at any given time. While psychology and spirituality are closely related, it is important that everyone know the difference between them. Psychotherapy alone cannot heal spiritual ills or bring spiritual growth, although it will help. Spiritual counseling alone cannot heal deep-set psychological ills or bring about psychological maturity, although it will help.

Here are two examples that show just how different psychology and spirituality can be. First, let's look at Freud's psychological image of God and compare it to Jesus' spiritual image of God. Spirituality owes a great deal to Freud, for example, for his discovery of the unconscious, which permits us to take a deeper look into ourselves, so we can get a better appreciation of how the Spirit permeates our entire being. Freud's view of God and religion, however, was not friendly to religion or spirituality. He saw God as a father who had been murdered by his sons, so they could get his power. The sons, however, instead of enjoying the power they stole from their father, live in a state of constant guilt and fear, anxiously expecting their father to come back and punish them. Religion, said Freud, is our childish, neurotic "protection" against our guilt and fear as we anxiously await to be punished for our sins by an avenging God. In truth, Freud does describe some Christians. But his description of God is a neurotic one. It could not have been otherwise because he took it from the unconscious minds of his neurotic patients. Broken humans, like broken mirrors, create broken images. Christians who have this neurotic image of God can be so anxious or depressed (I have met many such people) that they could benefit from psychotherapy. But more deeply, they need to find a healthier, more mature image of God. If they don't do this, their psychotherapy will not be successful.

Jesus saw God in a very different way. In his famous story of the prodigal son (Lk. 15:11-32), he also images God as a father. This father has two sons. Instead of being murdered by his sons, however, this father is fully alive. He is also exceedingly generous—far beyond the social norms of his day. In fact, he gives his inheritance to his sons before he dies. In Jesus' time, this would have been an unthinkable embarrassment—a gigantic social error. One of the sons goes out and wastes his entire inheritance. When he returns, bankrupt, broken and hungry, the father does not do the "Freudian thing" and make him fearful and anxious by punishing him and threatening to destroy him. Instead, he runs out of his house—another social embarrassment that shocked Jesus' listeners—picks his son up out of the dirt, embraces him, takes him home and gives him a party. When the other son complains that he, himself, has always kept all the rules, the father also gives him his full love and wisdom.

In contrast to Freud's image of an avenging God—an image that has influenced psychology and psychiatry for many years—Jesus' image of God is one of a father who is generous, forgiving, wise and all-loving. He is a God who is wasteful with his goods to the point of making a love-feast of them for his children. (The story should really be entitled, "The Prodigal, i.e., Wasteful, Father.) Here is a God who is more than ready to forgive us if we ask him, and who thereby inspires not fear and anxiety but hope, joy and love. Jesus' image came from his own healthy imagination, mind and heart, and is a beautiful, inspiring joy for us. It is a clear expression of the loving union he enjoyed between his humanity and divinity. It also explains what gave him the strength to face his demons and carry his life forward to its saving goal.

Our second example comes from M. Scott Peck's famous book, *The Road Less Traveled.* In it, Scott picks up Allan Bloom's imaginative description of Freud's discovery of the unconscious mind. In *The Closing of the American Mind*, Bloom says that Freud discovered that our minds had a "basement," and that psychology quickly ran down into the basement and found all sorts of fascinating and seductive things stored and hidden there. That's fine as far as it goes. Peck also goes down into the basement of our minds, but there he makes a mistake. He mistakes our unconscious mind for God within us. That, of course, is not true. Our unconscious mind is simply an aspect of ourselves—albeit an important psychological one. Peck is following the Modern World mindset of fragmentation between the secular and the sacred, and therefore cannot go deeper than our psychological selves, or our secular selves. For him, psychology is all there is; there is nothing more, nothing deeper. There is no indwelling Spirit and no spirituality. He cannot see our luminosity and therefore cannot see God within us. In the end, he makes us less than human.

Finally, we have to face our spiritual demons. We set out on the hero's journey because we sense our spiritual hunger, which is the sign that the Spirit is calling us to herself and to greater life in her. As we begin to approach her, however, we can be impeded by an unexpected demon—our fear of the Spirit. In calling us to herself, the Spirit is calling us, as she called Abraham, to leave our "secure home" and travel to a "new land." She is calling us to die to our "old selves" and become "new selves." She is calling us to grow up to a new level of life as spiritual adults, to take responsibility for ourselves and to try to make a difference, however small, in the world. The traditional religious understanding of Adam and Eve tells us that they were ejected from the Garden of Eden after the Fall. Another way to look at this story is to see that the Spirit tossed the newborn human community out of their "nest" of childhood and into the challenge of adulthood in the world. As we approach the Spirit, we can be tempted to remain on the level of past immaturity and not move forward toward new maturity. Such fear shows itself psychologically, for example, in a neurotic dependence on parents or other authority figures, or in a destructive identification with entertainers, cult leaders, et al. It can also underlie such disorders as anorexia and bulimia. It can show up when people blame others for their problems and refuse to take charge of their own lives.

In essence, the Spirit is calling us to grow up and be free, and this takes us to our next spiritual demon—fear of our own freedom. From the very beginning, we humans became aware of our freedom and its terrible, i.e., terrifying, power. To become human, we had to freely acknowledge ourselves as human and as not divine. Deep within ourselves, we know that, along with our ability to understand and to love, our freedom is the power that makes us human. It is the power to make decisions, take responsibility, accept and assign blame, be participating citizens, choose mates, and build the world. Our freedom makes us so God-like that we can be tempted to step into absurdity and think of ourselves as God. If this terrifying possibility were not built right into us, we would not be truly free. We are all haunted by the fact that the entire human community did step into absurdity and think of itself as God. The echoes of the Fall and the aftermath from which we still suffer can frighten us into rejecting our freedom and the responsibilities that come with it. We can give it away, for example, to our parents, church authorities, politicians, military authorities—to anyone who can take the burden of responsibility from us. As we approach the Spirit, we know ever more clearly that she is calling us to greater freedom and to greater responsibility. Christ set us free, but we can falter as we walk our way to express him more clearly.

Our freedom permits us to love—ourselves, one another and God. If we were not free, we would not be able to love but would be puppets on divine strings. This brings us to our ultimate spiritual demon—fear of love. Fear of love is the fear of God himself, who is Absolute Love. Love puts us in intimate touch with ourselves, others, the world and God. Through love, we open ourselves fully to who we are and to one another. To say, "I love you," makes us vulnerable to others. It is never a one-way statement. It is always a request to hear the response, "I love you, too." We can be refused, rejected, and even humiliated.

We've already seen how the word "love" has often been replaced by the word, "relationship." A relationship protects the two people from love; it protects them from revealing themselves to one another and making themselves vulnerable to one another. It protects their individuality by guaranteeing that they can break off and assert their unique individualism anytime it suits them. If love of others binds us to openness, vulnerability, commitment and responsibility, how much more so does love of the Spirit bind us?

To help overcome our fear of the Spirit, we can remember that it is the Spirit who opens herself to being refused, rejected and even mocked by loving us first. She has bound herself to us first, and invites us to bind herself back to her. The word, "religion" is made up of the Latin word, *ligare,* to bind, and the prefix, *re*, back. In religion, God initiates the act of love and invites us to bind ourselves back to him in love. If we need examples of God's being refused, rejected and mocked, we need simply look around the world at the poverty, famine, injustice and wars that mock and humiliate God every day. We need simply look at Jesus bleeding on the cross.

Jesus faced and conquered his demons when he was tempted by Satan in the desert. Here we see a passionate young man, about to embark on nothing less than the saving of the world, and facing the fear that he can mess things up. Despite the fact that he is God, he can, in his humanity, give in to temptations to aggrandize himself by doing tricks, like turning stones to bread, or by taking political/economic power. At this moment of his life, he reminds us of David before him, whom Michelangelo sculpted as a young man on the brink of saving his world. In David's eyes and in the tension in his entire body, we see a youth who is facing the possibility that he can mess things up. He only has one shot at Goliath. He has to pull himself together and act in a way that will change his life and the life of the world, forever. He took his one shot and made it good. Jesus had this "one shot" at overcoming his demons. He took it and he also made it good.

I bring my problems, fears and anxieties
with me on my journey.

Give me the courage
to face myself clearly and honestly,
and to open myself to the new fullness of life
that you are offering me.

Alone, I will lose my way;
With you
and with the help of others
I will find my way.

Step 6: The hero encounters dragons and fights them:

Our dragons are all the external forces that fight against our personal growth and development. They are all the corrosive forces that mark today's society, e.g., pathological individualism, broken families, sexism, racism, consumerism, child neglect and abuse, collapsed education, quick recourse to violence, mediocre politics, greedy corporations, polluters, non-credible religions, etc. These are all self-imposed human problems—problems of the human spirit that we have brought down on ourselves. As we condemn them and fight against them, we must humbly admit that each of us is partly to blame for them ourselves. One of our most effective demons is our ability to create our own dragons, and then to feel helpless to overcome them.

As we saw earlier, Philosopher Martin Heidegger named three of the "dragons" that keep today's society shallow. First, we are caught up with the gossip of the day instead of serious conversation. Second, we are caught up with noise instead of thoughtful silence. We are a "boom box" culture who take noise with us everywhere we go—into our streets and parks, into our politics, economics and even into some of our churches. Like anxious people, we are afraid to be silent because we don't want to "hear" just how anxious and nerve-wracked we are. Third, we have replaced true thinking with mere data processing. There is so much information coming at us at all times that we can get caught in the treadmill of just trying to keep up with it, and never take time to think critically about what it all means. How many people can rattle off a thousand pieces of data about how to operate a computer but don't know how to understand or judge the material they get from the computer?

Jesus encounters the hostility and corrosive values of the wealthy and powerful of his society, who are oppressing the poor, and of the political and religious authorities, who feel threatened by him. He also faces his people's mistaken expectation that he become a political/military savior.

<blockquote>
The corrosive values of society
tempt and attack me and others every day;

As the mystic that I am,
open my eyes and heart to see
your presence within me.
In your light, let me see
how much I live by the world's corrosive values myself.
Let me see what you expect of me.

As the prophet that I am,
give me the strength and courage
to collaborate with you,
to work to fulfill your intentions and expectations,
to face the corrosive values of society
and help bring understanding, healing, peace and love
to myself and others.
</blockquote>

Step 7: The hero is wounded, falls and bleeds:

Old habits and old fears die hard. In our fight against our demons and dragons we inevitably suffer frustrations, setbacks and failures. We can become demoralized and be tempted to give up and fall back to our old level of life. Or we can allow our old habits and fears to be crucified and "bleed" out of us and die.

Jesus is crucified, dies and is buried.

The journey is not easy.
I stumble and fall often.
I am afraid.

Give me the courage to allow you
to crucify my old habits and fears.

When I fall and bleed,
let me know that you are on the ground with me,
bleeding and crying with me.

Step 8: The hero rises.

In the strength of the Spirit, and with the help, encouragement and support of others, we get up after every fall. We find new strength to keep going along our spiritual path.

Jesus rises from the dead.

After every fall, you lift me up,
you heal my wounds.
In my every darkness,
you shine new light and hope upon me.
You open new horizons to me;
you show me who I can become,
you put new possibilities for new life ever before me.

Step 9: The hero finds a sunlit clearing in the forest. There he meets a fair maiden and he marries her.

In the light of the Spirit, our masculine aspect finds our feminine aspect, and marries her. We achieve new wholeness and discover new aspects and depths of our spiritual self. We meet the

Spirit in a new way—with new freedom, joy, intimacy and love. We discern the Spirit's presence and intentions more clearly and we commit ourselves more deeply to collaborating with her. We pray with greater familiarity and intimacy, and we are more easily able to gather up ourselves, others and the world and offer all to God in worship, with greater gratitude and love.

Jesus rises and now lives in a luminously transformed way.

Through you, the blessed victory is mine;
In giving a greater richness of your life,
you enrich my own life and make it more full.

You fill me with new light and new strength
to live and work for justice, peace, freedom,
hope, joy, gratitude and compassion,
for myself and others.

To you I give thanks, praise and worship always;
May you be blessed and glorified forever.

Step 10: The hero returns to his people to call and inspire them to set out on their own hero's journey to a new level of wholeness of life in the Spirit.

Our new life in the Spirit strengthens the inter-connections and oneness we enjoy with all others and God. In American mythology, when the hero in the white hat finishes his work in one town, he leaves and rides off into the sunset. E. T., the Extra-terrestrial, who is an updated version of the Lone Ranger, gets into his space ship and goes home. But they don't really leave the people they've met. The Lone Ranger always leaves behind a silver bullet to remind the town folks of him, and E. T. touches the forehead of a child and promises to always be "right here" in the child's memory.

In the spiritual hero's journey, the story is the same. When we meet the Spirit and achieve a new level of life, we may be tempted to forget where we came from. The hero's journey is not for ourselves alone. The Spirit calls us to go back to the people—back to our world (even if we go to a new geographic location)—and tell the world what the Spirit has done for us. By our words, and better, by the new way we live in the Spirit, we invite and encourage others to join us as we begin the hero's journey all over again in response to the Spirit's new call. Some will refuse to take the journey with us. We leave it to the Spirit to send them the person or persons who will attract them to take the journey.

As long as we live on earth, we will always be on our way to greater personal growth and development in the Spirit. We will always be discovering new aspects of our spiritual self. And we will always be sharing our experiences with others—and learning from others. We will always be gathering up the world and offering it to God in worship in and through Christ.

The Risen Christ shows himself in his luminous glory to his friends and apostles. He gives them his Spirit and offers her to all the world so that he could be with us always. He sends his apostles out to teach the world the greatest and most heroic of spiritual truths—to love God with our whole heart, mind and soul and to love ourselves and one another completely and unreservedly in God's loving Spirit. As our spirituality grows, we continue to grow, and Christ continues to grow. In and through the hero's journey, cosmogenesis continues to be Christogenesis. In this way, Christ gathers up the world and brings creation, which flows forth from our Creator Parent, full circle back to our Creator Parent.

> God, loving Creator of the universe,
> I thank you for my new life.
> I know that it is not for myself alone,
> but also for others and the world,
> and most deeply, for you.
>
> You show yourself to me and the world
> as, "I-Am-With-You-Always."

May I always have the light
to see your Spirit dwelling within me and the world.
May I always have the strength and courage
to collaborate with your Spirit
for myself and for the world.

May I live my life as a luminous expression of Christ,
gathering up my part of the world
in your Spirit of love,
thanking you and worshipping you,
as I return myself and others
to You, in and through Christ.

I pray to you,
our loving Creator Parent,
in the Spirit of Christ,
who dwells within me,
and as an expression of Christ;
to whom be all honor and glory,
now and forever.
Amen.

Today, as it will always be, it is the time for heroes.

FIFTEEN

Our Luminous Oneness

Mythologist Joseph Campbell told a story about two policemen who were patrolling in their car along the edge of a cliff, when they saw a man about to jump off and commit suicide. As the driver brought the car to a screeching stop, the other policeman jumped out, ran over to the man and caught him by the wrist just as he fell over the edge of the cliff. For a long moment, until the policeman's partner arrived to help pull the man up, the first policeman held on to the man's wrist. Afterwards he said that although he was a married man with children and had everything to live for, he knew he would not have let go of the man, even if he had to go over the cliff with him. Something in him would not allow him to let go.

Campbell pointed out that in that moment of crisis and heroic action, the fundamental oneness of the human community shone forth in all its luminosity. At that moment on the cliff, all radical, isolating individualism disappeared and the policeman was ready to die for another person—one he did not even know. This oneness also shows up, Campbell noted, among soldiers on a battlefield, and among all those who give up their lives for others for whatever reason. We could add that it shows up whenever someone makes any kind of sacrifice for others—anywhere from giving up time, money or goods for someone else, even to hitting a sacrifice fly in baseball. It is at times like these, that we show ourselves and others a special aspect of what it means to be a human person.

In today's mindset, however, when we say, "I am a person," we very often use the word, "person" to describe our unique individual self. The new spirituality fills out the meaning of person. It shows us that, as a person, each of us is a unique-individual-self-with-others. Each of us forms parts of a whole, which is a unity in diversity. "No man is an island," said John Donne (c. 1571-1631). Everything we do affects the whole.

When we are young, we naturally focus on ourselves. We say, "I will first become who I am; I will do my own thing and set up my own career. Then I will get married and have children. Then I will join with others and give back to society some of what I have received." This is good and true, as long as we don't get lost along the way. The pressure to establish our own personality and to make good financially in competition with others, can separate us from others and destroy the quality of our lives. Young people go out on their own for their own sake and also so they can come back to the community and share their humanity with others—just like the hero goes back to his/her people to share what he/she has received from the Spirit. How many divorces, for example, are due to the fact that husbands and wives continue to live the individual lives they lived before marriage to such a degree that they don't, or can't, find time for each other—for their oneness with each other and with their children.

The ancient Greeks had a word for people who operate so much on their own that they separate themselves from care and consideration for others. They called them idiots. The word comes from *idio*, which means "self," such as in "idiosyncrasy," which means something pertaining to oneself alone. Sadly, we have developed a society that contains a significant number of idiots.

The new spirituality calls us to constantly keep in mind that we are basically members of our families, local communities, and the global human community. It is only within this wholeness that we are free to discern our unique possibilities and work to develop them. Yet spiritually, we are required to put ourselves first. "You shall love your neighbor as yourself," is the second greatest commandment that Jesus gave us, after the first commandment that we love God with our whole heart, soul and mind (Mt. 22:37-39). In practical terms, we have to love ourselves first because we can't give what we haven't got. We love ourselves first, by recognizing who we are, namely, images and likeness of God, who is love. We enjoy the presence of God within ourselves in a way that makes each of us an expression of Christ. Part of loving ourselves is recognizing what St. Paul recognized, "I live, no longer I, but Christ lives in me." (Gal. 2:20). Our self-esteem is our Christ-esteem. Our self-love is our Christ-love. All of our growth in our personality, career, marriage, friendships, etc., takes place within the context of ourselves as expressions of Christ.

Like Christ, we love ourselves first by recognizing that love is truly what we are. To be who we are as fully as possible is to love others as fully as possible. In the alchemy of spirituality, the more we relate to and love others, the more we relate to and love ourselves. For example, the more the young relate to and love the old, the more the young appreciate and love their youth. The more a husband and wife relate to and love each other, the more the husband appreciates and loves what it means to be himself and a man, and the more the wife appreciates and loves what it means to be herself and a woman. The more we relate to and love flowers and animals and earth, the more we appreciate and love how human we are. And finally, the more we relate to and love God, the more we know and love who we are as humans—where we came from, why we are here and where we are going.

There are times, of course, when we go off by ourselves for rest or retreat, to contemplate and be alone. But even then, we are not totally alone. We go off by ourselves to free ourselves from distractions so we can be closer to earth, to others and to God. Even on an everyday basis, there are those who prefer to be more removed from others. Some writers, composers, and introspective people operate better away from "the crowd." This is good, as long as they keep in touch with others interiorly. The most isolated monk, for example, lives in interior communion and oneness with others. If he had to live in the everyday world, he would be unable to operate. On the other hand, if he broke off his interior communion with others, he would go crazy. Interior separation is part of the definition of psychosis. The "Unibomber," who lived in a cabin in a remote area of Montana, was an example of psychotic separation and isolation. At the other end of the spectrum, there are those who need to be among many people on a regular basis. They love the hustle and bustle of the world and operate best that way. If they were alone too often, they would be uncomfortable. In either case, we find our place according to what best permits us to be ourselves and to keep in touch with others.

Here we can also mention the extreme opposite of pathological aloneness, namely, the pathological over-identifying with others. Actor-director Woody Allen expressed this extreme in his movie, "Zelig." Zelig was a man who had absolutely no unique individuality. He was so pathologically dependent on others for his very identity that whenever he related to someone, he became that other person. If he related to a women, he became a woman; if he related to an African American, he became an African American, etc. "Zeligs" are those people for whom oneness is blind conformity; they include overly-dependent hangers-on such as cult members, hate groups, and Christians and others who rely almost exclusively on authority for their identity.

A special challenge to our oneness arises when the Spirit moves us to fight against the prevailing values of our society. In areas such as social justice, education, politics and economics, there is ample opportunity to stand against the prevailing mindset. Here we have to be especially careful to preserve our oneness. The rebels of the 1960's acted very much outside their oneness with others. But, despite some good intentions, they helped break society apart without giving it a basis to come back together again. Their break with oneness turned out to be a destructive one. In the new world, the new spirituality will move us to break apart the old oneness. It will move us to work against some of society's prevailing values, but we will act with the goal of setting ourselves and others free to discern the Spirit and collaborate with her in building a new, more luminously whole society.

Our final concern is the oneness that binds Christians together with people of good will who are members of others religions, or who have no religion. In the new world, how will Christians be able to work with others in the fields of social justice, education, politics, etc., while showing them full respect and not trying to impose Christianity upon them? Can Christians acknowledge that others are part of the luminous wholeness of good will and still continue to teach that Christ is the savior of the world?

The new spirituality shows us that recognizing Christ as the savior of the world is not a matter of requiring that people be members of a Christian church in order to be saved. It is a matter of requiring that people (beginning with ourselves) live a life of love and compassion.

> I give you a new commandment, love one another. As I have loved you, so you also should love one another. This is how all will know that you are my disciples, if you have love for one another.
>
> Jesus, as quoted in John 13:34-5

> Owe nothing to anyone, except to love one another . . .
>
> Romans 13:8

Some Christians, however, disagree that love is the sign of salvation. They point to
the following texts, which they interpret literally:

> There is no salvation through anyone else, nor is there any other name under heaven [except the name of Jesus Christ] given to the human race by which we are to be saved.
>
> Acts 4:12

> Amen, amen, I say to you, no one can enter the kingdom of God [i.e., be saved] without being born of water and the Spirit.
>
> John 3:5

In the view of these Christians, anyone who does not explicitly and consciously accept Christ as his or her savior, and who is not explicitly baptized, is condemned. To them, Jews, Muslims, Hindus, Buddhists, Animists, agnostics and atheists, are automatically destined for hell. There can be unity only in uniformity and not in diversity. The new spirituality disagrees. It shows us that the Spirit of Christ lives in the whole world (Gen. 2:7). She blows where she will throughout the world (John 3:8) and offers herself to everyone in the world. What is the sign that someone has accepted the Spirit? It is love. "God is love, and whoever remains in love remains in God and God in him (1 John 4:16). In people whose lives are marked by love, the new spirituality sees Christ and salvation, even though the people themselves may not see Christ. Those Christians who require that people *literally* say that Christ is their Lord and savior should keep in mind, "Not everyone who says, 'Lord, Lord,' will enter the kingdom of God" (Mt. 7:21).

When we read the Bible spiritually and thus see its luminous wholeness, we get a clearer view of how God is present in the people of the world and how God saves people of all religions. Many Christian churches are now seeing with greater clarity that God calls people to himself in many ways and that people answer God's call in many ways. The word "church" is from the Greek word, *ekklesia*, which means, "the people who are called." While the various Christian churches hold on to their own principles and traditions, they see that the global people of Christ extend beyond their own boundaries. Many Christians now see people of other religions as members of the one, global people of Christ—to one degree or another—even though those people don't accept what Christians see.

In the view of the new spirituality, the sign of the luminous wholeness of the global people of God is a life that is marked by consistent good will, love and compassion. The word, "consistent" is important. Anyone can show good will or love here and there. The old Soviet Union, for example, provided full employment and financial security—such as it was—for its people. Many American slave owners shows some random acts of kindness toward their slaves. In the beginning of Dickens' "Christmas Carol," Scrooge gives Bob Crachet Christmas Day off—albeit reluctantly and grumpily. But when a person's life is marked by consistent good will and compassion, Christians see the Spirit of Christ present and active in that person, without whom such a life is not possible. They see the person's love and compassion as the love and compassion of Christ, and as the sign of salvation for that person, even though the person may not see himself or herself as saved in and by Christ .

When Scrooge learned to keep Christmas better than anyone else, he thought he was doing it in response to three ghosts who visited him. Christians see, of course, that he did it in response to the Spirit of Christ, who visited him. That example is easy to recognize. The story, after all, is a Christmas story. But can Christians really say that the Spirit of Christ lives and acts in people who don't accept that Christ is the savior of the world? Yes. Quite simply, what Christians see, Christians see. But what they see, they do not impose on anyone. Christians are learning new lessons on how to recognize Christ and how to treat people of other religions. For example, Christian missionaries are learning that they do not have to bring Christ to "pagan" lands. When they go out to "pagan" peoples, they now look to see how these people are already living lives of consistent good will, love and compassion in their own way. In learning this, the Christians are learning to recognize these people as expressions of Christ. They don't have to bring Christ to these people; they recognize Christ as already present, and as being expressed by them in their lives of consistent love and compassion. And the Christians see that Christ already recognizes these people as his disciples.

When Christians look at Jews, for example, they see that Jews are so sensitive to God's presence within themselves that when they pray, they sway like a candle flame to express the living, flaming Spirit within them. Christians see that Jews are a specially chosen people, who enjoy a special, loving union with God. In the Jews' prayerful expression of their loving union with God, Christians see Christ, who is the union of all humanity with God, while they respect Jews for being Jews. In fact, it was through the Jews that God gave Christians and the whole world the magnificent commandment to love God above all else and to love our neighbors as ourselves (Mt. 22:34-40; Mk. 12:28-34; Lk 10:25-28, from Deut. 6:5 and Lev. 19:18). In this love, Jesus tells us, we are saved. All this does not make Jews Christians. It does make Christians more respectful of Jews and opens the way for Christians to work together with Jews in the new world in respect and trust. It also opens the way for Christians to learn from Jews new ways to love and serve God and one another.

With similar insight, Christians see Muslims as recognizing God's loving presence within themselves in the Islamic commitment to bring justice and peace to the world. The word, "Islam," means, "the peace that comes through submission to God." Is this not precisely a Christ-like attitude? Hindus and Buddhists see themselves and the visible world as windows that open to the Invisible Transcendent. Christians see Jesus as the "window" to God, and also see the whole world as the window to God. The Buddhist view of "self-emptying" is a strong reminder to Christians of Christ, who emptied himself of his divine majesty to take on human form (while remaining God). Taoism teaches that the various ways to God are like different wells. If we dip deeply enough into our own well, we will reach the common water that feeds all wells. Trappist monk, Thomas Merton went to the East to learn how we could blend eastern spirituality, especially its depth of contemplation, with our more active western mindset. With his Christian eyes, he too saw the common well from which East and West draw their spiritual water. To Native Americans, all nature shows us the presence of the Great Spirit. Christians can take this teaching as a reflection of Jesus, who is all creation in loving union with God. To agnostics and atheists, the Golden Rule is a valid criterion for living a life of consistent good will, love and compassion. Christians can share the Golden Rule with them in the golden love of Christ.

Does the new spirituality, with its new ecumenism, lead Christians to conclude that it doesn't matter what religion people profess, as long as they live lives of consistent good will, love and compassion? No. It does not lead Christians to indifference. Among all peoples, Christians will always proclaim that Christ is the savior of the world. They will do this in words, and more especially, by serving the peoples of the world in humble, Christ-like, self-giving love, and never by any "triumphalistic" imposition of Christ upon other peoples and cultures. By their own lives of consistent good will and love, they will show the world the fullness of life in Christ and thereby work to attract people to Christ. In the new world, their relationship with people of other religions is one of peace, service, love and compassion, not of competition or hostility. If any deficiency of Christ-like love of God and neighbor becomes apparent among any people, Christians will look first to themselves and examine the humility, clarity and persuasiveness with which they are expressing Christ in their own lives.

Most emphatically, in the new world Christians will never force anyone to accept Christ—not politically, or economically, or militarily, etc. The days of killing for Christ are over; the days of sacrificing and dying for Christ through humble service to others have dawned anew.

The new world and new spirituality require new eyesight and new insight. It will be good here to look again at the new view of ourselves that the new world and the new spirituality are giving us, so we can keep our full meaning in mind as we move along the path of our new spiritual journey.

We are not homo sapiens or some enfleshed machine. We are Adam-Eve—unique, individual members of the human community;

God's beloved daughters and sons; sisters and brothers to one another. We are God's image and likeness; God's specially created and endowed human word, special expressions of Christ. In us the Spirit of Christ—God, One and Trinity—dwells, in creating, healing and transforming intimacy and love.

Like God our Creator, we are creative—filled with galaxies of possibilities, able to know ourselves, one another, earth and God with loving intimacy, free to build the world into a more luminous expression of Christ. Like Christ, our Redeemer, we are humble healers and peace makers. Like God, the Spirit, we are capable of loving in a way that can reshape and refresh the face of the earth and transform the world.

We are artistic, passionate, poetic, story tellers and dancers, painters, sculptors and singers. We are mythic, insightful, intellectual and reasoning, understanding, philosophical, wise, skillful, cultural, believing, hoping, joyful, prayerful, morally free and responsible, visionary, mystical, prophetic, and worshipful. We are endowed with space/time and eternal dignity, integrity, meaning, purpose and destiny.

The Spirit is ready to open our eyes even more and show us how to rediscover ourselves as the everyday mystics and prophets we already are. As we proceed, our prayer will be, "Lord, teach us to see."

SIXTEEN

Rediscovering Ourselves as

Everyday Mystics and Prophets

Very simply, a mystic is someone who knows how to see, and a prophet is someone who knows how to act on what he or she sees. Our ability to see mystically is our ability to see, or discern, the Spirit dwelling within ourselves, others and the world, and to discern her intentions. Our ability to act prophetically is our ability to collaborate with her in fulfilling her intentions in our everyday lives in the everyday world.

In this world, no one sees the Spirit directly. We have to learn how to see the signs of her presence and intentions. Christian faith tells us that the Spirit is dwelling within the entire universe—within every person, thing and event, to some degree of brightness. We learn to "see" or discern her presence by learning to see everyone and everything as luminous. For example, we can focus our attention on people, animals, flowers, trees, the night sky, and on our public schools, governments, corporate board rooms, etc., and then use our faith and imaginations to see them all as luminous—as I saw the students in the lectures I gave. In some cases the luminosity will be bright; in other case, it will be dim or even almost dark. The students, for example, were brightly luminous. The Holocaust, on the other hand, was one of the darkest events in human history. Yet the Spirit was there, suffering with its victims, and even with its perpetrators. No matter who the person or what the event, some luminosity will always be there. The Spirit never leaves anyone or anything. If she did, that person or thing would cease to exist. In the case of the Holocaust, which was an irruption of hell into the world, we could say it would have been better if it didn't exist. The Spirit would agree. She was there to show the world how to foresee it and prevent it. At the time, the world didn't know how to see her, and so it didn't know how to collaborate with her to prevent the horror. Yet, she remained in the Holocaust, screaming in pain for people to come and stop it.

The luminosity of the Spirit shines most brightly, of course, in people and events that are expressions of justice, peace, freedom, generosity, hope, joy of life, and love and compassion. In a government, luminosity shines brightly when peace and justice are widely practiced. In a corporation, we can see the Spirit shining in the efforts to make a good product without polluting the environment, to sell it at a fair price, and to share the profits fairly with all the employees. We learn to see that the luminosity within the world is the sign of the Spirit who is animating us and directing us—while keeping us free—toward fulfilling our greatest possibilities in creativity, healing and love. The luminosity of the Spirit opens our eyes and energizes us to get involved in working for our personal growth and fulfillment, helping others grow and fulfill themselves—and according to our talents and interests, getting involved in our schools, government, businesses, the ecology, movements for peace and human rights, etc. In cases such as these, we are assured that we are carrying out the intentions of the Spirit and collaborating with her because we are working to make ourselves and others more just and peaceful, more free and joyful, more whole and compassionate—in sum, clearer expressions of Christ.

Our mystical ability to discern the Spirit's presence and intentions, and our prophetic ability to collaborate with her are already alive within each of us. The new spirituality moves us to rediscover ourselves as the everyday mystics and prophets we already are. For the most part, we are not great mystics and prophets—although we should not quickly sell ourselves and our possibilities short. We are ordinary, everyday people who do ordinary, everyday things—that could change our lives and the world. Miss Manton, a first grade teacher in a public school, will give us an everyday example of how she saw her students—especially one named Michael—come to mystically discern the Spirit and prophetically collaborate with the Spirit on a first grade level—without getting involved in religion.

Each morning, as Miss Manton's pupils entered her classroom, they heard music. Though they didn't know the name of the music—and didn't ask—it was Tchaikovsky's, "Nutcracker Suite." Miss Manton played it softly and never even mentioned that it was playing. When the time came to start class, she would turn the music off, and then, after the pledge of allegiance to the flag, she would gather the students around her on an area rug. For a moment she simply gazed at them. Being the everyday mystic she was, she took in their young, open faces, saw the expectancy in their eyes, felt the joy of life that filled them, and stood in awe and wonder at the luminosity that glowed within them. Being a Christian, she (privately) saw her students' luminosity as the sign of the Spirit's presence and love within each of them—a presence and love that made each one of them sacred. She saw each student as a loving union between the Spirit and themselves, that is, as a luminous expression of Christ—the young Christ, full of new life and ready to learn about himself and the world. In each of them, she saw galaxies of possibilities for being creative, for learning and for helping others learn, for loving and being loved. Silently, she thanked God for them, and then she focused on teaching her students the basic skills of reading, writing, arithmetic, art, etc., on increasing their knowledge and understanding, and on helping them gain an ever deeper appreciation of what they were to learn and of who we were as human persons.

She began by saying to the children, "Good morning children. Today is a new and wonderful day filled with wonderful possibilities. The world has waited many years for this day, just as the world has waited many years for you to be born. And the world is happy that you are here to enjoy all its wonders. Now let's all say together . . . " The children then joined in. "We stretch our bodies to wake up to this wonderful day, we open our eyes to see, we open our minds to learn, and we open our hearts to love." The students then formed a circle, held hands and concluded, "We will not say bad things to one another or hurt one another. We will help one another and love one another."

Throughout the day, Miss Manton treated each child—and saw to it that the children treated one another—with the dignity and respect that their luminous humanity called for. In grades and in discipline, her children flourished.

From some other classrooms, she could hear teachers yelling and scolding their students. One day she asked some of them how they saw their children. They told her that they themselves were Christians, and as Christians they saw their children as fallen and corrupt persons who have to be whipped into shape if they are to learn anything—and if they are to be saved. The principal agreed with them. The children needed to have the devil beaten out of them.

When the principal noticed that Miss Manton's class was very free from discipline problems and was scoring significantly higher than the other classes, he made a special trip to her classroom to watch her teach. In his report, he wrote that Miss Manton was very well prepared and stayed very much on task. He then added that she also gave her students some extra attention, which he officially described as "fluff."

Miss Manton knew, of course, that her students were not perfect. No one is. When they misbehaved, she corrected them with a discipline that was alive with justice, fairness, and love. She also worked to form them in the aspects of internal discipline, fostering in them the qualities of justice, peace, trust, true freedom, hope and love.

Here it will be good to point out again that Miss Manton was an everyday mystic. To many of us, the word "mystic" calls to mind such great mystics as St. John of the Cross, St. Theresa of

Avila, or George Fox. We also tend to look at mystics as people who have exotic visions or experiences of God. Some of the great mystics have indeed had exotic experiences but they are not at all required for mysticism. The mysticism enjoyed by the great mystics is the same as Miss Manton's, the same as ours. The only difference is one of degree. Each one of us can discern the Spirit according to the ability that the Spirit gives us. Also, today many people use the word, "mystic," to denote people who, for example, channel the spirits of the dead, or have trance experiences, or use crystals and pyramids to evoke a supernatural atmosphere. Much of this is associated with the so-called, "New Age" movement. Some Christians even put "mysticism" together with Satanism. I mean none of these things.

I mean that as mystics, we enjoy an intimate, loving union with God because we *are* an intimate, loving union with God. What we are, we can experience. We can learn to experience our loving union with God. This experience, in all its loving intimacy, is the basis for our spirituality. It is the basis for our ability to discern the Spirit dwelling within ourselves, others and the world. The spiritual hunger that so many people feel today is arising from their deep felt desire to experience God personally and intimately, and their hunger is often accompanied by their frustration at not having been taught how to experience God personally and intimately, and how to discern the Spirit and her intentions.

The word "mystic" simply means "hidden." The mystic is a person who can see what is hidden from ordinary sight. Miss Manton saw in her students what was hidden from some of the other teachers and her principal. As mystics, we look at people and see the Spirit present and shining in their everyday work, in their hopes and dreams, and in the ways they are trying to move forward in life.

We can now see more clearly the mistake of other-worldly spirituality when it moves us to look away from ourselves, others and the everyday world to see God. If we look up into the sky to find God, we will have to "send" our prayers up there and ask God to "come down" and be with us. Praying in such a mindset does not bring us the inner peace that true prayer brings, even in our deepest troubles. It serves, instead, to make us anxious and even frustrated, if God doesn't hear us from "way up there." Even St. Augustine, who helped give us the other-worldly spirituality, saw God as always within us and the world. In his deeply spiritual insight, he said that God is closer to us than we are to ourselves. As everyday mystics, we can discern God's presence within ourselves, others and the world and know that the Spirit, who is our intimate, indwelling companion, knows our needs before we do and hears even our faintest whisper. We rediscover ourselves as the mystics we already are by looking *into* ourselves, *into* others and *into* the everyday world, and seeing the luminosity that shines there. As we learn to see the light of the Spirit in everyone and everything, we take time to focus upon it. We gaze at it. We contemplate it. We open ourselves to it and let it come through to us. We let it touch us. In the Spirit's light and love, we let ourselves, others and the world simply be who we are. We can then see our own, and others', deepest possibilities, hopes, dreams and aspirations, and we can help ourselves and others fulfill our possibilities.

How do we know that what we are seeing is truly the light of the Spirit and not, for example, the glare of our own ego, or someone else's ego? We apply this test. The Spirit is the Spirit of life, justice, peace, true freedom, joy, hope and love. If we see ourselves or others moving toward these qualities, especially if we are moving toward them with humility and not arrogant pride, we can be sure that we are seeing the Spirit and that we can collaborate with her in moving ourselves and others forward.

Mystics are not naïve. In the light of the Spirit, we learn to see both the great possibilities and also the corrosive darkness that lives within ourselves, others and the world. This darkness weakens our ability to see ourselves and others in the light of the Spirit. In the 1950's, Thomas Merton, who lived in a Trappist monastery, foresaw the riots that would break out on the streets of American cities in the '60's, and he warned the religious leaders and urged them to try to prevent the trouble that was coming. The non-seeing, or dimly seeing clergy who lived in the cities chided their brother for being an alarmist. Then, when the cities began to burn, they apologized to him for not having seen what he saw.

To be the mystics we are, we don't have to see as clearly as Merton saw, and we don't have to be super-intelligent or super-artistic. God gives us all the wisdom to see in our own way. Wisdom is simply our everyday, practical, common sense way of knowing. In Latin, the word for wisdom is *sapientia*. It comes from the verb *sapere*, which means to taste. It is our "taste" of the Spirit, and it "flavors" every moment and every action of our lives. In the "taste" and light of the Spirit we can see what possibilities the Spirit has given us for our own education, career, marriage, family, and service to society. We can see how we can inspire a young person to make a life-enhancing decision, how we can console someone who is hurt, how we can be with someone who is lonely. We can see when politicians are serving themselves instead of the people, even though we don't know the details. We can know that trashy TV programs hurt us and our children. We can find out how to get involved in our schools, how to influence the entertainment industry, how to make a political impact, how to help move our economic system to create fewer poor people, how to foster full human equality for women and all races, and how to nurture the earth. And we can learn how to get involved in collaborating with the Spirit to fulfill her intentions in all these areas.

Having a "taste" for the Spirit permits us to experience her presence all day, every day, even when we are not paying attention to her. Miss Manton prepared her lessons and taught them well, paying attention to them and to her students, all the while enjoying the "taste" of the Spirit's presence, encouragement and love, dwelling within her and her children. Another example—a negative one—will help us understand the importance of being able to taste the Spirit and experience her presence always. At a dentists' convention, I offered an address on "Spirituality for Dentists." To my surprise, a good number came to hear me. I spoke of the need for them to recognize the Spirit in themselves and in their patients, and of the need to carry the experience of the Spirit with them as they worked. One dentist spoke up, "You mean, if I'm filling your tooth, you want me to be thinking of God?"

"No," I quickly answered. "I want you to be thinking of filling my tooth. But I want you to be working in an internal atmosphere of peace, joy and even love, that comes from your being able to "taste" the Spirit while you're paying attention to filling my tooth. In that way, you'll be as free as possible from distractions, you'll be directing your best energy into your work, and I'll be assured that you'll do the best possible job of filling my tooth."

The dentist replied that he couldn't see how that was possible considering all the practical details of dentistry that he had to keep in mind while he was filling my tooth. I couldn't get him to see more than the mechanical details of his profession. Later, one of his colleagues came over to me and said, "I wish he could have understood what you said. He's so up-tight over the professional details of his work. He has to be perfect. He doesn't know how to be free and joyful." Then he added, "In fact, he's often depressed."

I sympathized with him and prayed that his colleague might some day learn to see himself and his work as alive with the Spirit, whose calm, peace, joy and love he could "taste," all day long.

As we learn to see like the mystics we are, we will begin to see the Spirit acting in ever new situations and places. We will learn to see just how "everyday" our mysticism and others' really is. Rosa Parks was an everyday person whose feet hurt on the day that the Spirit called her to see and act in a new way. That day she walked into history by walking onto a racially segregated bus and refusing to give up her seat to a white person. Segregation was certainly a darkness that contradicted humanity and the Spirit. Ms. Parks, of course, already knew that. At that special moment, however, the Spirit broke through to Ms. Parks in a special way. She discerned the Spirit's intention in a way that gave her a special insight and a special strength, and she then acted in a new way. In that moment of mystical insight and prophetic action, she changed the world and moved it one big step forward toward being more luminously human. We ourselves are the ordinary, everyday mystics who can also be moved by the Spirit to move ourselves and society forward—and do works even greater than Jesus himself did! (John 14:12)

What we see as everyday mystics, we do as everyday prophets. The ordinary notion of a prophet is of someone who can foretell the future. This ability is reserved for a few special people. Here we will focus on the way we are the everyday prophets that we are. The word, "prophet" comes from the Greek, *prophemi*, which means to "speak for." A prophet is a person who speaks for God—not merely by uttering words but by acting in collaboration with the Spirit to fulfill her intentions. The mystic is the prophet at prayer, and the prophet is the mystic in action. The new spirituality requires that we be both mystics and prophets. If we are mystics without being prophets, we will be pious onlookers in a world that desperately needs our help. If we are prophets without being mystics, we will be enthusiastic activists who create heat and confusion instead of justice, peace and love.

To pray as a mystic is to do "research," the way scientists and artists do research. Scientists and artists "ask" reality to disclose to them what possibilities are available for insight and expression. They then take the necessary steps to bring their research to fruition, as a new discovery or a new work of art. To Christian eyes, they are not only asking reality, they are really asking the Spirit, who dwells within reality. When we pray as mystics, we "research" the Spirit by asking her to show us our best possibilities. We then ask her to show us the necessary successful steps we need to take toward fulfilling our best possibilities. Praying to see and take successful steps, one at a time, is spiritually important. As mystics, we don't pray immaturely or frivolously. If we want to buy a house, we don't pray to win the lottery; we pray to know the successful steps to take to ensure that we can eventually buy a house. An academically poor student should not pray for a scholarship but should pray to see the successful steps he or she can take toward improving his or her understanding and grades. By taking one successful step after another, researchers and pray-ers grow in the assurance that their goal is reachable. This is the way the Spirit calls researchers and pray-ers to herself—one step at a time.

A woman who was a member of Alcoholics Anonymous had a friend who was lost in alcoholism. She spent many difficult hours, working one step at a time, to get her friend into a hospital for treatment. Finally, the friend agreed to have the woman drive him to the hospital. On the way, he begged her to stop for one last drink. His pleas were so strong and heart rending that she soon began to feel the temptation, not only to stop for his sake, but also to take a drink herself. She kept saying over and over again, "Just one more block, one more block. We are getting to the hospital. Just one more block." One block at a time, she drove her friend to the hospital without stopping.

This example also shows the importance of living our spirituality in community with others. This woman belonged to a community of people who go out of their way to help others. As she liked to say, "AA is not a self-help organization, it is a help-somebody-else organization." Prophetic Christians need the same kind of organization. Very often, they see opportunities to act prophetically but they find themselves "out there" alone and on their own. Most Christian churches are not organized to permit their prophetic people to act in unison to make a difference in society. Prophetic action makes many churches uneasy. Prophetic activist, Jim Wallis, of "Sojourners," in his book, *Lessons from the Life of an Activist Preacher* (Random House, 2000), recognizes the need for more organization and suggests how prophetic people can do a better job of acting in unison.

Prophetic action almost always puts prophets at some risk. Our social ills are deeply entrenched—or "genetically encoded"—and the people who benefit from these ills will fight anyone who wants to change the way things are set up. In some societies, e.g., in Central and South America, prophetic action puts people at risk of their lives. In our society, corporation "whistle blowers" risk their jobs and financial security. For the most part, however, the great risk in our society is frustration and the temptation to give up the fight. This is another reason why it is so important that prophetic people work within communities, and that church members work to get their churches to add their weight to prophetic activity in today's society. In later chapters, we'll see some opportunities for mystical insight and prophetic action in our institutions. For now, we'll go back to Miss Manton's classroom and see how her everyday prophetic encouragement worked with her students—and with one in particular.

A few weeks before Christmas, without any announcement, instead of playing the usual audio tape of the "Nutcracker" before class began, she began to play a video tape of the "Nutcracker" ballet. Her students immediately recognized the music they had been hearing from the beginning of the term. As they watched dancers put new life to the music, some became enthralled, but others—actually a few boys—began to mock the dancers. Especially vociferous was a boy, whom we'll call Michael, who was a rough and troubled child. Miss Manton let the boys make fun of the dancers for a while, and then she suggested to Michael that he try to do what the dancers were doing. True to form, Michael jumped up, tried a step and fell down. The class laughed, but Miss Manton stopped them and encouraged Michael to try again. Again he fell. Miss Manton encouraged him, explaining to him and the class that the dance was very difficult. She then invited others to try the dance, and they too, learned by experience how difficult it was. Encouraged by Miss Manton, the students also learned it was fun to face such a difficult challenge.

Day by day, Michael made a special effort to study the dancers' movements very closely and continued to try to imitate them. Even after the other students had stopped trying, Michael persevered. One day, as Miss Manton was about to turn off the tape to begin the class work, Michael cried out, "No, wait! Turn it back on!"

"Why?" she asked with great curiosity.

"The ballerina," Michael replied, "She's doing this." As he spoke he stretched out his right arm and pointed his finger. All the students turned their attention to Michael.

"Yes?" Miss Manton asked him.

"You turned the tape off right before she does this." He extended his hand as far as he could and then he gently bent his wrist and pointed his finger downward in a wonderfully exquisite movement.

Miss Manton turned the tape back on and the whole class watched as the ballerina did exactly as Michael had indicated. The rough and troubled boy had learned to see very deeply into the dance, to the point of coming to appreciate a very small, delicate hand movement. As he spoke, Miss Manton saw new and joyful life shining in his eyes. He had seen more than a dance movement. In his own way, Michael had become a mystic. He had learned to see the beauty and luminosity of the dance. He had touched the Spirit and the Spirit had touched him. Then he turned to the class and said, "Everybody do it." All his classmates extended their arms, pointed their fingers and bent their wrists. "See how that works?" he explained. "That's how we have to do it." In the light of the Spirit, he had learned that he was one with the dance and one with his classmates, and he was now imparting the beauty and luminosity of the dance in new-found, joyful oneness with them. In his own way, Michael had become a prophet.

SEVENTEEN

A Little Help from the Spirit

One day a fellow psychotherapist asked me to have lunch with him because he had something very important to tell me. In fact, he added, he had something frightening to tell me. We often had lunch together and enjoyed discussing matters of the world, and especially matters of the spirit. One of our favorite topics was the Hero's Journey. He was even teaching a course on the psychological characteristics of the hero in today's society. Today, however, my friend's tone sounded ominous.

Unable to image what I was about to hear, I ordered my food and braced myself for the worst. He started by saying he hoped I wouldn't think he was crazy. I waited. He then told me that on the previous Sunday morning, he had gotten up before dawn and gone to a beautiful park near his home. At the time, he was living alone. His social life wasn't great, but he did look forward to marrying some day and having a family, although he openly wondered if his focus on his individual needs would permit him ever to fulfill his dream.

With no one near him in the park, he sat on a rock by a stream and watched the sun come up—its newborn rays shimmering through the trees and bouncing off the water of the stream. Totally captivated by the scene, he sat there in deep silence. After a while, the sun, the trees, the water, even the air—all began to glow with a new brilliance. Colors became brighter; fragrances, sweeter; sounds, more soothing; textures, more palpable. Everything around him glowed with translucent richness and the world grew luminous. Then it happened. Suddenly he felt sprung loose from time and space. Caught up in a wondrously rich and peaceful freedom, he was no longer sitting on a rock in a park, but felt himself floating in eternity and infinity. There were no boundaries, no obstacles, no images of himself or the world, or of God, just a beautiful sense of being embraced by infinite peace and love. Within this embracing presence, everything was one, everything fit together with ease; everything was good; everything and everyone was luminously transparent and beautiful; everything was all right. Feeling supremely alive, he simply basked in unbounded simplicity, beauty and love.

Then he "came back to earth." Once again he saw the sunlight dancing amidst the trees and on the water of the stream. He could hear the birds chirping and feel the cool morning air carrying to him the sweet freshness of the morning. But now everything was different. The experience of the all-embracing presence was still with him. That presence now filled the sunlight, the trees and stream, the song of the birds and the freshness of the morning air. It made everything newly peaceful and alive, deeply luminous and beautiful. With deep certitude he knew that the richness, simplicity, peace, beauty and love he had just experienced as being outside of space/time, were all present here in space/time—within the sunlight, within the grass and the trees, within the water—within the whole world and universe—within himself. In a special moment, he had gained a whole new and deeper way to see himself, others and the world.

He recounted the experience to me with awe and wonder. Then he said, "Now tell me if I'm crazy or not."

"You're a psychotherapist," I quipped. "Do you feel like you're crazy?"

"No," he replied, smiling. "In fact, I feel more sane—more alive—than I have ever felt. And I certainly feel more peaceful, and even more able to help people."

I knew from previous conversations that he was not religious. He had grown up in a religion but as his experiences and education grew, he felt his church had not kept pace. It did not address the questions he faced—either personally or professionally. To him, religion had become irrelevant. Yet, he had retained some kind of belief in God—a belief that he described as the belief that there was some spiritual presence in the world that was greater than himself. It was this belief that attracted him to the conversations on spirituality that we often had at lunch. He expressed his belief by saying he wanted to be spiritual but not religious.

With this in mind, I said, "It looks like your spirituality is alive and well."

"What happened had nothing to do with religion," he shot back.

Disregarding his comment for the moment, I said, "Let's look at what happened. You say you felt like you left this world behind and found yourself in a new place."

"Yes. It was beautiful—even though I didn't see anything, or anyone. But I'm sure I was in some beautiful presence."

"And when you came back, you felt more alive."

"Yes."

"And you felt more confident that your possibilities and dreams could be realized?" I suggested.

"Yes. That's a good way to put it. I do feel more optimistic about myself."

"Do you mean, for example, that you're more confident that you really can find the right woman, get married and have a family?"

"Yes," he replied quickly.

I pushed him a little further. "Do you think your wife and children will simply fall from heaven?"

He looked at me quizzically and than laughed. "O. K.," he conceded. "I know what you're getting at, and you're right. Come to think of it, what happened to me Sunday makes me realize that I have to change my attitude. I have to tone down what you call my almost pathological individualism and find the necessary successful steps to reach my goal. If I do all that—yes, I can do that— I can attract the right woman and get married and have a family."

Encouraged by his answer, I assured him that he wasn't crazy. "As far as I could tell", I continued, "you had a mystical experience."

"Mystical!" My colleague recoiled at the word. He would have preferred that I said he was crazy. As a psychotherapist, he was familiar with various forms of psychosis, and at that moment, mental illness was more acceptable to him than mysticism.

I held up my hand and told him to calm down. "Mystical experiences", I explained, "are very common. Just about everybody can remember having had such a special moment. They could have been at work, or reading a book, or nursing a baby, or balancing a checkbook, or worrying about a sick relative, or in church. Suddenly, for a moment, they were in another place where they were in a special presence that made everything peaceful and good."

"Come to think about it, " he interjected, "I think I felt that way before."

"It's the Spirit's way of reminding us that she's there. You could say it's her way of inviting us to move forward on the hero's journey. Especially if we're stuck along our way, she likes to give us a nudge and build our confidence."

"Is that what you mean by a mystical experience?"

"Yes."

"Well, that I can accept."

"Good. Let's take it from there. On Sunday morning, the Spirit took your regular experience of yourself and flipped it over."

"Flipped it over? Like a pancake?"

"If you want to put it that way. You live constantly in the presence of yourself and in the presence of the Spirit within yourself and the world. Ordinarily, your experience of yourself is in the foreground and your experience of the Spirit is in the background. Given the noisy, thing-driven way we live, we can easily crowd out our background experience of the Spirit. On Sunday morning, the Spirit flipped your experience around, so for a moment, you experienced her presence in the foreground and yourself in the background."

He thought for a moment, struggling with what I said. "Why did she do that?"

"It's her way of letting you know that she's there."

My colleague hesitated. I could feel him fighting off my explanation. "No . . . Hmm . . . I'm not too sure." Then he sat up straight. "Wait a minute!" he said strongly. "Abraham Maslow and his 'Peak Experience!'" He was referring to psychologist Abraham Maslow (1908-70) and Maslow's 1964 book, *Religions, Values and Peak Experiences,* in which he wrote about a special experience that many of his patients reported having. In this experience, his patients said they suddenly perceived the whole universe as an integrated and unified whole, with all the fragmentations of life reconciled. Fear and anxiety were lost, and they felt that they were closer to reality and to their real selves. In this "new presence," they were more free, more creative, more loving, more graced, more whole. They became unattached from their everyday concerns and less desirous of everyday things. They found themselves to be more self-forgetful and unselfish, more understanding, more forgiving and less condemning—perhaps, a little more God-like. Everyone and everything became sacred, beautiful and good, and life became more worthwhile. They felt humility, wonder, awe, reverence, surrender and worship. Even death became acceptable. Maslow considered this experience to be a purely natural and healthy one, and one which was open to anyone.

"That's it!" my friend exclaimed. "I had a peak experience. It's purely psychological and has nothing to do with religion." With a sigh of relief, he added, "I'm not crazy—and I'm not mystical."

"Not so fast," I said. Maslow was a psychologist and he saw his patients' experience strictly from a psychological point of view. The mystical experience certainly has a psychological component, but psychology doesn't come close to explaining it all. Sunday morning you could also have had a change in your blood pressure, but that doesn't explain what happened to you."

My colleague calmed down. "Well, actually, I do feel that what happened to me Sunday morning was more than just a psychological experience." He hesitated and then said, "Yes, I really be-lieve I was in the presence of something spiritual."

"Or Someone spiritual," I suggested.

"But I didn't see the Spirit. I didn't see anything or anybody."

"No. Nobody sees God in this life. That's what Maslow missed. Psychology today can still be so separated from religion and spiri-tuality that it can't really account for God's presence—though it's learning fast how to do it. If some psychologists can't see God, they shouldn't make the mistake of concluding he's not there."

My colleague pondered what I had said and then noted, "You know, Freud spoke of a consciousness that is above consciousness. I wonder if he was getting at what is behind the experience that Maslow's patients had—and that I had."

I took a bite of my lunch and then continued. "That could be true. Freud spoke of an 'oceanic feeling,' or a 'feeling of eternity' that his friend, Romain Rolland, told him about. But he didn't go into it too deeply. Rolland had tuned in on the experience of a presence that is hidden behind our ordinary awareness. Spiritual-ity calls it the experience of Mystery.

"Well, it's a mystery to me," my colleague quipped, with his mouth full.

"No," I corrected. You just said 'mystery' with a small 'm.' I mean Mystery with a capital 'M'." Small 'm' mystery is ignorance. In a murder story, the identity of the killer is a mystery. We are ignorant of his or her identity until we find out 'who done it.' Then the mystery disappears. With small 'm' mystery, the more knowledge and understanding there is, the less mystery there is."

I sipped some coffee and continued, "I'm talking about capital 'M' Mystery."

"All I know is that I had this fantastic sense of being in some presence . . . "

"Yes. And that presence you experienced had no image. It wasn't even the luminosity that we talk about—that we "see" shining in everyone and everything. It was just an invisible background to the whole world. Is that right?"

My colleague thought for a moment. "Yes," he said reflectively, "that's right. The presence was invisible. It was everywhere, it filled the whole scene. Even afterwards, I could still sense it in the sun and the trees and the air. . . ." He looked around at the other people in the restaurant. "I can still sense it now. It makes me feel closer to everybody."

"Yes, it brings everyone and everything together. It's the invisible presence out of which everything that we can observe is emerging."

"What does that mean?"

"Here's one way to explain it," I offered. "When we watch television, we see the picture and hear the sound, but we don't see the electricity that's making the picture and sound possible. We can say that the picture and sound are emerging from the invisible electricity; they are the way the electricity is showing up. We are in the presence of electricity but we can't see it directly. We can only see it in the ways it's showing up. And we know that if it wasn't there, the picture and sound wouldn't be there."

I paused as my colleague ordered more coffee, and then continued. "In fact, if you could see the electricity, it would distract you from the picture and sound. It's better that the electricity remain invisible and live in darkness." I raised my hand to signal a break in my thought. "Here the metaphor of electricity breaks down. In the case of the Spirit, you were aware of her presence, and your awareness was not a distraction. In fact, it made your experience of trees and sunlight, of people—of your whole life— all the more rich and meaningful."

"Yes, you're right," he agreed.

"I mentioned earlier that your experience was different from seeing the luminosity we see when we look at people and things with the eyes of faith. You experienced a presence that had no image, not even light. You were in the presence of someone who we can say is living in darkness. Remember how we described the Biblical picture of earth, with God living in darkness above the blue metal dome? Mystics often describe God as darkness, or

Mystery, who shows himself within every observable thing and person that make up the universe. Some mystics have described God as the 'pregnant void' who births forth all the observable universe. In any case, we begin the see the difference between small 'm' mystery and capital 'M' Mystery. The more we know and understand, the less small 'm' mystery there is, but the more capital 'M' Mystery there is. In everything we know and understand, for example, about science, or psychotherapy, or ourselves, or baseball, we diminish small 'm' mystery. But at the same time, we are also learning a little more about God, from whom science, psychotherapy and everything else ultimately emerge, and our knowledge and understanding of God can never be exhausted. Capital 'M' Mystery just goes on and on.

My colleague continued eating in silence for a moment. Then he said, "Let's get back to the darkness. Darkness sounds more like sin than like God."

"True, darkness is used to symbolize sin. We call Christ the light of the world because he overcame the darkness of sin. Darkness can also mean ignorance or confusion or chaos. The Bible speaks of the process of creation as the ongoing movement from darkness, confusion and chaos to light and order. But in spirituality, darkness is also used to symbolize God himself, as the Absolute Incomprehensible and Inexhaustible Mystery. In the Biblical image of the earth I just mentioned, God is depicted as darkness, because God is beyond all human images—all human imagination, language and understanding, and even beyond all human references of male or female—despite the fact that the Bible refers to God as male. This is the sense in which we can describe God as Absolute Darkness." I paused for some more of my lunch and then said, "There was a great mystic named Meister Eckhart, who lived in the 14th century, who prayed to God to rid him of God."

"What kind of a prayer it that? It sounds like he was praying to become an atheist."

"What he meant was that he wanted God to remove every image that he had of God, like a king, or a shepherd, or an old man. He saw his images of God as obstacles to his closeness to God, and to his ability to experience God in everything and everyone. He was afraid that any image of God would interfere with his full experience of the presence of God. He wanted God to be totally invisible, so he could see his presence in everyone and everything as directly as possible. His odd prayer helped give us the expression that many mystics use, 'The best image of God is no image at all.'"

"Wow!" my colleague exclaimed.

"Some people even get hung up on the fact that Jesus was a man. Their image of Jesus traps them in his masculinity so they can't see women as true expressions of the Christ-reality that Jesus was. When God became human—while remaining God—the result, of course, had to be either a male or female. Given the culture of the first century Jews, the result had to be a male. But we have to look at Jesus with the eyes of spirituality, and see him as the all-embracing, luminously transparent, human expression of the invisible God, who is fully expressed by men and women, as well as by all the earth and universe. If you want something crazy, look at how Christians don't mind referring to God as a rock, as in Rock of Ages, and yet won't refer to God in the feminine."

"Wow!" my colleague exclaimed. "But what does that have to do with me?"

"On Sunday morning you experienced the presence of God as darkness, as the darkness or pregnant void out of which everything emerges. Your experience set you free to experience God's presence more sensitively in everything and everyone. As you said, you can still sense God's presence right now. That's an important step in your spiritual journey."

"All that happened to me!?"

"Yes."

"What did I do to deserve something special like that?"

"Well, as I said, everybody has experiences like the one you had. They're special moments in our lives in which the Spirit gives us a special 'peek' into her presence. What's that old Beatles song,

'A Little Help from my Friends?' In those special moments, the Spirit gives a little help to her friends. Those moments are so impressive that we can live on them for a long time."

My colleague ate quietly for a while. Then he said, "Do the churches talk about this?"

"No," I answered. They talk about morality but not spirituality—at least not this kind of spirituality. Mostly they talk about piety and devotions but not about our personal experience of God. In fact, Carl Jung once described a patient who came to him and related that he had had an experience just about the same as the one you had. The patient was a Catholic, and after he finished telling Jung what had happened, he said he would probably have to leave the Catholic church, because he thought the church would never tolerate such an experience in one of its members. Jung lamented the fact that the patient had come to him in the first place, instead of going to a priest, and further lamented that the priest would probably not have known what to do with him anyway."

"From my experience," my colleague mused, "I agree with Jung and his patient." He sat quietly for a while, and finished his lunch. Then he became excited. "I'm going back there again this Sunday so I can have the same experience."

I cautioned him not to try that. "The experience doesn't come on demand. If you try to force it to happen, I can guarantee that it won't happen. It doesn't come from us; it comes from God. The great mystics enjoy this experience almost all the time. God's Spirit keeps coming through to them constantly. We on the other hand have these experiences infrequently. But we're also mystics. Everybody is a mystic. We should constantly dispose ourselves to experience the Spirit's presence as you did Sunday morning, whenever she decides to come through to us in this particular way."

"How do we do that?"

"Well, we do it by doing such things as praying and meditating regularly, taking walks in quiet places, appreciating something beautiful, loving someone, and even going to a park at dawn—not to force the Spirit to come through to us, but to be ready if she does. We do it by learning to see the luminosity that is shining in everyone and everything—which nurtures our sense of God's presence and helps make us habitually aware that, as Teilhard de Chardin said, we live in the divine milieu."

As the waitress gave us our checks, I added, "Artists are naturals at disposing themselves to experiencing the Spirit in the form of Mystery. They let all sorts of luminosity flare forth from the pregnant void into their hearts, minds and imaginations. To Christians, Mystery is God himself, or the "seat" of God's presence. To artists—and others—Mystery can mean God, or it can mean simply the inexhaustible natural energy that is the source and wellspring of art, beauty and creativity. The different meanings of Mystery always make for a good and lively discussion."

We finished our lunch and paid our checks. As we were walking back to our office, my colleague brought up a thought that I had let drop in our conversation. "What has any of this got to do with religion or church?"

"Well," I answered. "You felt you had to tell me about your experience, didn't you."

"Yes. And I feel a lot better that I did."

"And you feel closer to people, don't you."

"Yes, I do."

"So you just joined a church."

"What!? What church?"

"It's a very small one. In fact, it only has two members—you and me. And possibly others you feel close to. That's what religion and church are all about, aren't they—people getting together to share and enjoy their experiences of God, and to thank God by living ever fuller lives."

We laughed together and went back to work.

That evening, I thanked God for the help he had given my colleague. I picked up the Bible and looked for a psalm that described the Mystery of his all-embracing, all-loving presence. I found one and read it slowly,

LORD, you have probed me, you know me:
you know when I sit and stand;
you understand my thoughts from afar.
My travels and my rest you mark;
with all my ways you are familiar.
Even before a word is on my tongue,
LORD, you know it all.
Behind and before, you encircle me
and rest your hand upon me.
Such knowledge is beyond me,
far too lofty for me to reach.

Where can I hide from your spirit?
From your presence, where can I flee?
If I ascend to the heavens, you are there;
if I lie down in Sheol, you are there too.
If I fly with the wings of dawn
and alight beyond the sea;
Even there your hand will guide me,
your right hand hold me fast.
If I say, "Surely darkness shall hide me,
and night shall be my light"—
Darkness is not dark for you,
and night shines as the day,
Darkness and light are but one.

(Psalm 139: 1-12)

About a year later, my colleague met a wonderful woman. They married and have two sparkling daughters.

EIGHTEEN

The Luminosity of Art and Poetry

An art professor once told his students, "When you paint, I want you to look deeply into what you are painting. I want you to get to the point where you see the Mystery from which the beauty of your painting is emerging. Go into the first moment of creation when all was darkness. Then pull out of that darkness all kinds of luminous expressions of reality, truth and beauty. I want your paintings to be like the light that illumined the newborn universe as it flared forth to form all the beautiful galaxies of the night sky."

His students laughed. "Is that what we have to do to pass this course?" one asked.

The professor continued. "I am talking not only of your paintings but more importantly of yourselves. I want you to touch the first moment of your own creation and ask yourselves, 'Who am I? Where did I come from? Why am I here? Where am I going?'" I want you to answer those questions in every painting you create. I want your work to be luminous with the creative beauty of the universe and of yourselves." Then he looked at the student who had asked the question and said, "If you don't do this, you may possibly pass my course, but you will spend your lives decorating people's houses and other buildings, and you will never become an artist."

The professor was calling upon his students to go deep into the infinite Mystery, the pregnant void that is the primary source of the universe and of all creativity and beauty. From the depths of Mystery, beauty calls us to find her, express her and celebrate her—in paintings, poems, dances, music, etc. As part of Mystery, whether we see Mystery as God or as natural energy, beauty is inexhaustible. The more we find her, express her and celebrate her, the more there will be to find, express and celebrate—forever. Some people once asked an Italian pastor why he was permitting the beautiful frescoes in his church to deteriorate. They wondered if he did not have the money to maintain the works of art. To their surprise, he answered, "It is the nature of beauty to reveal herself in these frescoes for a while and then have them die. It's all right. Beauty will reveal herself elsewhere. The frescoes are mortal, beauty is eternal."

Beauty makes art luminous with truth and with the Spirit who lives within beauty and truth. Earlier we took a look at Michelangelo's statue of David. Let's look again at this wonderful example of beauty and truth. The great sculptor shows us a youth on the brink of becoming luminously alive as a man and hero. David is facing Goliath. He has one shot of his sling. If he misses, Goliath will kill him, and the Philistines will kill or enslave David's people. There are so many ways he can mess up. He can become overwhelmed by his challenge. He can lose his nerve. He can give in to fear. He can get distracted by the crowd around him. He can swing badly. He can hit Goliath in a spot that will not kill him or even hurt him. The intense look in David's eyes and the electric energy in his muscles tell us that he is pondering all these contingencies. The situation has pulled him totally into himself. He is asking himself, "Who am I? Where did I come from? Why am I here? Where am I going?" Am I alone? Is God with me? Can I collaborate with the Spirit within me in this great challenge? In this way, he foreshadowed Jesus, who also had to answer the same questions.

In David's intense expression and in his strong muscles on the brink of action, we see that he is about to answer, "Yes. The Spirit is illumining me. I know who I am and what I must do. I can do this." As we gaze in wonder at this marble statue, we become one with this young man who is at a very powerful spiritual moment in his life. We become one with the Spirit, of whom he is a luminous expression. With him we ask ourselves the same deep questions he is asking himself. As the Spirit is enlightening and strengthening him, we wait for her to enlighten and strengthen us.

The statue is a great work of art. It is deeply human, luminous with transcendence and open to eternity. We ourselves are great works of art. We may never face a challenge as deep as David's; we may never accomplish what he went on to accomplish. That is of no matter. We are called by the Spirit to become great works of art by making ourselves luminous with transcendence and open to eternity, so the world can see how we and all people and things are in their own way, luminously beautiful works of divine art.

The following two poems are examples of the beautiful luminosity of art. Let's look at how they shine with transcendence and open us to eternity. The first is the famous poem by Robert Frost, "Stopping by Woods on a Snowy Evening."

Whose woods these are I think I know.
His house is in the village though;
He will not see me stopping here
To watch his woods fill up with snow.

My little horse must think it queer
To stop without a farmhouse near.
Between the woods and frozen lake
The darkest evening of the year.

He gives his harness bells a shake
To ask if there is some mistake.
The only other sound's the sweep
Of easy wind and downy flake.

The woods are lovely, dark and deep.
But I have promises to keep,
And miles to go before I sleep,
And miles to go before I sleep.

Written in ordinary, everyday language, the poem shows us how our ordinary, everyday lives are luminous with the Spirit. A man is driving his sleigh home on a snowy evening. He has been to the village, perhaps to do his day's work, and is now returning home to his wife and children, to supper and bed. How very ordinary. How very special. He is involved in the ordinary moments and movements of his life, which go on and on from day to day—almost like perpetual motion. We see this motion in the rhyme scheme that Frost has set up for the first three verses. In the first verse, the word, "here," doesn't get a rhyming word until the second verse. The word, "lake" in the second verse doesn't get a rhyming word until the third verse. Each verse sets up the need for another verse—with no end in sight. Like life in today's society, Frost has set up a pattern of never ending movement. Yet, as we read the poem, we discern deep within its movement a living, silent peace. The poem's luminosity is beginning to show.

Spirituality requires that we find such peace in the never-ending movements of our everyday lives. We find this peace in two ways. In the first way, we actually stop what we are doing for a while and turn away from our everyday routine. We go for a walk in the woods, or we enjoy a sunset, or read a good book, listen to good music, spend time gazing at a baby's smile, say a prayer, or join a group for prayer, meditation or discussion. Such stops, or retreats, are good for us. The new spirituality warns us, however, that when we stop for these moments, we not try to pull the world back to an earlier time and an earlier security. This temptation is one of the demons we must overcome on our hero's journey.

In the second way, we find peace, i.e., we experience the Spirit, without stopping our everyday activities. We learn to be in the presence of the Spirit no matter what we are doing. We can think of my colleague, who learned how to do this after that Sunday morning in a park, and of the dentist, who could not do this while he was drilling people's teeth. St. Ignatius called our experiencing of the Spirit during our everyday activities, "Contemplation in action." In our own time, mystic-poet, T. S. Eliot, in his "Four Quartets," said we find the still point of the swirling universe. Note that Eliot did not say the still point *in* the swirling universe, but the still point *of* the swirling universe. We and the world do not stop so we can see the Spirit dwelling within it. We and the world are in constant motion, just as the poem is. It is within our very motion that the still point lies—the still point where all is vibrantly alive and quiet, all is connected, all is one, all is peaceful, all is beautiful. It is the "background" in our everyday lives and in the everyday world, where the Spirit lives.

In the poem, the man comes upon some woods, out in the middle of nowhere, away from the everyday world. He stops to look. In stopping, he can find the peace that lives within the woods—and within himself. The evening is dark. The man can't see anything except the snowy woods. For a moment he thinks of the owner of these woods, but then he puts that thought away. He is alone with the woods and the snow—and the dark. Here he puts away his everyday sights and sounds, smells and movements, thoughts and desires, and enters into Mystery, into the pregnant void from which shines the light to let him see who he really is and why he is alive. This man is not used to being in such a place. His senses and thoughts want to know why he put them aside. He wonders that his horse must think it queer that he has stopped here. His horse represents his senses, and his horse's wondering represents his mind. The horse even shakes his harness bells, as if trying to awaken him, to bring him back to everyday life. But the easy sweep of the wind and the soft, downy snowflakes keep his attention fixed on the deeper reality, on the pregnant, peaceful, life-giving darkness, where the Spirit lives. Though his senses and thoughts are uneasy, his soul is at rest—at home in the darkness of the pregnant void. "The woods are lovely, dark and deep." His soul likes being there. He is in the still point of the swirling universe, where the Spirit lives.

> Your imperishable Spirit is in all things.
>
> Wisdom 12:1; cf. 1:7

While he is at home with the Spirit, yet he is still in touch with the woods and the snow and with his horse—with the everyday world. For the moment, though, his awareness of the Spirit is in the foreground and his awareness of the everyday world is in the background. Then the jingle of the sleigh bells gets through to him. The everyday world calls him back, and he remembers, "I have promises to keep." He has everyday obligations and responsibilities. He must move on. It is time to get home.

"I have miles to go before I sleep." The man knows how far from home he is, how many miles he must travel to get there. He knows his wife and children will be waiting for him, with supper ready. He will then go to bed and get a good night's sleep in preparation for a new day.

We are now ready for one of the most wondrous, mystical lines in all of poetry.

And miles to go before I sleep

Frost repeats the very same words that the man used to describe his everyday responsibilities in his everyday life. But now these words are brightly luminous. The same man, the same horse, the same sleigh, the same family waiting for him with the same supper, now shine with the eternal meaning that dwells within them. The man's everyday life—his work, his family, his horse, his home, the woods, etc.—does not have only space/time meaning. It also has eternal meaning. In a stroke of poetic genius, Frost shows us that the man's everyday life is also a promise of eternal life. By his deep involvement in his family, home, work, and even in his horse and the woods and the snow, he is building his life in eternity—a life that is built of the love he creates and experiences in this world. He has miles to go in space/time and "miles" of eternity to create before he dies. In that one repeated line, the whole world becomes transparent, and the luminosity of eternity shines through the most common, everyday activities.

In repeating the last line, Frost also stopped the poem's "perpetual motion." There is no need to find another rhyme, no need to say more. He has said everything in this one, poignant expression of beauty. The poem is over; this particular evening, this particular sleigh-trip, is over. Frost has stopped the world for a moment to see eternity. Now the world can start up again. There can be a new poem, a new day, a new opportunity to express the beautiful transparency of the world that lets the Spirit shine through it.

The poem is made up of language and scenery that we can easily imagine and understand. In this way, it gives us an easy way to look into our everyday experiences in order to see the Spirit living within them and the eternal promise that lives within them. The language of the poem also shows us how we can discern the Spirit when our lives are going along as usual. But what about when something occurs that breaks up our usual routine—when we get sick, or when the kids get out of control, or when the boss makes impossible demands to have a job done yesterday. More deeply, how do we find the Spirit when we lose our jobs, get divorced, lose a spouse or child through death, or experience poverty, oppression or violence. On these occasions, the everyday world becomes opaque and the luminosity of the Spirit can hardly be seen—or cannot be seen at all. In times such as these, we need another way to see into the world and find the Spirit there.

Mystic-poet, E. E. Cummings wrote a poem in language that is as confused and opaque as the world can become for us at times. Yet, the Spirit shines through the poem in a very beautiful way.

i thank You God for most this amazing

i thank You God for most this amazing
day: for the leaping greenly spirits of trees
and a blue true dream of sky;and for everything
which is natural which is infinite which is yes

(I who have died am alive again today,
and this is the sun's birthday;this is the birth
day of life and of love and wings;and of the gay
great happening illimitably earth)

how should tasting touching hearing seeing
breathing any—lifted from the no
of all nothing—human merely being
doubt unimaginable You?

(now the ears of my ears awake and
now the eyes of my eyes are opened)

In this stunningly mystical poem, Cummings befuddles our ordinary perception and challenges us to find the "glue" that holds the poem together. He challenges us to find the luminous meaning that shines through the broken grammar. How do we do that? More to the point, how do we put our lives back together when they have fallen apart? How do we see the Spirit when all goes dark? The Existential philosophers tell us that sometimes our lives break into pieces—a situation they describe as "Shipwreck." The pieces are scattered all over the beach and we don't know how to put them back together again. We scream—from our very souls—in pain and fear from within the darkness into which we have been cast. From out of the darkness itself comes the answer. It is a choice. We can settle for our brokenness and grow depressed, or angry and bitter. We can blame ourselves or the world for what has happened to us and then live a life of dark emptiness. Or we face the darkness, go into it, embrace the pregnant void and search for the light that shines forth from it. Cummings' poem invites us to do just this. It calls us into itself and challenges us to see the light that is shining within it. If we go deep into the poem, we can see the Spirit dwelling there in the midst of the chaos, and we can put the pieces of the poem—and of our lives—together in a new way that makes luminous sense and opens us to a new life:

> I thank you, God, for this most amazing day:
> For trees, whose green spirits leap with life.
> I thank you for the blue sky, into which I can
> look and dream of a better life.
> I thank you for everything that is natural, that
> is space/time, and that shows me the supernatural,
> the infinite and eternal.
> I look at your world, your creation, and see that
> all of it is saying, "Yes," to life.
>
> My life was broken apart, some terrible force
> killed the way I was,
> But I am alive again!
> The sun has come out again, as if for the first
> time—as if for its birthday.
> My life is reborn; love is reborn; I can fly again;
> The earth and the world are reborn with all their
> unlimited life and possibilities
>
> I feel and know that I was born out of nothingness,
> though I can't even imagine or understand how
> you do this.
> Yet how can I ever doubt that you exist:

How can all that I taste, touch, hear, see and breathe
ever doubt you?

In and through the brokenness I suffered
I have come to hear you in a way deeper than
my ears hear,
I have come to see you in a way deeper than
my eyes see.

Cummings' way of finding meaning and the Spirit is also the
way of unconventional and abstract artists, such as Picasso, George
Braque or Juan Gris. It is the way of those architects, researchers,
explorers, scientists, mystics, prophets and others who dare to break
old patterns and to travel new paths in order to discover and express the deeper, hidden truths of reality. It is the way, for example, that true statesmen take to improve the world when it
seems to be hopelessly lost in confusion, as in the Marshall Plan
after World War II, or the Civil Rights bills of the 1960's. It is the
way that African Americans saw through the horror of their history of slavery and began improvising on the regular beats of music, creating the joyful spontaneity of Dixieland jazz, the plaintive
soul-deep cries of the Blues, and the cool exuberance of the Modern Jazz Quartet. It is the way Jesus took, when, contrary to the
law of the Sabbath, he picked grain to feed himself and his disciples (Mt. 12:1-8). It is the way he lived his entire life, choosing
to break the old, set patterns of his culture and religion to bring
out the great possibilities that lived within them—and to expand
those possibilities to all the people and cultures of the world. It is the
way of many Christians today, who are breaking the old traditions—
leaving behind the old ways of thinking, believing and acting, in
order to find new depths of faith and life in a new spirituality.

It is the way of the ballerina, who leaps with exquisite motion
and total trust that her partner will be there to catch her. It is the

way of living in and with Mystery. In the words of dancer-choreographer, Agnes DeMille,

> Living is a form of not being sure, not knowing what next or how. The moment you know how, you begin to die a little. The artist never entirely knows. We guess. We may be wrong, but we take leap after leap into the dark.

In a newly rising world that is still feeling the effects of the Modern World's fragmentation, it is the way of the new dance of Christ.

NINETEEN

The Luminosity of Science

Einstein had an experience of Mystery similar to the one my colleague had that Sunday morning in the park. My colleague tried to explain his experience by appealing to Maslow's psychological view of the "peak experience." Einstein tried to explain Mystery through his scientific view of the universe. Like Maslow, Einstein missed the presence of God in his scientific experience of Mystery—at least as Jews and Christians understand God. He saw Mystery as the natural, inexhaustible energy source of the universe. Yet, by giving us a new way to see the universe and ourselves, he enabled us to develop a new and persuasive way to see God's presence in the universe and ourselves. In his own way, therefore, he made a very important contribution to the new spirituality.

Einstein's goal, of course, was scientific knowledge and understanding, and in this context, we could say he was an atheist. As a scientist, he did not believe in a personal God, i.e., a God who is a person and who rewards and punishes people. True to his roots in classical science, he saw the universe as complete in itself, and he saw the laws of the universe as purely natural. There was no need to appeal to any personal God for explanations. Also, in his view, nature has no purpose or goal. As Newton before him, Einstein saw the universe as a giant machine.

But then he went on. The more he observed and understood the universe, the more he recognized a magnificent order and harmony that moved him to experience profound feelings of awe, wonder and humility, (which Christians recognize as the religious emotions). All scientists see this order and harmony and all have these feelings, he said. Religious geniuses also recognize the universe's deep harmony and luminosity. But, he added, no church bases its central teaching upon it. Its appreciation is left to "heretics" such as Francis of Assisi.

The luminous order and harmony of the universe, he concluded, reveals an intelligence that is extremely superior to human intelligence. This intelligence calls scientists to overcome all notions of fragmentation and to work to experience the universe as a single whole. Because of the superior intelligence that is revealed by the universe, no matter how much scientists understand the universe, he said, they will never completely apprehend or comprehend this intelligence and so, they will never completely understand the universe. The superior intelligence will always offer more to be understood. It is inexhaustible. In his own way, Einstein had discovered Mystery, not as God, but as the inexhaustible natural energy source and wellspring of the universe and of all knowledge and understanding. His appreciation of Mystery was so deep and clear that he declared it to be the source of all science and art. He even said that the most important function of science and art is to awaken in us the notion and appreciation of Mystery.

Though Einstein did not have a Judeo-Christian view of God (I wonder how he came to terms with his Jewish soul), nevertheless, his notion of Mystery opens the way to a new and persuasive way for us to discern and appreciate God as present and active in the universe. In the light of the new spirituality, we can discern the divine presence in terms of the luminous order and harmony that science has discovered, and we can experience in a new and contemporary way, the feelings of awe, wonder and humility as we contemplate the magnificent order and harmony of the universe.

Einstein's view of the order and harmony of the universe and the feelings it inspired was so suggestive of the experience of God that it evoked strong resistance among those who reject any connection between science and God. One scientist firmly noted that science has made it possible for people to reject religion—something that he considered to be one of science's great accomplishments. This kind of resistance, however, pales before the ever increasing interest in the connection between science and religion, and especially between science and spirituality.

Later scientists such as Heisenberg, Schroedinger, Pauli and Hawking, built upon Einstein's insights and opened the way for an even clearer scientific view into the magnificent and baffling order and harmony of the universe. For example, they have overturned the old view that the universe is a dead, mindless machine and that we, who are alive and have minds, stand outside the universe and objectively understand it. In the contemporary view, the universe itself is alive. When scientists say the universe is alive, the notion becomes more acceptable to our scientifically oriented society. Scientists also make it more acceptable to say that we are not standing outside the universe but are part of the living universe. We are its human mind. Along with some philosophers and theologians, scientists can now also say that we *are* the universe having become conscious of itself in a human way—able to see itself and appreciate its own intelligence and beauty. (I say the universe became alive and conscious in a human way. It may also be alive and conscious in an "alien" way, but we don't know that, so we will have to wait and see.) Today's science permits the new spirituality to say that with our arrival the universe became able to discern the Spirit dwelling within it, and became able to freely collaborate with the indwelling Spirit in taking human responsibility for its own evolution and for its space/time and transcendent destiny.

The number of scientific insights that are luminous with exciting spiritual possibilities is growing daily. Here are some wondrous examples. We'll start by borrowing a snowflake from Frost's poem. I'm sure he won't mind. In simple scientific language, we can say that a snowflake is made up of water molecules that have crystallized into a six pointed symmetrical figure. The crystallizing process begins at a central point and moves outward in six directions. In each case, the water molecules crystallize in all six direction in exactly the same pattern. How does this happen? Why does it happen? Scientists look for some kind of communication that is going on among the six developing "arms" of the snowflake. They note that on the human scale, the distance between the arms is very small, and so some communication might be possible. But on the molecular scale—the scale on which the snowflake is working—the distance between the tips of the snowflake's arms is very large—so large that no communication known to science is possible. So how and why do all the arms of a snowflake crystallize in exactly the same pattern?

Today's scientists give us a wonderful answer that resonates clearly with spirituality. They say that the snowflake we see is not the whole snowflake. We see only the way the snowflake is showing up to our human senses and understanding. There is more to the snowflake than that. There is an invisible shaping force that is directing the six arms of the snowflake to crystallize in exactly the same pattern. This shaping force is pure energy that is making itself observable as a snowflake. The invisible shaping force itself is hidden from us—and will always be hidden from us. We have no direct access to it, but only indirect access to it through the observable snowflake. One thing we do know for sure—if the snowflake's invisible shaping force were not present, the observable snowflake would not be present.

The snowflakes' invisible shaping force is pure energy that has been focused and individualized into "snowflake" energy. Pure energy can be focused and individualized into any kind of energy in the universe. It can show up as a snowflake, or as an electron, a planet, a flower or a tiger. It is also free to show up in any place at any time. Not only is it beyond our ability to directly apprehend or comprehend, it is beyond the limitations of space/time. It bears the mark of eternity/infinity.

Thanks to today's science we can see two points that are very important to a contemporary understanding of spirituality. First, we can say that pure, unformed energy is one of the ways we understand capital "M" Mystery, and helps make Mystery more plausible to today's society. Pure energy exists in a "darkness" that we cannot penetrate, but which shows itself as the observable expressions, like snowflakes, that emerge from it. While we cannot understand pure energy directly, we can understand it indirectly, in the ways it shows up. We can never be sure, however, that pure energy has completely shown up as our snowflake. The more we understand about our snowflake, the more we have to say we will never finish understanding it because we can never be sure what new possibilities live within the pure energy from which the snowflake is emerging. In contrast to early 20th century scientists, who thought they would soon understand all there is to understand about the universe, today's scientists agree that they will never fully understand the universe. The same is true of our scientific understanding of ourselves. Science does not have all the answers and never will. With humble insight, scientists now see that all the certitude of their field is ultimately based in pure energy, the Mysterious source of all observable reality, which they will never fully understand. They know now that they are living with Mystery and always will. Of course, scientists have a working certitude on many levels, e.g., in medicine, mechanics, etc. But from now on, they know they will never be *absolutely* certain about anything. This is especially true when scientists try to tell us what it means to be human.

Now for our second point. In the case of the snowflake, what science calls pure energy, that has been individualized into "snowflake" energy, spirituality calls the soul. We can say that the snowflake's invisible shaping force is its soul. In this sense, a snowflake has a soul, and so does a flower, a tree, a tiger and everything else that exists. This is not animism, that says everything has a living, conscious spirit, but science, that says everything has its own invisible shaping force, from which it is emerging. To complete the thought, when we say that humans have a soul, i.e., their own individual, invisible shaping force, we mean something different from every other soul. The human soul includes the special infusion of the Spirit's own energy into each individual shaping force, which makes humans qualitatively different from all other creatures on earth.

It is not correct to say that the Spirit creates the soul and the parents create the body. The parents are collaborators with the Spirit, who takes the energy that the parents put together and forms it into the individual, invisible shaping force that shows up as a soul, mind and body. The human body and mind are the observable ways that the soul is showing up. If we take away the soul, the body and mind cease to exist. This is important to remember when scientists, or teachers, or politicians treat us as if we have no soul and say we are nothing more than our genes, or our relationships, or our body.

All this from a snowflake!

Science is giving us much more. Today's scientists tell us that we are not static beings. Being made of energy, which is dynamic and always in motion, we are dynamic and always in motion. We are an *energy event*—always the same person and yet always becoming who we are. Here again, science gives us a contemporary view of ourselves as images and likenesses of God, who is described as always at rest and always in motion. In scientific terms, energy oscillates. We can say that it turns itself ON and OFF trillions of times a second. This means that we are literally being recreated trillions of times a second. We are not only constantly happening, we are constantly being re-created. We are always new. We are always coming alive, always coming into observable form as expressions of Christ, with all the "Christmas" gifts and possibilities that live within us. This is important to remember when we reach that point of the hero's journey when we have to face our demons and dragons—especially when they get us down. We can die a trillion times and rise again a trillion times—always renewed! Possibilities and hope are being born in us trillions of times a second!

In arriving at the insight that we are constantly in the process of being created, today's scientists concur with the writers of the Bible, who saw creation not as something that happened billions of years ago and is now over, but as something that started billions of years ago and is still going on. According to the Bible, creation is an ongoing process. It is still happening, ever evolving from confusion to order, from darkness to light, and it will continue to do so until the end of time. Every time we finish our hero's journey, we are inspired to start a new journey from confusion to greater clarity, from dark disorder to greater light and beauty. Until the moment we die, our growth and development never stops. This scientific insight helps bolster the spiritual insight that we always live in hope that we can create a better society, rather than live in despair and look forward only to the end of the world.

Because of our human condition, we can, however, fall back to an old, lower level of living or to old habits. Since energy is in constant motion, there is no standing still. To keep from falling back, we have to keep calling upon the Spirit to give us the energy to keep moving forward.

I have already referred to the universe as being alive, conscious and free, and I have described evolution on earth as the Spirit-directed, living movement toward human life. As we noted earlier, for centuries, classical scientists have asked the question, "Where does life come from? "How can life on earth arise from a ball of dead dirt?" We can now look at contemporary science and answer that life did not come from anywhere. It has always been here. The universe was created as a living universe, with life already built into it. The energy that moved evolution forward to create living beings was living energy, that was endowed with the seeds of consciousness and freedom from the very beginning. When living energy arrived at the point where it was able to be infused with the Spirit's special energy and make itself observable as human life, it did what it was capable of doing from the very beginning of creation.

There's still more. Let's look at an electron. In ordinary language, an electron is that part of the atom that dances around the atom's nucleus. But what is it? The answer baffles scientists and will always baffle them. To begin with, an electron, like everything else in the universe, is the emergent, observable expression of its invisible shaping force, or soul. We have no direct access to the electron's invisible shaping force; we can only access it indirectly through the way it is showing up. Here's where things get baffling. An electron shows up as a particle and a wave. We can describe a particle as a dot of energy that is in a particular place at a particular time. We can describe a wave as a motion of energy that is not in any particular place at any particular time. How can the same electron be in a particular place and not be in a particular place at the same time!? It is showing up as a rational impossibility that defeats the human mind and understanding. Yet, it happily exists, showing up as both a particle and a wave. No matter how much we learn about the particle and wave, we will never fully understand the electron's invisible shaping force, or soul.

The electron tells us something spiritually important about ourselves. We'll begin by taking another look at our soul, or our invisible shaping force. Our soul emerges into observability as our body and mind. To turn the notion around, our body and mind are the way our soul is showing up. Our body is like the electron showing up as a particle. We can directly observe our body with our senses, and see that it is made up of atoms, bones and muscles, organs, feelings, drives, imagination, etc. Our body is always in a particular place at a particular time, and in this way we are always in a particular place at a particular time. Our mind (we'll consider only our conscious mind here) is like the electron showing up as a wave. We can directly observe our conscious mind with our understanding, and see that it is made up of our thoughts, ideas, reasoning, intuition, etc. Unlike our body, our mind is not bound by space/time. We can think of the past and the future; we can think of ideas that have no set place or time, like the idea of a tree, which covers every tree that ever existed or ever will exist anywhere in the world. We can mentally place ourselves anywhere in the universe and even outside the universe. We can mentally conceive of eternity and infinity. So while our body puts us in a particular place at a particular time, our minds frees us from all restrictions of place and time.

Our soul is like the electron's invisible shaping force. We cannot directly observe or understand it. We can only get to it through the ways it is showing up—as our body and mind. When I speak, my soul is showing up as sound and verbal meaning; when I see, my soul is showing up as sight; when I give a drink of water to a thirsty person, my soul is showing up as compassion. The old saying goes, "The eyes are the windows to the soul." Actually, our entire body and mind is a window to our soul. We can "see" our soul in our eyes, our speech, our walk, our work, our relationships, our values, our peacefulness, our hope, our joy, our love, etc.

No matter how much we learn about our body and mind, we will never fully understand our soul. It lives in the realm of Mystery, and so do we. We will never, therefore, exhaust our understanding of ourselves. There will always be more to a person than what is showing up as the body and mind. We have no way of knowing what new possibilities for creativity, healing and transforming love live in every human soul. This is what we mean when we say a person is a whole that is greater than the sum of his or her parts. One of the person's "parts" is the soul, which is filled with the inexhaustible possibilities of Mystery. Like the electron, we are immersed in eternal Mystery.

Some scientists, however, refuse to accept the scientific awareness of Mystery. One day, for example, when I mentioned the Mystery of the electron to a physicist, he grew quite angry and said there was no Mystery to it at all. He pointed out firmly that physicist Otto Schroedinger had figured out the mathematics that fully explains the electron as particle and wave and therefore removes all Mystery from it. He called Schroedinger's discovery, "The principle of complementarity." Schroedinger, he said, had figured it all out. There was no ignorance of the electron left to dispel. The mystery had been removed. But then the physicist added that Schroedinger's principle didn't work unless he played a mathematical trick on it. Otherwise, he said, it kept running off into infinity. At first I was a bit intimidated by the physicist. He certainly knew his field and his mathematics. But then I realized what he had said. Unless Schroedinger played a trick on his mathematics, his calculations kept running into inexhaustible *infinity*! In claiming to do away with the inexhaustible Mystery from which the electron is emerging, Schroedinger actually gave us a persuasive mathematical example of it. Later, another physicist chided the first one for not seeing the whole picture.

We too, keep "running into infinity" and eternity. Because of our soul we are already free from the restrictions of space/time and already living in inexhaustible eternity/infinity, although in a preliminary manner here on earth. Here it will be good to emphasize that our soul is not supernatural but natural. The body, mind and soul are all made of the same "stuff," namely, energy—natural, created energy. Our soul, however, is naturally immortal and it makes us immortal. Once we come into existence, we live forever. The concept of the immortality of the soul first arose in ancient Egypt, and then was greatly developed by the Greek philosophers. Religion, of course, has developed the concept of immortality very deeply, and this fact often leads people to mistakenly conclude that the soul is not only immortal, but also supernatural. This is not true. The soul is as natural as our mind and body—as natural as a tree or a flower or a tiger—since it is made of the same energy that they are made of. (We must always keep in mind that the human soul is qualitatively different from all other souls because it is the special dwelling place of the Spirit's own energy.) In its natural, philosophical aspect, our soul has a legitimate and important place in every phase of our life on earth, not only in religion, but in medicine, law, psychology, public schools, politics, economics, and today, in science.

Though we cannot see our soul directly, psychologist Carl Jung said we can "glimpse" it when we "jostle" our body and mind together. We do this by putting our bodies and minds together in a way that permits our soul to move us forward toward greater and richer life. Inevitably, our body and mind will clash, or jostle, over a decision or a need. For example, whenever I am in our local mall and pass the pharmacy, I can smell the chocolate bars that are seductively displayed right up in front of the store. My body comes alive and I want the chocolate. My mind tells me I'm already a bit chubby and shouldn't have it. My body and mind jostle against each other, and I would be stuck in indecision unless my soul took over. It tells me to walk faster so I can get out of range of the aroma. I know it's my soul talking because my body wants the chocolate and my mind is busy arguing. If I listened to them, I'd be stopped in my tracks. So I walk past the pharmacy. My desire abates and my mind stops arguing. I've glimpsed my soul. Sometimes however, my soul, being benign and knowing what life is all about, directs me into the store and I buy and savor the beloved chocolate while my mind gives me a conditional O. K. In more serious cases, we jostle our body and mind together when we choose a job or career, when we choose between money and certain values, when we decide to marry, have children, choose schools for them, vote, go out of our way to help the poor, etc. Our body may tell us one thing and our mind another. If we let our body alone lead us, we will suffer from the inability to reflect on what we are doing and we will fall into emotionalism, consumerism and even greed. If we let our mind alone lead us, we will suffer the inability to get passionately involved in our own lives and in the lives of others and we will isolate ourselves in our thoughts and become judgmental dilettantes. In either case, we fragment ourselves and experience a form of death. If, however, we jostle our body and mind together, we will be able to look more deeply into ourselves, glimpse our soul, where we can discern the presence and intentions of the Spirit, and we will be able to make the right decisions and carry out the right actions that move us forward toward order and harmony and life in abundance.

Here we can take a moment to look at death. Death is the final space/time separation of ourselves into parts. We are one person and we are meant to be one person forever. In death, however, our body and soul are separated. Our mind is a function of our soul, so it stays with our soul. Death is an unnatural, wrenching experience that constantly has to be explained. Christianity and many other religions are aware that we were not meant to die. Christianity has concluded that our dying is not the intention of God but the result of something we did that caused us to deserve dying. We will discuss death more fully, along with our resurrection, in the final chapter. For now we can simply point out how spiritually imperative it is never to allow ourselves to separate our body from our soul by choosing one against the other, and never to allow anyone to treat us as if we had no soul—and therefore no mind. For in either case, we would be permitting others to treat us as if we were dead.

The new understanding of our soul as our invisible shaping force that is making itself observable as our body and mind, also shows us that each of us is unique and unrepeatable. We appear in space/time only once. Christianity teaches that there is no reincarnation. To use a show business expression, this is our only ride on life's merry-go-round, our only time to catch the brass ring of life in abundance.

All this from an electron? Yes, and more. Scientists tell us that electrons always work in pairs. They have what is called, "spin," and in every pair of electrons, one spins in one direction and the other spins in the other direction. If you change the spin of one electron, the spin of the other electron will automatically change. Scientists conclude that somehow, each pair of electrons communicate with each other, and "tell" each other which way they are spinning. One day, some scientists got an idea. They decided to figure out what would happen if they took a pair of electrons and separated them as far as possible—placing each one at opposite ends of the expanding universe. Would the separated electrons be able to communicate with each other, and if so, how? The fastest possible communication that we know between two objects or people occurs at the speed of light. Now if one electron is at one end of the universe and the other at the other end, it would take 15 billion years for the one to communicate with the other. The experiment, of course, would have to take place in the scientists' minds—which, as we noted above, are not limited by space/time. So they took one electron and separated it from its partner by mentally—and mathematically—placing it at the other end of the universe. To their amazement, when they reversed the spin of one electron, their calculations showed that the spin of the other electron *immediately* reversed.

There is no known physical way the electrons could have communicated with each other at that speed. The scientists came to the only conclusion they could come to—they realized that the universe itself "knew" that the spin of one electron had been changed and so it immediately changed the spin of the other electron. Being alive and conscious, the universe knows all at once exactly what is happening throughout its unimaginable expanse of space and its entire 15 billion year history. It can act at once, at any time in any place. This scientific insight gives us an amazingly new and clear view of the universe as the image of God.

An even more amazing example of the living, conscious universe is found in the work of physicist Raymond Chiao. He shone two photon beams, i.e., two beams of light, from the same distance, at a wall. The photons started out at the same time and, as expected, traveled at the same speed and hit the wall at the same time. Then he put an obstruction in the path of one of the photon beams. To his surprise, some photons arrived at the wall anyway. His first conclusion was that some photons—some light—had somehow passed through the obstruction and continued on its way to the wall. But then, to his amazement, he discovered that the photons that he thought went through the obstruction, had arrived at the wall *earlier* than the photons from the unobstructed beam. After much study, he realized that the photons had not gone through the obstruction at all. The obstruction had stopped them. Instead, new photons had instantly materialized themselves on the other side of the obstruction and continued to the wall. They arrived at the wall earlier than the photons from the other beam because they had skipped traveling the thickness of the obstruction. The thicker he made the obstruction, the earlier the obstructed photon beam arrived at the wall, because the new photons had that much less distance to travel. As an old hymn tells us, something's up in the universe. It's alive and it knows what it is doing. It is a wondrous image of God.

Experiments such as these also show us how sensitive the universe is, and how sensitive earth is. Earth too "knows" everything that happens to her. She feels spring rains and great earthquakes, human love and horrible wars. The messages she receives don't have to be loud or hard. Mathematicians tell us that a butterfly flapping its wings in the Amazon forest will affect the weather in Chicago a few weeks later. On our living earth and in the whole living universe, all is interconnected and interdependent, and all is sensitively alive, even to the shudder of a butterfly's wings. Indeed, as a poet said, no one plucks a flower here on earth but that a star in heaven shudders. All that we feel, think and do, earth and the universe *instantly* feel, think and do. And of course, so does God. What does this say of how sensitive the indwelling Spirit is to earth and to ourselves? Today's science is showing us in wondrous new ways that the Spirit can act anywhere and at any time, in response to even the most quiet action or whispered prayer.

For our final example, we'll look at a pendulum and see how it gives us a scientific way to understand how we experience ourselves in space/time and in eternity/infinity, and how our experience can "flip flop," as we saw in the case of my colleague that Sunday morning in the park. Mathematicians tell us that as a pendulum swings back and forth, its location can be mathematically determined at every point except two—at the end of each swing, when it stops before reversing its direction. At these two points, the equation for the pendulum's location runs into infinity. Mathematically, we can say that while the pendulum is swinging, it is in space/time, but at the end of each swing, it leaves space/time and goes into infinity/eternity.

Like the pendulum, we too "swing back and forth." We are made of Spirit-filled energy that oscillates, turning itself ON and OFF trillions of times a second. (When we are OFF we don't cease to exist, because the Spirit is in us—and the whole universe—and turns us back ON.) When we are ON, like the swinging pendulum, our "up front" experience is of ourselves in space/time, here and now, in this place, in this situation, at this job, etc. When we are OFF, our "up front" experience is of ourselves in eternity/infinity, in the presence of the Spirit. Our energy oscillates so quickly that for all practical purposes we are always open to experiencing ourselves in both space/time and eternity/infinity at the same time. We can live every moment of our lives in the experience of the creative, healing and transforming love of the eternal/infinite Spirit within us. We can always be aware that we are immersed in the divine milieu.

Today's science is giving us amazing and wondrous ways to see all the way into eternity/infinity, even as we pay attention to ourselves and our lives here in space/time. It is showing us how much we can learn about ourselves—and God—not by turning away from ourselves and the world, but by looking as deeply as possible into ourselves and the world and gaining as much knowledge and understanding as we can. It is helping us realize that there is no foreseeable end to the possibilities and opportunities that live within us and the world, possibilities and opportunities that we can use to develop into more luminous humans and clearer expressions of Christ. Science is showing us contemporary ways to see how we are mystics and how we can be prophets.

Before we leave this chapter, we should return the snowflake we borrowed from Frost's poem. In its place I will leave a poem I wrote that celebrates the luminosity of science.

A Genesis Carol

In the beginning was the word, "Become,"
And the atom became—
The atom,
Spinning, whirling, whizzing, buzzing,
Hissing, sizzling, fizzing, fusing,
The snapping, crackling, popping breakfast of the
universe.

Electron sparks in swirling motion,
Shimmering halos of devotion,
Circling, circling round their center,
Never colliding, never exploding,
Never intruding, never imploding,
Dancing, dancing, do-si-do and change your orbit,
Hear the call and dance the song,
Become! Become! Become!

In the center of the dance the proton yoke,
Egg-stuff of the universe, embryo of life,
Atom's Eve,
a-move and a-dance to her own special tune,
Up quark, down quark, strange quark, charm quark,
Muon, one-step; gluon, two-step,
Photons, neutrons, life-fantastic.
Dance! Dance! Dance! Dance!
Become! Become! Become!

Deep beneath the throbbing heartbeat of the dance
There lives a peace,
That glows within the heart of every atom's pure alloy,
A virgin, pregnant peace,
That in a silent, holy night
Transforms the dance into a healing psalm of joy.
Become! Be loved! Be whole!

And in response the universe explodes in cosmic bloom;
Stars skip to grand polyphony
Through pinwheel galaxies in newborn skies,
And holy antiphon abounds from sphere to sphere.

While oceans sing and mountains chant
Their Gloria's to God on high,
Man and woman dance to life,
Rising, growing, working, loving,
Wedding, birthing, dying, rising,
Caroling the universe's song of praise,
I am! I am! I am!

The blessed offspring of your fertile Word,
Crescending proclamation of your love,
Loud, macrocosmic praise of Boundless One,
And softly allelu-ing cradle of your Son.

TWENTY

A Spiritual View of What Went Wrong
with Public Education

Public education, like everything else in the world, is luminous. When we look for the luminosity of our public schools, however, we see that something has gone wrong. The luminosity of public education is frightfully dim. From the time a report concluded that educationally, we are a nation "at risk," much has been done to try to improve our public schools. Yet, so much still remains to be done. We should immediately point out that in the midst of the darkness, we can see the light of many dedicated teachers and administrators, who are working—over-working—to do a good job. But they are working against a system that stymies them at almost every turn. In the light of the new spirituality, we can identify two great obstacles that counter-act all the best work of the dedicated professionals.

The first obstacle is our society's collapsed value system. The corrosive values that live in everyday society are the same values that our children bring to school. Our society is significantly marked by an almost pathological individualism and competition, by broken family life, by a frantic chase after goods, and by a commitment to superficiality instead of to deep thinking and understanding. In the everyday adult world, these corrosive forces are bad enough, but when our children bring them to school and concentrate them there, they go beyond the children's and the teachers' ability to handle. It is no mystery, then, to see so many distracted children disinterested in learning and behaving badly. In recent times, the corrosive forces have even exploded into the tragic scenes where children are killing children.

Teachers and administrators are lost when society asks them to handle, if not solve, all the ills of society—while educating our children at the same time. In my contacts with teachers, I constantly hear the lament, "How can we even talk about educating kids, when we're trapped into making sure they simply survive!" They relate how they are expected to handle such non-educational work as disciplining undisciplined children, maintaining security, watching for guns, drugs and alcohol, and trying to anticipate violence—as well as being expected to provide psychological and social counseling. In some cases, they even have to worry about giving some kids breakfast. Such chaos has reduced our schools to fortresses, or mental health centers, or social engineering centers. Even in those schools that may be considered to be reasonably safe for our children from a physical viewpoint, the corrosive values of society are still present and still militating against a good education.

Restoring our social values—to society and to our schools— will take nothing less than revolutionary mystical insight and prophetic work. It is difficult to think of a more pressing spiritual need than to rescue our children from the dangers they face every school day—not only to their personal safety but to their educational safety.

The second great obstacle is the collapse of educational values. The new spirituality shows us what it means to be luminously human—and luminously educated, and moves us to get involved in our schools for the sake of the best possible education for our children. Two questions immediately come to mind. First, given the separation of church and state, what right do we have to get spiritually involved in our public schools? Second, even if we have that right, how can we get spiritually involved in our public schools without imposing our religion upon them? Both questions, of course, need to be answered before we can proceed.

To answer the first question, the founders of our country clearly expected all citizens to participate in our society. While they wisely ruled out that any one church would become the official American church or religion, they just as wisely expected all citizens to use their moral and spiritual sense of humanity to contribute to the public good.

This leads to the second question. Some Christian churches are trying to impose their particular brand of morality upon American society and upon our schools. This contradicts what America stands for. The spiritual challenge of getting involved in our public schools is deeper and more mature than forcibly imposing any religion upon them. Our involvement must be true to our spirituality and yet be acceptable to the educational community and to all the people. The new spirituality does this by speaking, not religion to public schools, but education. It gets involved not for the purpose of making our public schools Christian, or any other religion, but for the purpose of making them more academically excellent and therefore, more luminously human. We do this by getting involved at the spiritual level, i.e., at the deepest level of education—the level of the academic and human "soul" of education. So many efforts to improve education have fallen short because they have not gone deep enough. To use an old cliché, they amounted to rearranging the deck chairs on the Titanic. It is time to re-envision a whole new ship.

To begin, public schools must learn how to teach our children the *wholeness* of knowledge, and they must teach them what it means to be a *whole* person. Today's schools and curricula are still caught up in the fragmented Modern World mindset. They present a fragmented picture of knowledge and a fragmented picture of the students themselves. Actually, some picture of wholeness is visible in the beginning of a student's years in school but it gets lost along the way. In elementary schools, the children have the same teacher all day. This makes it possible for the teachers to get to know their students well—to know their strengths and weaknesses, how they learn best, and how they can best develop the social skills necessary to form a classroom community within which they can participate. The teachers, to the extent they know how, can also show their students how the various subjects fit together to form a whole. But many schools suffer from breaks in coherence from grade to grade and teacher to teacher. Teachers tell me how material they taught in their grade was left behind or forgotten in the next grade. For example, when one teacher taught the parts of speech in second grade, she knew that her students wouldn't hear about them again until fourth or fifth grade. By that time, they had to learn them all over again, because they had lost years of consciously making them part of their academic development. In such a fragmented program, students cannot accumulate and deepen their knowledge and understanding. Rather, they move from lesson to lesson, from grade to grade, without building a coherent fund of knowledge. Their fragmented learning tends to be superficial and easily forgotten.

In middle and high school, fragmentation comes to full bloom. Despite increasing efforts at team teaching, the curriculum is designed as an array of individual subjects, usually taught in isolation from one another. Teachers see their students one period a day for one subject. For the most part, the teachers of the various departments hardly talk to one another, and they make little, if any, effort to relate their subjects to one another. When they come together for team teaching, the challenge is often how to fit their separate material into the time allotted rather than how to unify their material into a coherent and meaningful whole. The result of this is that students, when they talk about their high school studies, will talk about this subject or that subject, but never about the wholeness of knowledge they are gaining, or what the program is doing to form them as whole persons. Where linkages are not made, critical thinking gets lost and is replaced by scattered data processing. Such a fragmented and superficial array of subjects easily gives the students a fragmented picture of education, of knowledge, of themselves, of the world, and of life. Reflection, depth, coherence and wholeness fade from interest.

In 1998 I wrote a new vision of education for a new charter high school. I based the vision on human and educational wholeness, on the scientific and artistic notion of Mystery, and on the galaxies of possibilities that are living within our young people. The "Atlantic City (NJ) Press" wrote an editorial about my work and about the state of education today. It said in part:

> "The most beautiful thing we can experience is the mysterious. It is the source of all true art and science." So said Albert Einstein, and Anthony Massimini concurs.
>
> . . . There is a fragmentation in public education that tends to produce students who possess bits of specialized knowledge but who lack any unified vision of life. Increasingly, the larger questions are never asked, or it is assumed that answers don't exist. Technical information is acquired and pressed into service to obtain a paycheck, but intellects hang useless when confronted with the most fundamental problems of human existence.
>
> Many students leave school with no integrated system of values, no decided purpose. When confronted with the thornier problems of living, they can only extemporize and hope for the best. The results are often personal tragedies hidden beneath the veneer of economic success.

Some people would object to the editorial and point out that our schools are producing successful people. "Look at all the scientists, physicians, engineers, business leaders, and others that our schools produce!" This objection is valid only if education is nothing more than training for the professions or for the workplace. Our public schools are certainly responsible to prepare students to make a living. The new spirituality shows us that our public schools are also responsible to academically prepare students to make a life. It shows us the difference between education and training. Successful professionals or workers may be very highly trained in one area of life, but that does not necessarily mean that they are educated—formed—in the totality of life. To show what I mean, let's ask some professionals to use their training to answer the great human questions, "Who am I? Where did I come from? Why am I here? Where am I going?" I once asked a bio-geneticist these questions. She told me I was once a tumor in my mother's womb. Even if I could try to accept that repulsive notion, I wondered if she had been educated to know that I was once part of a star. Did her training account for the fact that I have a soul and a transcendent meaning and destiny? She was trained to know that it took me nine months to be born. Did her training account for the fact that it took me millions of years to be born—even billions of years? She was trained to see me as a nothing more than a conglomeration of genes. Did she know that I am an emerging, observable expression of Mystery, in whom the Spirit dwells, and that this fact has a great deal to do with how she was trained to see me? Training all too easily narrows down one's view to "nothing but," e.g., we are nothing but a tumor, nothing but a fetus, nothing but our genes, or nothing but our responses to our environment. Education takes all the aspects of who we are, interconnects them and puts them into a totality, a whole that is greater than the sum of its parts. It presents to students a wholeness of knowledge that opens us to transcend every particular view of who we are, and see ourselves as space/time, eternal persons. While specific training in specific fields is good and necessary, education ensures that the training does not reduce itself to a "nothing but" view of human persons or the world.

Education, for example, would prevent a politician I once spoke with from holding this "nothing but" view. A new family moved into his district. A short time later, sadly, their house burned down and they moved away. The politician lamented the unfortunate event saying, "What a shame, I just got them to register in my party." Training can reduce corporate executives to viewing their employees as dehumanized "profit centers." Our society's values can even train parents to narrow their focus down to providing "nothing but" material things for their children, while they fail to get to know their children as human persons—or to know that their children are out in the garage making bombs so they can kill their classmates.

The difference between educating students and training them causes teachers to shake their heads in frustration. At conferences I give to teachers I constantly hear them say, "You're talking about educating kids instead of training them, and about academically forming the whole student. That's two new ideas at once. We're not prepared to do either." Teachers constantly point out to me that their own "education" consisted mostly of being trained in the techniques of teaching. They know how to teach, but, for example, they have no idea whether they are teaching in the Modern World mindset or, for that matter, in any coherent mindset. Most have no idea what a coherent mindset, or paradigm, is. They were not taught to discern how their own world fits together, so they cannot see how the school program fits together, and they cannot help students see how their world fits together—and how it can continue to fit together in new ways as they mature. They have no coherent whole into which to place their subjects. In fact, they fear trying to achieve a coherent whole for fear they will impose some unacceptable coherence on their students, or that one subject will dominate the rest. They have little or no sense of a transcendent wholeness into which every subject fits with its full uniqueness and which is free and open for all students to accept in their own way. Coherence and wholeness are worked out by our minds; when they are lost, the mind, i.e., critical thinking, deep understanding, tends to get left behind and the educational program tends to direct itself more toward the students' bodies, e.g., their various mechanical skills, their behaviors and feelings. In the face of this disintegration, even the best teachers struggle hard to avoid presenting the subjects of the curriculum as if they were so many individual, non-matching carpets strewn about on a floor. Even allowing for the problem of collapsed social values that afflicts our schools, the loss of the educational values of coherence, wholeness and depth, forms the root cause of the collapse of education and of the widespread disinterest in education that is the mark of so many students, especially in middle and high school. Also, during the middle and high school years, interest in the opposite sex explodes upon the scene and our culture's frantic chase after money kicks into high gear. Working after school and on weekends now adds its own, often lethal, distraction to studying.

The collapse of educational values and the loss of wholeness also lead students to feel isolated. In over-individualized, competitive and "body" directed schools, true community is lost. When students are asked what they would like to have in their schools that they don't have now, a significant number of them answer, "Relationships." They want to feel that they belong—not merely to their peer groups but to a community that includes a close, guiding and caring relationship with their teachers. The teacher who cares is a life long memory and treasure, and again it is necessary to point out that there are many such teachers. But given the system's prevailing values of individualism and killing competition in a frantic race for making "good money," and given the fragmentation of the curriculum and the school community, teachers are forced to operate within a human vacuum that young people all too easily fill in with anxiety, depression, irresponsible behavior and even violence. Along with our collapsed social values, the collapse of educational values has led to a fragmentation that is separating our young people from their own humanity.

Ironically, while our public schools clearly teach the dehumanized values of radical individualism and consumerism to fragmented students in a fragmented world, they continue to protest that they do not want to teach values. Ignorance of philosophy and the fear of religion are probably the two basic reasons why our public school teachers and administrators won't look at the values question. The ignorance of philosophy prevents today's educators from seeing that the public school program actually is based on a particular philosophy and on values arising from this philosophy. The curriculum and the entire program are based on the philosophy that is called, "Positivism."

Positivism was founded by Auguste Comte (1798-1857). Very simply, Comte said that knowledge has gone through three stages of development. The first stage was the Theological Stage, in which people explained the universe in terms of God. If an object fell, for example, it fell because the gods, or God, caused it to fall. The law of God ordained that things fall. This stage lasted through the Middle Ages, when theological reasons were included in all explanations. The next stage was the Philosophical stage. In this stage, when an object fell, the fall was explained in terms of reason and science. The law of God was replaced by the law of gravity, which scientists could work with and understand. Comte said that this stage has also passed. In his time, philosophy began to recede into the background, and the science that he saw as passing away was Modern World science. Today, we are in the Positive Stage. We explain things not by faith, philosophy or Modern World science, (or today's science, which he did not know about) but by our senses and emotions. The only way to know if something is real is to be able to see, feel, taste, smell or hear it, and thereby measure it. If we cannot sense or measure something, we cannot say it exists. God, the soul, morality, cannot be sensed or measured so we cannot say they exist. Things are right or wrong according to the way we feel about them. Murder is wrong to many people because it is repulsive. Sex is right because it feels good and satisfied a bodily appetite. The only "sin" in any activity is getting caught.

Intelligence also is an abstraction that cannot be sensed, but in this case the educational community has figured out a way to "measure" intelligence. Admittedly against much opposition from good teachers, people use I. Q. tests to try to give the impression that the mind can be measured. The value of sensing and measuring as a test of reality, is pushing public education down the road of improving test scores in order to see how "educated" the student are. Teachers "teach to the test" without having the time or opportunity to teach deliberation and depth of understanding and judgment. The value of measuring easily spills over into the mindset of judging the worth of human persons by how much money they can make or how much prestige they can accumulate.

Positivism, by its emphasis on the senses and emotions, is the philosophical basis for moving education away from the soul and mind (which is a function of the soul) and toward the body, as we saw above. This movement is clearly exemplified in the "sex education" that most schools offer. They teach sex very much as a body function. Students are taught to identify their body parts and are told how the parts work. They are also taught about the bodily dangers of irresponsible sex, such as sexually transmitted disease, pregnancy and AIDS. These lessons are most often given by teachers who are in the "body" departments of the schools, e.g., the gym teachers or the nurse. Very little, if any, attention is paid to the concerns that deal with the mind or soul, e.g., whether or not

irresponsible sexual behavior is bad thinking, or bad judgment, or contrary to one's individual freedom, or one's transcendent integrity, dignity, destiny, etc. Also, in such a sense oriented atmosphere, teachers are hard pressed to mentally motivate students to learn. They are forced instead to stimulate their students' senses with ever more exciting techniques and presentations—none of which can really compete with the intense sense stimulation of TV, video games, movies and popular music.

Finally, Positivism gave birth to Pragmatism, the prevailing mindset of our society. In a word, Pragmatism judges the worth of anything or anyone by their usefulness, or their "cash value." Ideas are judged on their practical value, i.e., on whether they can be put to use, especially to make money. Pragmatism is a powerful motivation for training students instead of educating them. Teachers lament, "Our kids don't want to be educated, and their parents don't want them educated. The parents just want their kids to be credentialed. As long as their kids have a diploma, or letters after their names so they can compete and make money, they're happy. Why should the kids learn history, or a language, or the Pythagorean theorem, if they're not going to use them to make money?" The fact that these disciplines help our children see and appreciate what it means to be human is not a value.

The final demise of educational values came when our schools added psychology to the philosophy of Positivism and Pragmatism. At one time, the word, "psychology," (psyche—logos) meant the study of the soul. But then it lost its soul and became the study of the mind. Today it has lost its mind and has become the study of behavior. Much of the psychology that guides today's school programs is behavioral psychology, which at times, cannot tell the difference between a pigeon and a human person. Together with the "body" focus of Positivism, the focus on psychology reduces knowledge to mechanical skills to be practiced and learned. While students can, of course, learn the rules of logic, thinking is not a skill to be acquired, it is a deep and vital activity of the entire person. My body doesn't think, my brain doesn't think. *I* think. With the loss of the "I," critical thinking is impossible, because students are treated, not as human persons to be educated but as animals to be trained. Even worse, the pressure for better test scores has now reduced students in some schools to computers to be programmed so they can "print out" test answers.

The superficiality of behavioral psychology and the philosophy of the senses as opposed to the mind, pulls our public schools into espousing shallow, politically correct views, for example, of "self esteem" that is gained by dumbing down subjects so everyone can pass; and "the right to choose," which permits students to abuse their human freedom by justifying what they do simply because they have chosen to do it, without having to apply any standard of right or wrong—other than that it feels good—to what they choose to do.

Can our schools once again teach the luminous wholeness of education and the luminous wholeness of the person and community? Can they learn once again to educate students instead of merely training them? Can they learn how to teach students how to make a living and also how to make a life? The new spirituality answers, "Yes," and in the next chapter, we'll take a detailed look at how all this can come about. We can begin here by noting that a new world is now being born and with it a new mindset is arising that sees every subject and every person—body, mind and soul, individual and member of community—as living, participants in an interconnected web of luminous wholeness. Picking up from this mindset, the new spirituality addresses our public schools and says that their job is to academically form the whole person—body, mind, and soul, individual and member of community—in the context of the luminous wholeness of knowledge. Along with all the subjects, and in all the subjects, they can teach the full 3000 year long, ever developing concept of what it means to be human, without imposing any conclusions upon the students, but leaving all conclusions to the students and their parents. Academic formation means giving students as much material as possible so they can make clear, informed decisions throughout their lives.

The new spirituality is not naïve, nor does it offer a road to Utopia. It opens to us a new world and new vision—a new mindset—within which we can dream and work for a higher level of academic excellence for our schools. Developing and implementing this new vision will not be easy—or readily accepted. To begin with, our colleges will have to change their programs, and our teachers will have to be re-educated. The vision will challenge the vested interests of those teachers and administrators whose positions depend on maintaining our present system. No matter what the difficulty, it is time to restore full luminosity to our public schools. Let's begin building a new vision.

TWENTY ONE

A New Spiritual Vision for Public Education

The new spirituality moves us to get deeply involved in our public schools in a way that fosters academic excellence without interfering with anyone's religion (or atheism). In 1998 I used the new spirituality to create a new vision of education for a public charter high school that was being founded. I will use this vision as the basis for this chapter. With age and grade appropriate adjustments, it will also work for elementary and middle schools. Instead of using the name of the school, I will uses the expressions, "our school," or "our schools." In this way, I invite every reader to think of his or her local schools as we go through the vision.

Our School
sees every student
as an ever developing work of art,
filled with galaxies of possibilities.

Our program is designed
to help each student discern his or her best possibilities
and to nourish and form them
so that each student may become
a life-long, self-actualizing work of art
in his or her career and life.

We offer an educational program
that is fully and joyfully alive, scientifically correct,
intellectually clear, emotionally moving, poetically a-dance,
artistically poignant,
and practical and applicable in the everyday world.

Our school will provide a truly liberal education, i.e., an education that *liberates* students from ignorance and from as many restrictions as possible that inhibit their ability to discern and fulfill the possibilities that live within them.

Our school will academically form the whole student—body, mind and soul—as a unique, individual member of the local and wider communities. It will open our students to the fullest possible range and depth of knowledge and understanding, and to the clearest way to make informed judgments—with full respect for parental authority. The goal of our school's educational program will be to set our students free to become the luminously human, beautiful works of art that they already are and are always in the process of becoming, despite their human failings. Our goal will also be to teach our students how to make a living and how to make a life—leaving the choices on both careers and life to the students and their parents.

Following are the features of our new educational vision:

Our Schools will teach every field of knowledge.

The curriculum will be whole and universal. For the most part, this is already true. Today's "core curricula" are being increasingly designed to introduce students to every field of knowledge—language, math, science, art, philosophy, politics, etc. We envision a curriculum that is modeled after a hologram, i.e., it will show how mathematics, art, literature, social studies, etc., are all individual expressions of the whole of human knowledge—to the point where the whole curriculum is contained in each individual subject. Teachers will show, for example, how poetry contains mathematics, how physics contains awe and wonder, how sports contain science, and how languages contain history and culture.

Our schools will teach
what it means to be human.

The teachers will show how every subject shows our students what it means to be human. Education is *human* education; it is the academic formation by which we learn about ourselves, others and the world in the way that only humans can learn. Behavioral psychology, for example, has often mistakenly applied animal behavior directly to human behavior and education. It may seem silly, but we still have to point out that if a monkey selects a particular food to eat and a person does the same, there is an infinite difference between the two actions. Today's evolutionary psychologists show almost no insight into what it means to be human. They are teaching the evolution of a sub-human flesh-machine.

Also, in accord with the insights of today's science and of 20th century philosophers like Martin Heidegger, students will learn that "purely objective" knowledge is no longer a valid premise. We do not stand outside the universe and objectively understand it, as Modern World scientists taught us. We *are* the universe, understanding itself. When the human community arrived, the universe woke up, saw itself, was able to know itself and love itself, and it became able to act, consciously and freely, on its own accord. (For the moment, we'll disregard the possibilities that there are other intelligent beings in the universe.)

In the same light, our students will be given the insight that they do not stand outside their subjects and learn them objectively. They *are* their subjects. Mathematics, for example, does not exist in itself; people exist who do mathematics. If there were no people, there would be no mathematics. When students study mathematics, they are studying a particular aspect of themselves; they are learning a particular way of being human. The same is true for poetry, language, biology, ecology, business, politics, psychology, etc. Students *are* poetry, language, biology, ecology, etc., all of which are various aspects of themselves and of their luminous humanity.

Our schools will teach every aspect of knowledge in every subject.

The Artistic Aspect

Our schools will teach our students to see the way artists see—all the way to the Mystery that is the living, creative source of the observable universe. Every person is first and foremost an artist—a poet, dancer, singer, story teller, painter, musician, sculptor, etc. At heart, we express ourselves artistically and beautifully—in the way we walk and talk, play and work. We especially love to express ourselves beautifully by telling our own story—our individual history and dreams, and the history and dreams of the human community. This is the basic way we see ourselves and appreciate who we are and why we are here. Our students will be taught that it is only after we acknowledge ourselves as artists and are free to tell our story, that we can then go on to become farmers, thinkers and philosophers, healers and teachers, scientists and mathematicians, technicians, and finally, politicians and business people—while we never let go of the basic fact that we are artists. In all that they learn and all that they do, our students will learn to hold on to the deep well of creativity that lives within them, and to the sensitive appreciation of who they are and where they are going. Our students will be made aware that in today's society, we have turned our identities—and, it appears, our destinies—upside down and given primacy to the financial, commercial, and technological aspects of our lives. We have made our country the land of the marketer and consumer. In the process, our artistic aspect has been trivialized, e.g., in TV programs and rank entertainment, and our humanity has suffered. We have very much forgotten who we are and why we are here.

Our students will be taught to appreciate the artistry and beauty of every subject in the curriculum, and to see how each subject tells us something beautiful about who we are. Their eyes will be opened so they can enjoy the way numbers and quantities dance mathematically, the way literature reveals the stirring beauty of language and life, the way a football wide receiver moves with balletic grace, and they will gaze in awe and wonder at computer generated images of Fractal Geometry, that reveal the awesome, mystical beauty of the universe. Our school will open our students to beauty and allow beauty to touch them deeply in every aspect of their studies.

Every subject will be presented as a human drama, an artistic adventure in search of truth. For example, math teachers will not teach the Pythagorean theorem as an accomplished fact, but will involve their students in Pythagorus' great search to understand the triangle. They will immerse their students in the stories of how people dreamed and asked questions, how they faced challenges and set-backs, and how they found answers. They will show how the discovery and development of each subject is the on-going story of the hero's journey. This approach will help motivate students to learn by developing their own imaginations and sense of adventure, along with their creativity, spontaneity, inquiry, reflection and contemplation, their deep emotions, and their sense of awe and wonder.

The Scientific Aspect

We have already seen the luminosity of science in an earlier chapter. Our teachers will show our students how every scientific insight moves the students deeper into themselves and the universe—all the way back to the pure energy from which all is emerging. They will show our students that the certitude of science is ultimately based in Mystery, which we will never be able to fully apprehend or comprehend. The students will see that while science has so many answers, it does not have all the answers and that, like art, it is emerging from Mystery and giving us the best information and understanding that we have at this time. The more we know, the more there will be to know—always. New possibilities will always attract our scientific curiosity—as they will always attract our students as they make their living and make their lives.

The Poetic Aspect

Poetry brings us closer to reality than prose. Our students will be taught how poetry puts us in specially sensitive touch with Mystery and the source of all meaning—especially with the Mystery and source of our own meaning. Poetry opens our hearts and minds to see how all reality dances and sings of life, e.g., how science resounds with the music of the spheres, and how technology embodies the flowing beauty of design. Teachers will show how every subject "talks" in prose, and "sings" in poetry at the same time.

The Cultural Aspect

Our teachers will show our students how every culture is an expression of the one human community. While American education will inevitably be Western based, there will be no arguments over whether the curriculum should be male centered, or female centered, or Afro-centered, or Native Culture centered. The education will be human/earth centered and will have full room for all aspects of culture. Nor will there be any arguments over which discipline will dominate the curriculum. The curriculum will be centered in the transcendent, creative Mystery from which all the disciplines flow—and from which all cultures flow. Each culture and each discipline will be taught as giving a different view of what it means to be human. Students will learn how to evaluate various cultures, e.g., their politics and economics, their art, their acknowledgment or denial of human rights, etc., and how the various aspects of the cultures fit—or don't fit—into the wholeness of our luminous humanity.

The Psychological Aspect

Our teachers will employ the best principles and techniques of learning psychology, e.g., using both left brain and right brain presentations, and taking advantage of the students' various intelligences and their visual, auditory and kinetic learning skills. Our students will be taught to "listen" deeply to their subjects and let their subjects "happen" to them, so they can become their subjects and let their subjects form them academically, instead of their gaining merely a superficial knowledge of them.

The Sociological Aspect

Our students will be taught the history, structure and dynamics of the various institutions of today's societies—local, national and global—and they will see how they participate in their various societies.

The Intellectual Aspect

A. Knowledge

Our students will acquire a thorough and coherent knowledge of the past and present "story" of the human/earth community and the universe. Our teachers will develop their students' **reasoning abilities**, showing them how to attain and work with clear ideas, and how ideas are brought together to form patterns. Our students will be taught the various mindsets or paradigms of history, and they will know what paradigm they are living in as well as what paradigm forms their curriculum, e.g., the Modern World fragmented paradigm, the Positivistic paradigm, the Einsteinian paradigm of interconnected wholeness emerging from Mystery. They will be encouraged to envision new paradigms. They will be taught to see how the various paradigms and philosophies have arisen and passed away.

Our teachers will develop the students' **intuitive abilities**, showing them how to recognize underlying interconnections and patterns in all their subjects.

Our students will be shown that every subject brings its own answers to the **philosophical questions**, "What is real, true, good and beautiful?" From the simple truth that in base ten, 1 + 1 = 2, to the blueprints for a jet liner, to the workings of a computer, to the beauty of a job well done, every subject shows our students something about reality, truth, goodness and beauty, and about themselves.

B. Understanding

Our students will be taught to see and comprehend the deeper meaning that "stands under" the literal knowledge they acquire. One apple plus one apple equals two apples. One of anything plus one of the same thing equals two of those things. It is an historic fact that Hitler invaded Poland in 1939. What reasons motivated him to do it? Why do people declare war, while others work for peace? Why do hurricanes hit the Atlantic coast from June to September? Why are we human and not machines?

C. Deliberation

Our students will be given time to reflect upon their knowledge and understanding, to gather their learning into an interconnected, coherent whole, and to communicate their knowledge and understanding clearly and persuasively to one another and to their teachers and parents.

D. Judgment

Our students will be taught to do **critical thinking** as they learn the logical, epistemological and ethical principles for making informed judgments as to what is right and wrong. They will learn how to judge such controversial questions as the conflict between pathological individualism vs. healthy individuality; between false self esteem in seeing ourselves as money making machines vs. true sense in seeing ourselves as luminously human.

They will learn how to use their knowledge, understanding and deliberation to make practical judgments concerning their careers and relationships. They will be taught how to justify their judgments, decision and choices—under the due authority of their parents.

The Physical Aspect

Our schools will give full attention to developing students physically and emotionally. This includes the full opportunity for our students to use their imaginations and express themselves in every subject and at every grade level. It also includes sports programs, shows and presentations. The physical aspect will be seen and treated as one aspect of the whole person—body, mind and soul—and will never be separated from the mind and soul of our students.

The Vocational Aspect

Our schools will be true centers for education and not merely for job training. While education goes far beyond job training, it fully includes preparing students for success in the workplace and the professions. The question has arisen as to how far our schools should go in preparing students for jobs, as compared to how much corporate America should do in this area. There is a rising awareness that our schools should give students a wide and deep basic education, especially in thinking and communicating skills and in their appreciation of what it means to be human, and leave the everyday, practical training to the business and professional world, and to later college years and graduate schools.

The Religious Aspect

Public schools do not teach religion, but they are professionally and academically required to teach that religions exist and to show their influence on people, culture and history. Our schools will learn to overcome their mistaken notions of the separation of church and state and learn to present the fact of religion in a professional way that does not foster any particular religion, or religious view such as Deism, or interfere with anyone's religion, or atheism.

The Aspect of Values

As we have seen, our public schools already teach values, especially the values of Positivism, Pragmatism and behavioral psychology. In general, values begin to show with how the school is physically set up, e.g., with well lit or dimly lit classrooms, with a full supply of good textbooks or with worn out, out of date textbooks, with labs, playing fields, etc. Values also begin to show in the way teachers dress and speak and relate to their students.

Our school will teach our students' the full value of their luminous humanity as it is expressed in all the aspects of our program. Our teachers will also point out that some particular values always remain the same and some change. For example, in base 10, 2 + 2 always and everywhere equals 4. Respect for one another never changes. Stealing and murdering are always wrong. On the other hand, our society once valued owning slaves and segregating the races in schools, stores, buses, etc. Only recently have we begun to value nurturing the earth. As Socrates taught, "The unexamined life is not worth living. Know yourself." Our students will be taught the value of knowing who they are and what are the prevalent values of society. They will be taught how to make informed judgments on these values—under the due authority of their parents.

The Timeless, Eternal/Infinite Aspect

Our students will be shown how every subject in the curriculum is emerging ultimately from pure energy, which art and science call Mystery. Emerging from the same source, all the subjects are variations of the same reality and so are ultimately one. In the same way, each student is one and the whole human/earth community is one. Also, since pure energy is not bound by space/time, it bears the mark of timelessness, or eternity/infinity. Every subject will be taught as emerging from timeless energy and as opening our students to eternity/infinity. Earlier we saw, for example, how the poems of Frost and Cummings open us to eternity/infinity, and how Schroedinger's mathematics regarding the electron ran into infinity. Our students will be taught that everything, as well as everyone, has both space/time meaning and eternal/infinite meaning.

The Aspect of the Human Soul

Our science department will teach our students about the invisible shaping force of the snowflake, flower, tiger, etc., and this will be one of the ways our school teaches about the human soul, which shows up, in human persons, as a body and mind. Our school will teach that while some religions take deep account of the human soul, the soul does not belong exclusively to religion. The soul has also been taught to the human community by Socrates, Plato, Aristotle, Michelangelo, Rembrandt, Darwin, Freud, Frost, Browning, Einstein, Rosa Parks, Nelson Mandela, and, although they probably don't know it, by every teacher, every physician, every politician, every corporate CEO and all others who treat persons with integrity, dignity and respect. These qualities are not qualities of the body or the mind but of the whole person. They arise from the person's very soul. The consideration of the soul belongs to the entire human enterprise, including, most certainly, public education. Our school will also teach about the human soul by teaching our students that every person is a whole that is greater than the sum of his or her parts, i.e., that each of us transcends the parts that make us up, and that the more we know about ourselves, the more there will always to be know.

Our school will recognize that the human soul is not supernatural but natural—as natural as the body and mind. When, for example, I speak, my voice is my soul making itself observable as sound; when I think, my soul is making itself observable as my thought or idea; when I give a drink of water to a thirsty person, my soul is making itself observable as compassion.

Our school will also teach our students the long academic tradition that says the soul is immortal. Philosophy, art and literature are replete with descriptions of immortality. Immortality means that once a person comes into existence, that person lives forever. Our school will show our students how immortality gives us transcendent purpose and hope, and how the counter notion that we are not immortal creates an existential mindset of pessimism and absurdity.

Our school will teach that the human soul gives each person the eminently human qualities that show in the joy of being alive, in giving service to others, in being able to knowingly and willingly submit to reality, in being able to forgive, to feel awe and wonder, and to search to see if God exists.

Internal Discipline

While our school will have disciplinary rules and regulations, it will work to develop the discipline that already exists *within* our students. Aspects of internal discipline include:

Order: Chaos to cosmos

Order is the dynamic movement from chaos to cosmos. Within the parameters of the natural vagaries of our youth, our students will be guided in an orderly growth through their school years. Our teachers will help their students see and appreciate their own growth and work to solve the problems they are having.

Justice: Mutual respect

Our teachers will treat everyone fairly and respect all their students, especially those who are in some way "different," e.g., slow, or awkward, etc. "Respect" means to take a second look at someone, to re-spect the other. The first look often leads us to think what the other can do for us. The second look leads us to ask what we can do for others. Our teachers will form their students to take that important second look and respect others—as well as themselves.

Peace: Mutual reaching out

Peace is more than the mere absence of conflict. It is reaching out to one another to help one another feel safe, be healed, and to become his/her full self. Our school will be one in which every teacher and student will work to make everyone feel accepted and safe. All harassment will be stopped in its tracks. By explicit teaching and example, and by vigilant monitoring, our teachers will teach their students to be sensitive to their own needs and the needs of others. Our students will be taught to help one another, listen to one another, encourage one another, heal one another (according to their ability) and forgive one another. Our school will be a community of peace.

Trust: A true sense of belonging

Our teachers will see to it that their students feel they fully belong in their school and in their world. Our teachers will always "be there" for their students. They will also know how to recognize signs of mistrust, anxiety and depression in their students, and move to solve such problems.

Hope: Firmly based confidence

Hope is not wishing. It is our confidence that we can achieve some degree of success in school, at home, in a career, and in life in general. It is confidence that is built upon reality, i.e., upon programs and activities that are designed to lead students to true success experiences. It is not, however, the false hope that students receive when their subjects are watered down to give them a false sense of success. Our teachers will personally mentor our students, helping them discern their best possibilities, and leading them through the steps necessary to fulfill their possibilities—which includes teaching our students to recognize and cope with their real limitations.

Freedom: Knowledgeable and responsible action

Freedom is not the right to do whatever we want to do, but the human ability to discern what is right, to freely and knowingly do what is right, and to get credit for doing what is right. It is also the responsibility to be held accountable for knowingly and willingly doing what is wrong.

Our school will teach true freedom and give our students grade-appropriate opportunities to express their freedom. Our students will learn that freedom and responsibility are always interconnected. They will be rewarded for their correct use of freedom and properly punished for their abuse of freedom.

Creativity: Discerning and expressing new possibilities

Creativity is the ability to discern and pull new insights and images out of the galaxies of possibilities that live within us and the universe, and then to express these insights and images in ways that give us a new and joyful appreciation of what it means to be human.

Our students will learn to discern the possibilities that live within their subjects, the world, and themselves. They will learn how to express and nurture these possibilities in new and joyful ways. They will develop a healthy sense of spontaneity, and will feel free to make safe, creative mistakes—and correct them. They will learn to make informed judgments as to what is creative and what is bizarre.

Joy of Life: The celebration of being alive

Joy of life is the celebration of being alive. It is different from happiness, which is the satisfaction of getting the things we want. In America, we are free to engage in the pursuit of happiness. Joy of life already exists within each person and is to be nurtured in our public schools.

Our entire school program will reflect the joy of life as it prepares our students to live as fully as possible in every aspect of their lives. Our teachers will show their own joy of life in a special way by showing their joyful commitment to being teachers and to academically forming their students.

Compassion: Self-giving service to others

Compassion goes the extra step beyond justice and peace, and reaches out to others, even to the point of some self-sacrifice for the sake of helping others fully become who they are. Our teachers will joyfully go that extra step for their students and teach their students to do the same thing. Our school will be a community of compassion.

Putting It All Together

Our school will not consider our students to be educated until they can take everything they learn and put it all together in a coherent web of luminous wholeness. Our teachers will meet often to discuss ways to unify the curriculum into a coherent whole. They will do their weekly plans together so they can "cross pollinate" their lessons. From time to time, extra classes will be scheduled in which our teachers will lead their students to see how their courses inter-relate and to see how the entire curriculum is unified into a coherent whole of knowledge and meaning. They will show their students how education helps the students appreciate themselves as coherent, whole, luminous human persons.

Mystery in Public Education

Being a public school, our school may not acknowledge Mystery as God. It is, however, professionally responsible to acknowledge Mystery as it is seen and appreciated by art and science, namely, as the inexhaustible, unformed energy that is the source of the entire observable universe, including all the subjects of the curriculum, and which we cannot directly apprehend or comprehend. Our school will teach not only that art and science acknowledge the existence and presence of Mystery but that people throughout history have understood Mystery in various ways. It will present these ways of understanding to our students as part of our full educational program—leaving our students free to accept or reject any or all of the following meanings:

Five Ways that People Understand Mystery

1. Atheism, Secular Humanism, and Modern World Science
Mystery is nothing more than natural, pure energy out of which the observable universe is constantly emerging. We understand Mystery artistically and scientifically in the various ways it is showing up. There is no need to look for any religious or spiritual meaning, or any other meaning in Mystery.

2. Agnosticism
Mystery can be an analogy, or image of God, or it cannot be. The question remains open.

3. Eastern Thought
Mystery can be a way of experiencing the incomprehensible "No Thing" that we can experience by attaining the state of awareness that some people call, "Nirvana."

4. Judaism
Mystery can be seen as an analogy, or image, of God, our Creator, who gives the world meaning and purpose, and whose chosen people teach global brother/sisterhood under one God in love and compassion, as they await the Redeemer.

5. Christianity
Mystery is one of the ways we experience God—as the Absolute, Eternal/Infinite, Inexhaustible Godhead. It is also a created,

natural analogy, or image of God, our Creator, Redeemer, and Loving Spirit. It is the fundamental dwelling place of the Spirit of Christ—God, One and Trinity—who is animating, shaping and directing the universe toward the fulfillment of its greatest possibilities—while keeping us humans free to collaborate with her or not. Finally, Mystery is the primary energy source of the universe, which is making itself observable as the universal, cosmic Christ.

*   *   *

The new spirituality calls for us to get fully and deeply involved in our public schools so we can help them achieve the fullest possible academic and human excellence. Our involvement in public education in one Christian way of serving the world in Christ-like, self-giving love, without imposing the Christian religion upon anyone. It is an important way that Christians can join with all people of good will in teaching that we not only give our children life, we also owe them life in abundance.

TWENTY TWO

A New Spiritual Vision

for Christian Schools and Universities

The new vision for public education that is outlined in the previous chapter applies to Christian schools as well. Christian schools have the same responsibility and goal to achieve the greatest possible academic excellence as they prepare our students to make a living and to make a life. Christian schools, of course, contain an essential difference from public schools. Christian schools offer their students an academic formation that explicitly expresses the mind, heart and soul of Christ. They explicitly teach that to live is Christ (Phl. 1:21) and to be fully educated as luminous human persons is Christ. While the new spirituality sees everyone as an expression of Christ, our spiritual vision sees Christian school graduates as being explicitly educated and formed to be expressions of Christ.

In our vision, we see every subject of the curriculum being taught as arising not only from the natural Mystery from which the observable universe is emerging, but from the Spirit of Christ who is dwelling within Mystery. As the subjects become observable and understandable, they become clearer expressions of Christ. Christian education is the formation of students in the mind, knowledge and heart of Christ. Christ is both the heart and mind of Christian education and also the "recipient" of Christian education. As the students grow in knowledge and understanding, so Christ grows. Cosmogenesis is Christogenesis.

Christian education is universal. Christ is the universal, global Christ, and Christian education embraces and celebrates all the humanizing knowledge and wisdom that has been accumulated by all the people and traditions of the human/earth community throughout history. By embracing and blessing the fullness of knowledge and wisdom, Christian education opens its students to their fullest and deepest possibilities—helping them see and take advantage of their best skills, abilities, talents, desires and opportunities in the light of the indwelling Spirit. Christian education opens our students to the fullest possible development of their minds, with no fear that ever wider and deeper knowledge and understanding of themselves and the world will ever interfere with their faith. In fact, the more they know about themselves and the world, the more they can enrich their faith and give greater glory to God.

Christian education is a holistic education. Today's mindset can make this goal of holism difficult to achieve. In the Middle Ages, for example, Christian education was clearly organized as a coherent whole. The lower subjects, e.g., mathematics, rhetoric, etc., were not considered whole in themselves, but were made whole by philosophy, which in turn was made whole by theology. In this way, Medieval Christian education expressed the one, harmonious body of Christ. But the fragmentation of the Modern World affected Christian schools as well as public schools. An increasing number of parents are complaining that Christian schools have become secularized. They see Christian schools teaching math, science, social studies, etc., no differently from the way these subjects are taught in the public schools. And these parents fear that the Christian schools are fostering the same values of an almost pathological individualism and consumerism that they see in the public schools. On the other hand, I know teachers in Christian schools who tell me that some parents *insist* that their children be taught the values of radical individualism, competition and consumerism. To offset the pull toward secularized values, Christian schools teach such courses as Biblical Studies, "Knowledge of Religion," or theology. But these courses tend to stand side by side with the "secular" courses, with little or no integration. Some Catholic universities say they are Catholic because they offer a full array of courses. This makes these school catholic with a small "c" and not Catholic with a capital "C." Instead of looking like the one body of Christ, many parents fear that their Christians schools are looking like Humpty-Dumpty.

The new spirituality sees Christian schools presenting a coherent and comprehensive, academically excellent educational program, that forms the whole student and expresses the whole Christ. Mathematics, reading, history, literature, etc., will be presented in the light of their own validity. In Christian schools, 2 + 2 still equals 4, in base 10. But the schools will explicitly point out that each subject is an example of what it means to be human, and what it means to be an expression of Christ. The wondrous order and harmony of mathematics, for example, is one expression of the wondrous order and harmony of the cosmic Christ. The entire curriculum will be gathered up in the students' humanity and in Christ.

All education, and all the world, is sacred. Christian education explicitly sees itself as sacred. Anyone entering a Christian school should immediately become aware that they have entered an academically oriented institution in which a sacred activity is going on. This does not mean that the students and faculty should be piously walking around as if in a medieval monastery or convent. Every Christian school should be making its own joyful noise unto the Lord (cf. Ps. 100:1) as it proclaims an age-appropriate celebration of life and learning. Being sacred does not mean being stodgy. The sacredness of education is expressed in the joy of life that is being experienced by young people who are learning how to make a living and how to make a life as luminous humans who are expressions of Christ.

Christian education incorporates the teachings of the Christian faith and of the Bible into its entire program. It teaches its faith and the Bible in accord with the best scholarship of the day. It shows students how to read the Bible with mystical eyes, so they can look into the words and see the timeless message of God that the words are carrying, and be able to carry the timeless message into today's language and culture. They will learn the truths carried, e.g., by the stories of creation, the mustard seed, the good Samaritan, etc., and learn how to these truths animate their subjects and the entire school program.

The new spirituality envisions Christian theology as updated to fit contemporary thinking. In the past, theology was very much the domain of the ordained, whereas today, lay people—especially women—have become prominent in the field and are "incarnating" theology in the everyday world of love and marriage, work, peace, human rights for all peoples, economics—with special concern for the poor and outcast. In Christian schools, theology can also "incarnate" the curriculum by showing how the Spirit is present and active in every subject, as well as in the students, teachers and administrators, and in the world at large—calling all into a living, ever growing wholeness. Theology teachers can work with all the other teachers to help the students see how everything fits together into a whole that is alive with luminous order and harmony. Theology can open students eyes so they can see themselves as the mystics and prophets they already are and they can see how they are called to contribute, through prophetic action, to the luminous order and harmony of themselves and the world.

Our vision must also examine the place of non-Christian or atheistic faculty in today's Christian colleges and universities. Certainly, they cannot be required to accept a faith they do not believe in. The must accept, however, that they have come to teach in a Christian school or university whose fundamental purpose is to form students academically as expressions of Christ in a world seen through Christian eyes. They will be required to teach that, even though they themselves do not see in this way, their school or university sees every subject, as well as all the students and faculty, and all the programs, as expressions of Christ. Academic honesty will permit them to do this. If, however, Christian schools face the loss of some faculty members, or the loss of grants from the government because of their clearly stated Christian vision and belief, so be it. How better to teach their students that it is better to lose the whole world than lose one's soul.

Many people will see this view of Christian education as hopelessly naïve. They will say that schools who teach and operate under this vision simply cannot survive financially in today's society. If this is so, then the Christian schools must face the challenge of persuading their churches of their worth, and they must question their Christian identity. No one ever said Christianity would be easy. Non-Christian and non-believing students will know that the Christian school or university they have chosen to attend lives by the luminous vision that all is Christ, even as they are assured that the school will not force this believe upon them.

Finally, Christian schools will periodically "gather up" all the students, teachers and administrators, all the learning and academic formation that is taking place—and mentally if not physically—the parents, the community and the world in general, and offer all to God, our Creator, in thanksgiving, joy, praise and worship. In this way, Christian education takes its place in the dance of Christ, which begins with creation, continues by gathering up the entire universe, turning it into luminous knowledge and love, and finally returns it to God, our Creator, in the Spirit of Christ, in and through Christ.

TWENTY THREE

A New Spiritual Vision for Politics and Economics

Rosa Parks was not a politician. All she did was refuse to give up her seat to a white person on a bus, because her feet hurt. This simple act by an ordinary person (who, at that time was actually considered even less than ordinary) graced our society with one of the most luminous political acts of our time. She not only saved her aching feet, she helped save the soul of our country.

Like everything else, politics is luminous. The new spirituality sees it as an emergent expression of Christ, who is making himself observable in the way a society works to assure the common good, i.e., freedom, education, economic opportunity, security, etc., for all the citizens of a society—with special concern for the poor and outcast. Rosa Parks' action and the changes it helped bring to our society are a blessed example of how politics can be made to show its Christ-like luminosity. In a beautiful way, she fulfilled the Beatitudes that guide us when we get involved in politics, and also in economics:

Blessed are they who hunger and thirst for righteousness,
for they will be satisfied.

Mt. 5:6

Blessed are they who are persecuted for the sake of
righteousness, for theirs is the kingdom of heaven.

Mt. 5:10

In the Bible's language, "righteousness" means "meeting the right and full standard." Righteousness challenges us to set our standards for politics and economics as high as possible. It moves us to aim for the stars, to aim for our best possibilities and brightest luminosity. In the new spirituality, we see who we are as hu mans with new fullness, insight and appreciation. We see our ability to be creative, healing and loving in a way that can refresh and transform our society and the world. With global communication inter-connecting everyone in the world instantaneously, the smallest act, like the butterfly flapping its wings in the Amazon forest, can change the way we see and do things. Physicist-mystic Brian Swimme said we are now in a position to reinvent the human person. The new spirituality can now get us involved in politics and economics in a way that can reinvent the world.

The new possibilities that are flaring forth from the new spirituality show us even more clearly the harm of setting our sights too low. Collapsed political and economic standards show themselves ever more clearly as our fall from our best efforts to achieve justice, peace, fairness and compassion in accord with today's opportunities. The new spirituality moves us to get mystically and prophetically involved in politics and economics as part of our sacred responsibility to work toward ever greater justice and peace for all people—with special consideration for the poor and outcast. Our spiritual vision sees us keeping our standards high and working to ensure that people may never be used by politicians or the corporate world for any purpose whatsoever. People do not exist for politics or money. Politics and money exist for people.

The new spirituality is not naïve. It does not expect everything to work out perfectly. In this world, nothing does. It says, however, that if we continue in the old mindset, with its standards of fragmentation, radical individualism and killing competition, we will dehumanize ourselves at an ever greater pace. The new spirituality gives us a better chance because it gives us a new mindset in which fragmentation, radical individualism, killing competition, secularism, materialism, and all that would degrade our humanity is programmed out, so that we have a view of a luminous inter-connected wholeness that can work for everyone's benefit. If we fail, it won't be because we don't have a good plan. In the new mindset, we can see more clearly, and with more confidence, that the Spirit expects us to aim and work for the highest levels of justice and peace even to the point of being persecuted and suffering for our efforts. Rosa Parks was ready to have the weight of the law come down upon her for her blessed action. Other examples of the search for righteousness under threat of harm include the work of the Rev. Martin Luther King, Jr., Gandhi, theologian Dietrich Bonhoeffer, the young man who stood in front of a tank in Tianenman Square, the martyrs—women and men—of Central and South America, and the intensely luminous example of Nelson Mandela in South Africa. In people like these, the luminosity of righteousness shines with special brilliance in a world that can grow very dark.

In our time, Christianity has begun to speak more clearly concerning our spiritual obligation to get involved in the everyday world of politics and economics. The Roman Catholic church, for example, in its Second Vatican Council, says:

> They are mistaken who, knowing that we have here no abiding city but seek one which is to come, think that they may therefore shirk their earthly responsibilities.

> . . . The split between the faith which many profess and their daily lives deserves to be counted among the more serious errors of our age.

> . . . The Christian who neglects his temporal duties neglects his duties toward his neighbor and even God, and jeopardizes his eternal salvation.
>
> The Church Today, No. 43

The problem lies in the fact that the Catholic church, and many other Christian churches, do not have the mechanisms in place for their members to be effectively involved in politics and economics in a way that can change our society in accord with this contemporary Christian vision of involvement. Those Christians who are working for justice and peace are still pretty much on their own, without the bulk of the Christian population involved with them.

Justice and peace always go together. Justice gives full respect to every person and sees to it that every person has what belongs to him or her in the context of order, safety, food and housing, education and health care. The more that justice is satisfied, the less hostility marks society. Peace becomes possible. Peace, though, is more than just the absence of hostility. It is the mutual reaching out of people to one another to help one another become who they can become. On both the individual and social bases, another word for peace is development. Peace occurs when individuals and society are free to develop their possibilities for the quality of life the Spirit intends everyone to have. It leaves no room for greed, racism, sexism, the growing gap between the rich and the poor, industrial pollution, unethical technology, etc. Whenever these occur, people of peace work to correct them. They also work to reconcile whatever differences or hostilities arise that keep people from being free to move toward life in abundance.

The peace of the new spirituality is the same peace that Jesus expressed in the Beatitude,

Blessed are the peacemakers,
    for they will be called children of God.
                                    Mt. 5:9

The principal Biblical word for peace is the Hebrew, *shalom*. It means completeness, fullness, perfection, i.e., lacking nothing. Christ expects all of us to be peacemakers by setting the highest standards of humanity that we can set and by working to live up to them in the light and strength of his Spirit. He calls us as peacemakers to ask one another, "What can I do to help you become more completely and fully yourself, i.e., the person God wants you to be?"

Another Biblical word for peace is the Greek, *irene*. It means order and harmony. Today's political and economic leaders can look to science and see the magnificent order and harmony that scientists see in the universe. They can work to make our political and economic life an expression of that same order and harmony, and even to foster the feelings of awe and wonder that order and harmony stir up in the human heart and soul. Without being too cynical, we can find it odd to imagine politicians and corporate executives feeling awe and wonder, as scientists do, but at least they have the scientists' example to follow. And they have Christ's expectation to live up to in their own way.

One expression for political justice and peace is "the common good." Again, we quickly see how the prevalent values of radical individualism and killing competition are a danger to the common good. For example, Rep. Thomas P. "Tip" O'Neill, former Speaker of the House of Representatives, once expressed a widely accepted truth that, "All politics is local." The astute politician knew that when people enter the voting booth, they tend to put aside thoughts of peace and justice for all, and vote for their own good—for the good of their wallets and pocketbooks. This brings up the spiritual question: Can Christians vote for their own good and still foster justice, peace and the common good? We can answer this question in two ways. First, the founders of our country asked themselves this question, not about Christians alone, but about the entire population. They had the wisdom to answer the question by setting up, not a true democracy, but a representative republic. Office holders have the responsibility to look at the needs of their districts or states and then balance those needs against the needs of the greater community. When Robert F. Kennedy was a senator from New York, he looked at this question and asked himself, "Am I a New York senator or an American senator?" He wondered if every vote he cast for the "local" good of New York was good for the whole country.

Sometimes, the common good could override the local good. On the state level, the tension between the common good and the local good arises, for example, when tax money is allocated to the various school districts. The richer districts, which pay the most in taxes, are often reluctant to see some of their money go to poorer districts. Christians can look to assure that their office holders make decisions in the best light of justice and peace, balancing local needs against larger needs, especially the needs of the poor. They can back up their leaders when the leaders are "persecuted" for a particular vote by taking political heat from their constituents. One of the principal political goals of Christians is to encourage their leaders to fulfill the Scriptures:

> . . . he satisfied the thirsty,
> filled the hungry with good things.
> [i.e., with justice, peace, their
> good reputations, etc.]
>   Psalm 107:9

> He has shown might with his arm,
>   dispersed the arrogant of mind and heart.
> He has thrown down the rulers from their
>   thrones but lifted
>   up the lowly.
> The hungry he has filled with good things;
>   the rich, he has sent away empty.
>   Mary, the mother of Jesus, in Luke 1:51-53

The second way to answer the question of whether Christians can vote for their own good and still foster justice, peace and the common good, is to look at particular Christian causes such as the legality of abortion. The new spirituality calls us to try to achieve a balance between the Fundamentalist efforts to take over the political power of our society and the false withdrawal from everyday society. If Christians want to influence society to see an issue their way—for example, to declare abortion illegal—it seems that the best way is to publicly state their position as clearly and persuasively as possible, until they achieve a majority opinion that making abortion illegal is the best way to achieve justice, peace and the common good. Violence against abortion clinics and doctors, and threats against Christian lawmakers who disagree with the Christian position, contradict the heart and mind of Christ. More to the point, in the matter of abortion, Christians should concern themselves with the fact that Christian women have abortions at just about the same rate as non-Christian women. Are Christians trying to use the power of the law to achieve what their own spiritual power (or lack thereof) cannot achieve? There's much homework to be done.

Political and economic justice and peace call Christian spiritual attention especially to the poor and outcast. If anything made Jesus angry, it was the way the wealthy and powerful of his society were oppressing the poor. When he preached about the kingdom of God, he knew that many of his listeners automatically excluded the poor from consideration. The poor were seen as hardly human; they had no place in society and would have no place with God. So when Jesus said, "Blessed are you who are poor, for the kingdom of God is yours" (Lk. 6:20), his words were shocking and revolutionary. Matthew's Gospel adds the phrase "poor in spirit." This emphasizes that the spirits of the poor people were deeply degraded and depressed by their poverty and by the way the wealthy and powerful were oppressing them.

Getting involved in helping the poor is a spiritual challenge that requires good information and a clear understanding of the political and economic processes. Christian groups such as Sojourners and Network are a good source of such information and understanding. Concerned Christians also need to come together to encourage one another. It is not always popular, for example, to favor votes that help the poor, or that reform campaign financing. Corporate whistle blowers can easily lose their jobs and careers just for telling the truth. Such people need a great deal of support and encouragement.

Our form of capitalism has created the greatest engine for economic growth in history. Spirituality shows us, however, that our economic system is especially prone to being influenced by what St. Paul called, "the principalities and powers" of the world (Eph. 1:21). This was his way of describing the corrosive forces that live within us and within the institutions of our society—the forces that constitute "the world" that hates Christ and that we must avoid. These are the same force that Christ has radically overcome. So our basic challenge in facing these forces is a spiritual one in which we work to overcome these forces and make our economic system more luminously human and a clearer expression of Christ. In our use of money, goods and services, we are caught in a fight for our very humanity—for our very souls.

A story is told of a corporate CEO who downsized his corporation and then gave himself a multi-million dollar raise. He justified his actions by saying that they were in keeping with the code of the market. The downsizing had saved his corporation, he said. As for the hardship that the downsizing caused the employees, he is reported to have looked down on them for being upset at losing their jobs. Didn't they realize that the market is cruel? The new spirituality is neither blind nor naïve. Spiritually mature people realize that some corporations have to be downsized in order to survive. (They also realize that some downsizing could possibly have been avoided by managerial foresight.) Our spiritual focus here is not so much on the downsizing but on the attitude of the

CEO. Somewhere along the line, he had managed to remove himself and his personal responsibility from his job. He was not personally responsible either for his raise or for the hardship that the downsizing caused the employees. "The Market" was responsible. While this is partially true, the deeper truth is that his humanity was absent. His attitude showed that he just didn't care. He had given himself over to the corrosive forces of "the world," and had made "The Market" his guiding divinity. It was to "The Market" that he sacrificed his employees, and it was "The Market" that rewarded him with a raise. We can see how far this CEO, and others like him, are from Christ's expectation of how we should conduct the affairs of our society:

> You are the salt of the earth. But if salt loses its taste, with what can it be seasoned? It is no longer good for anything but to be thrown out and trampled underfoot. You are the light of the world. A city set on a mountain cannot be hidden. Nor do they light a lamp and then put it under a bushel basket; it is set on a lamp stand, where it gives light to all in the house. Just so, your light must shine before others, that they may see your good deeds and glorify your heavenly Father.
>
> (Mt. 5:13-16)

There are, of course, corporation that are trying to be part of the "light of the world." These are the ones, for example, who make good products and sell them at a fair price—all without polluting the environment. They are the one who offer continuing education and training, so their employees can upgrade their skills and change jobs in accord with the changing needs of the company—or be prepared to get new jobs if necessary. We see luminosity in those corporations that sponsor community projects and environmental programs. Some stockholders are checking their portfolios and refusing to hold stock in corporations whose products endanger health or pollute the environment. All these expressions of Christ show that we can truly give to Caesar what is Caesar's and give to God what is God's (Mt. 22:21). The spiritual insight involved here, as Jesus well knew, was that even Caesar belongs to God.

How does Christ see our personal economic dreams? We want a good education and the best paying job we can get. We want to live in a nice house in a nice neighborhood. We like to have nice things. We want to give our children all the things that we have—and more. Does the Spirit approve of our values or condemn them? Is our American dream a true expression of righteousness, and of Christ, or a distortion of them?

Jesus tells us we have to answer that question for ourselves—and he shows us how to find the answer in the story of the rich young man The rich young man comes to Jesus and tells him that he already obeys all the commandments—he is already morally good. He then asks if this is enough for him to enter the kingdom of heaven. Jesus tells him he still lacks one thing. He tells him to sell everything he has, give the money to the poor, and then follow him. The young man refuses and walks away. Jesus then speaks some very dark words:

> How hard it is for those who have wealth to enter the kingdom of God. . . . It is easier for a camel to pass through [the] eye of [a] needle than for one who is rich to enter the kingdom of God.
>
> Mark 10:23-25

Jesus' disciples were astonished when they heard this. Biblical scholars explain that the, "The Eye of a Needle," possibly was the name of a narrow gate in the walls of Jerusalem, through which even the smallest camel could not pass. Jesus was expressing an impossibility. He was saying that a wealthy person cannot be saved. How could this be? Must we become poor—and therefore despised and oppressed by the wealthy and powerful—in order to be saved? Is that what, "Blessed are the poor" means?

The Biblical scholars go on to tell us that when Jesus told the rich young man to give up all his money and goods, he meant it literally. But Jesus' instruction applied only to this particular young man and was not meant to apply literally to all of us. Jesus is not telling us to give away all our money and goods, and become poor and despised. No, not literally. In a very special way, however, he *is* telling all of us to give away all our money and goods and to become poor. How can we do this?

> For human beings, this is impossible but not for God.
> All things are possible for God.
>
> Mark 10:27

In the case of the rich young man, Jesus saw that the youth not only had a great deal of money but that he was attached to it. It was his attachment that was his problem, not his money. He was basing his identity and self-image—today we would say, his "self-esteem"—on his money, and thereby blinding himself to his true sense of who he was as a person. He was saying that he was money and power, not a human person. So he did not know who he really was. If he did not know who he was, then he could not know he was the image and likeness of God, a luminous expression of Christ. He could not know who Jesus really was. In this mindset, he could not follow Jesus.

Jesus knew that the only way he could cure the young man of his lethal blindness was to have him literally get rid of all his money and goods, strip himself down to his "naked" self and thereby be forced to take a good, sincere look at the human person he really was. The word "sincere" comes from the Latin, *sine cera*, without wax. The young man had to wipe away the waxy gloss of his wealth and power, and probably of the arrogance with which his attachment to his money was covering him.

In and through this story, Jesus is giving us—and our economic system and dreams—the same message. He is telling us that when we get involved with money, we must take great care not to get attached to it and to the power it brings. It is all too easy to let money blind us to who we really are. Certainly, we must use our money for our goods and security, but always in a way that fosters fairness, justice, peace and compassion for all people—especially for the poor and outcast. It is up to everyone of us to work out what this means in our own lives and in today's society. Jesus did not despise the wealthy for their money but for the arrogant way they used it to oppress the poor. He wants us to accumulate and handle our money and goods in a way that respects and follows the needs of the poor.

As for our own money, how do we determine how much we need in order to collaborate with the intentions of the Spirit. In some circumstances, we may need tens of millions of dollars to live a good Christian life, e.g., if we are using our money for a charity or foundation, or if we use the position that money give us to influence the political and economically powerful in our society to be more fair and just to the poor and outcast. On the other hand, do our kids really need $125.00 sneakers? Christian Poverty shows itself in our hearts and in our spiritual maturity, not in our bank accounts.

Literal poverty is a curse that afflicts large segments of the world. Christians, together with all others of good will, are required to do all they can to overcome it. Getting mystically and prophetically involved in helping overcome poverty doesn't mean only giving money and shelter to the poor and outcast. This ministerial work is essential, but spiritual involvement goes all the way to working to assure that our society does not keep producing the poor and outcast. Christ's economic and political challenge to us is the same as Camus' was to the priests of Paris. "Maybe we can't make a world in which no children suffer, but we can at least work to make a world in which fewer children suffer." Our mystical and prophetic job is to help make a world in which fewer people suffer from poverty and the depression of spirit that poverty brings.

As for ourselves, Christ does not ask us how much money we have, but how honestly have we earned it—with special care that we have not earned it at the expense of the poor and marginalized around the world—and what are we doing with it. When we consider our money and goods and our attitude toward them, we can keep in mind what Jesus said,

> If you bring your gift to the altar, and there recall that your brother has anything against you, leave your gift there at the altar, go first and be reconciled with your brother, and then come and offer your gift.
>
> Mt. 5:23,4

In today's world of sweatshops where the poor of the Third World make our jeans, sneakers and baseballs, in a world of starving children in Ethiopia, and of all the horrors that poverty brings, these words should haunt us. They haunt me every time I enter a church and look at the altar. I hear Christ borrowing a slogan from the 1992 Presidential campaign and saying to me, "It's the economy, stupid!"

TWENTY FOUR

Where are We Going?

Our Final Destiny

Philosopher Martin Heidegger, for all his brilliance, could not see past himself and the world, so he settled for finding whatever meaning he could in this life, here and now. He even went so far as to declare that we are nothing more than, "Toward-death-beings." For him, no matter how we live, no matter what we do or what meaning we find here on earth, in the end we die and it all adds up to nothing. In his view, the agnostic Heidegger agreed with the atheistic Jean Paul Sartre, who taught that all is absurd and our lives come to nothing. Both men spoke for all secularized people.

Christianity offers a different insight. It tells us that even though we will die, we are not merely, "Toward-death-beings," we are, "Toward-eternal-life-beings." Once we come into existence, we live forever, and all the meaning we find during our lives in space/time carries over into eternity.

Many Christians understand eternal life as the life that will begin after we die. This is only partially correct. Our eternal life has already begun. From the beginning, the divine Spirit placed herself in the universe, and in doing so, placed eternity in the universe. It is a Christian insight that God does not annihilate what he has created, so the universe will live forever—though, as we'll see below, not in the same way it is living now. In our own case, the Spirit lives within us in a special way, so we are eternal in a special way. God will be I-Am-With-You to us forever. Here and

now, eternity lives within us and we live within eternity. As we saw
in the earlier chapters on our own spirituality and on the spirituality of art and poetry, science, education, and politics and economics,
we and the entire universe are already luminous with eternity.

Another way of saying that we are already living in eternity is
to say that we are already living in heaven, in a preliminary way.
Heaven is not a place where we will go after we die, as for example,
somewhere up in the sky or in outer space. It is no place at all. Nor
is it a very long time. It is no time at all. Heaven is a way of living
that is not restricted by the bounds of space or time. The word,
"infinity" means "not-space," and the word, "eternity" means "not-
time." Right now we are living in both space/time and eternity/
infinity. Since our experience of ourselves in space/time is so "up
front" we can only begin to imagine what it will be like to be free
of space/time and live exclusively in eternity/infinity. Our fleeting
mystical experiences, like the one my colleague had, and like the
ones everyone of us has at one time or another, give us hints as to
what heaven will be like. Most importantly, our life in heaven will
be a life of eternal happiness as we enjoy the sight of God, whom
we see only darkly in our present way of life.

Old spirituality moved Christians to put away considerations
of their life on earth and to look forward to leaving all behind and
going to heaven. It also taught us to offer up our sufferings here on
earth (with the implication that we are helpless to do much about
them), since all will be right in heaven. The new spirituality moves
us to get deeply involved in our lives on earth, to do all that we can
to make ourselves and our society more luminous so that fewer
people suffer in this life. It shows us that our Spirit-directed involvement with one another and in the institutions of our society
is the "raw material" that Christ will turn into gold in heaven.
While our eternal life in heaven is a pure gift of God, yet part of
the great respect God has for us and for our human dignity is to
permit us to contribute to the quality of life we will enjoy in heaven.
As images and likeness of God, and as expressions of Christ, living
in his Spirit, we can help build and enrich heaven. Whether God

gives us five talents, or two or one, he expects us to use them, develop them and then give them back (Mt. 25: 14-30). The return we make of our talents—of our prayers and Spirit-directed involvement in our own luminous development and in the luminous development of society—will be part of the measure of happiness we will enjoy in heaven. God will also add another measure, as he did to those who used their talents well. Also, the degree of intensity of the luminosity we contribute will be part of the degree of intensity with which we give glory to God. The more creative, healing and self-giving love and compassion we create on earth, the happier we will be and the more glory we will give God. The spiritual urgency not to waste any of heaven presses us.

At some unknown time, the world will end. Scientists tells us that in about 5 billion years, our sun will burn out. In its death throes it will expand and engulf the earth, burning it to a cinder. Our faith tells us that Jesus could return at any time. Despite the constant predictions that pour fourth from some Christians, the actual date of the last day of earth is unknown. Even Jesus himself did not know it (Mk. 13:32; Mt. 24:36). The best we can say is that the end of the world will come at any time between this moment and 5 billion years from now. Spiritually mature Christians who are involved with building heaven by using their talents and possibilities to build and serve the world in the Spirit of Christ, are content to leave it up to God to decide when the world will end.

On the last day, Jesus will return. While his first coming to earth was hidden from all but Mary, Joseph and a few shepherds, his second coming will be witnessed by the whole world. The Bible says he will come on the clouds with power and glory (Mt. 24:30; 26:64; Mk. 13:26; 14:62: Lk. 21:25-27). By this, the Biblical writers mean that Jesus will appear in the full manifestation of his divinity. The Christian view is that on that day, no one will doubt that Jesus is both human and God. In the Biblical language and mindset, the blue dome of the sky will open and Jesus will come down to earth from above. In our language and mindset we can say that Jesus will once again enter space/time. He now lives in eternity/infinity, unbound by any restrictions of space/ time. In his way of living he is in touch with every moment and every place in space/time. We could use the example of a sponge that is immersed in water. The sponge is space/time and the water is eternity/infinity. The water is touching the sponge at its every point. Jesus is touching space/time at every point. From eternity/ infinity, he is touching the first flaring forth of the universe, he is present at the beginning of earth and at the first appearance of oxygen on earth. He is present to Lucy, our special ancestor. He is present at the moment the human community was created as Adam-Eve, male and female. He is present to ancient China and Egypt, to the time he lived on earth and to the land where he lived. He is present to the artistic and human richness of the Renaissance. He is present to the horror of the Holocaust. He is present to Asia, Africa, America, Australia and both poles. He is present to every flower and animal, to every person who has ever lived, is living now, or who will ever live. On the last day of earth, he will travel no distance and take no time, but will simply appear in space/time at whatever point he chooses.

Those who are alive on the last day will die, because no one escapes death. Earth as we know it will be destroyed (2 Pt. 3:10-12), but it will then be re-created and rise again in a new, changed condition (2 Pt. 3:13; Rev. 21). It is necessary that our eternal life include the earth. Here in space/time our identity includes earth. We are "members" of earth—our bodies are made of her atoms, her water, her minerals, etc. Our life does not have complete meaning without earth's air, water, food, land, seas, mountains, light, sunsets, flowers, animals, etc. All will be changed beyond our imagination, but we are members of the human/earth community now and forever.

The entire human community of all history will be brought back to life—body, mind and soul—in a re-created condition on the re-created earth, which will be easily able to accommodate everyone. Right now, those who are dead are in a state of fragmentation. Their souls and minds are still alive but their bodies have disintegrated and returned to earth. The souls in heaven are not complete persons and they look forward to being complete again in their bodies. When the dead rise again on the last day, they will be complete again—soul, mind and body. In our new condition, we will be recognizable. We will be able to recognize ourselves, one another, and Jesus.

Jesus will then judge the world. He will gather up all the creativity, healing and self-giving love and compassion that we expressed in the Spirit of Christ, i.e., all the charity that we created, and he will turn it into eternal happiness. In his saving love, every good word that we spoke will be exalted; every drink of water that we gave to a thirsty person, every bit of care and love we gave to the sick, will sparkle with glory; every effort at justice and peacemaking, especially for the poor and outcast, will be rewarded a thousand times over; every pain we endured fighting our demons will be turned into joy, every effort we made to help our family and community grow in love will reflect the face of Christ, every sacrifice we endured fighting to reshape the world's corrosive forces and make them more luminously human will sparkle—all will glow before the entire world as golden expressions of Christ. In the view of the new spirituality, every person who lived a life of consistent good will and love according to his or her own religion or tradition will have their religion or tradition confirmed as a loving expression of Christ. They will recognize Christ and he will smile upon them and embrace them as his beloved disciples.

Christ will also look at all the missed opportunities to create the "raw material" of heaven—all the hero's journeys not taken; all the demons and dragons left unfaced; all the wasted energy given to power, greed, oppression and war; all the involvement for the sake of others and society that was declined. He will take them and toss their wasted luminosity into a burning heap. All those who knowingly and willingly rejected their luminosity and refused to be expressions of good will, love and compassion will have their choice eternally confirmed. God will condemn to hell only those people who knowingly and willingly condemned themselves to hell. (God eternally knows if anyone will condemn himself or herself to hell but he does not predestine anyone. The choice is entire up to the people involved.) The "hell and brimstone" attitude of many Christians makes it important to emphasize that hell is not for those non-Christians who lived lives of good will and compassion while honestly not knowing Christ. It is not for those who made mistakes along the way, or who stumbled and fell, and depended on God to pick them up. They will live forever in God's arms. It is only for those who choose to live in eternal separation from God. In its 2000 year history Christianity has acclaimed many people as saints, i.e., as living in heaven, but it has never judged anyone to be living in hell—not even Hitler. In the time we have on earth, we are called to pray and work so that hell will be the eternal condition of as few people as possible.

Christ will then embrace those who are saved and bless them with eternal happiness in the sight of God. They—let's say, we—will know and love one another in a wondrous new and unbounded way. Our faith and hope will disappear because they will be totally fulfilled. We will become pure love. Our emotions and intellects will be filled with every good feeling, imagination, thought and understanding that we are capable of experiencing. While husbands and wives will no longer be married, they will live in the magnificent fulfillment of their beautiful, creative, healing and transforming love for each other and for their children. Our love of our other relatives, our friends and of all people will be totally fulfilled. As a point of special joy, our pets will be returned to us in full vigor of life. I especially look forward to being reunited with my cat, Mopsie, and to rubbing her belly again.

A friend once asked me what about those who die young, even those who die before they are born, and those who are mentally handicapped. How will they be fulfilled? His question reminded me of a question someone once asked St. Thomas Acquinas. "How old will we be in heaven?" He answered that in his opinion we will all be the same age as Jesus—around 30 years old. In light of his answer, I would say that the people my friend mentioned will be brought into the condition they would have enjoyed if they had grown to the age of 30 without being in any way handicapped.

In heaven we will see God directly. As we now know, here in space/time we "see" God only as a dark, all-embracing and loving background experience behind our "up front" experience of ourselves, others and the world. Even in those special moments when the Spirit "flip flops" our experience and puts herself up front, we still do not see or experience her directly—we still experience her in the darkness of Mystery. In heaven, all the veils between us and God will be removed, and to the extent that humans can see God, we will see God in all the magnificence of the divine glory. The sight of God will magnify all the charity we have expressed during our life in space/time and our happiness will be multiplied many times over. Some pragmatic people ask, "What will we do in heaven for all eternity?" One European sports enthusiast imagined himself taking part in an eternal, perfect soccer game. We can only answer that we will be fully and luminously alive and active in a way we cannot even begin to imagine. In heaven there will be no sickness, no unhappiness of any kind, and of course, no death. In our resurrected state, we will be able to move about without taking any time or traveling any distance or bumping into any obstacles. Jesus himself gave us a hint of what our condition will be like in heaven when he appeared to his apostles and friends after he rose from the dead. He was able to enter a room without opening the door. He was able to speak and be heard. He ate. And when Thomas touched his side, Thomas could feel the wound in Jesus' body. Of course, in all this, Jesus was relating to people who were still on earth, so we are left to use our imaginations and to how things will go in heaven.

The crowning glory of heaven will be the glory we give to God. To begin with, to the extent that we were expressions of Christ during our space/time lives, we will be part of the eternal exaltation of Christ. It was in and through Christ that the universe was created (John 1). The universe is the cosmic Christ. Earth and we were created in and for Christ. It was as the saving Christ that

God came to earth in the person of Jesus. In his humanity, Jesus was one of us, our loving brother, who saw our sunrises and sunsets, breathed earth's air, ate her food and drank her water. He laughed and cried with us, felt as we do, thought and decided as we do, acted as we do, lived as we do and died as we do—and for us. He rose from the dead so that we too could rise from the dead and live forever in his blessed company, and he gave us his Spirit so we could be expressions of him throughout our lives on earth. In heaven, Christ will gather up all of us and earth; he will unify all in himself (Eph. 1:10) and give all to God, our Creator, for God's glory. In heaven, the purpose of creation will be completed. Creation flowed forth from our Creator Parent, was filled with the divine Spirit, was the cosmic expression of Christ, who joined with it, loved it and redeemed it, gathered it up and returned it to the Creator for God's glory. In heaven the dance of Christ will be complete but it will not end. Christ will always be dancing—forever.

To Christ, our brother and savior, in and for whom we were created, who joined us in our humanity, who gave his life for us and who gave us his Spirit in whom we fulfill the best possibilities of our integrity, dignity, meaning, purpose and destiny; to Christ, who perfectly fulfills the divine intention for the creation of the universe, and for the redemption and salvation of the human/earth community; to Christ, who gathers us up in his eternal dance of love so we can give eternal glory to God; to Christ be all honor and glory, now and forever. Amen.

MASS

Printed in the United States
25448LVS00005B/13

9 780738 827957